IMAGES
of America

FAIRFIELD CONNECTICUT

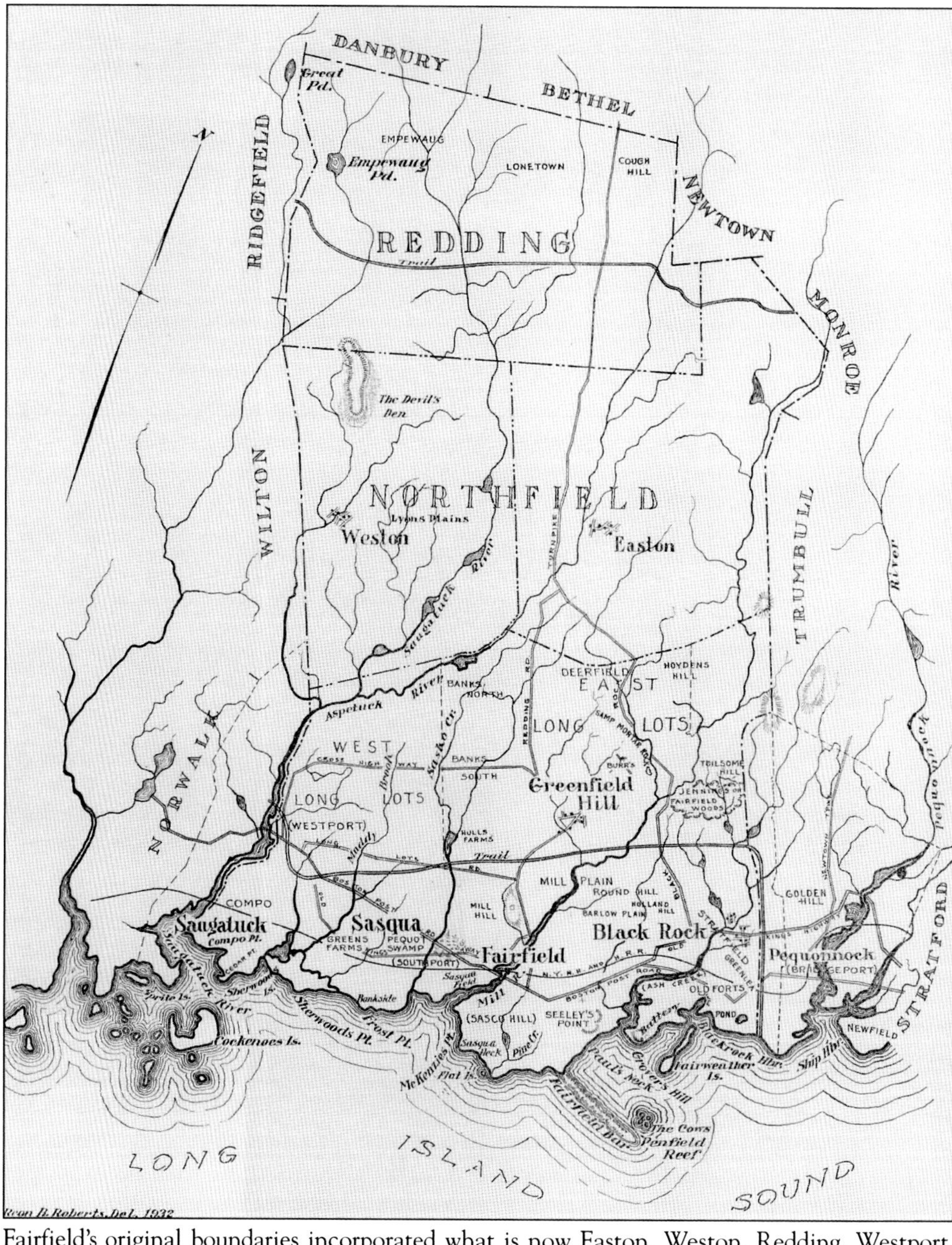

Fairfield's original boundaries incorporated what is now Easton, Weston, Redding, Westport, and part of Bridgeport.

On the cover: Alumni gather in 1904 for a reunion at Fairfield Academy.

IMAGES
of America

FAIRFIELD CONNECTICUT

Barbara E. Austen and Barbara D. Bryan

ARCADIA
PUBLISHING

ISBN 978-0-7385-3887-7

Published by Arcadia Publishing
Charleston, South Carolina

Printed in the United States of America

Library of Congress Catalog Card Number: 2005926945

For all general information contact Arcadia Publishing at:
Telephone 843-853-2070
Fax 843-853-0044
E-mail sales@arcadiapublishing.com
For customer service and orders:
Toll-Free 1-888-313-2665

Visit us on the Internet at www.arcadiapublishing.com

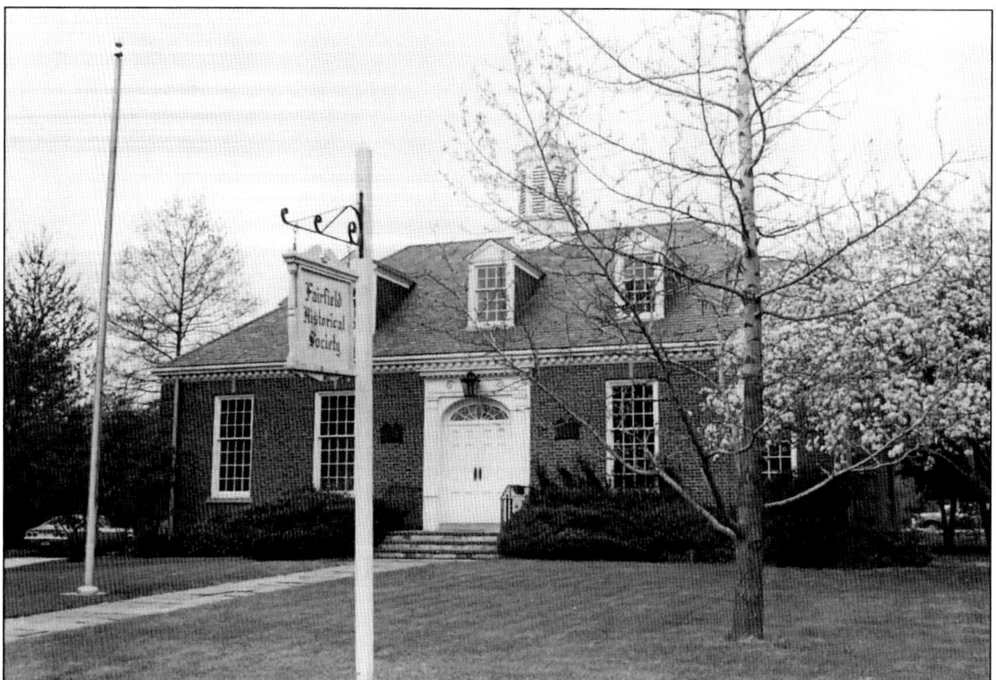

In 1955 the Fairfield Historical Society, founded in 1903, moved to a newly constructed headquarters on the Old Post Road. The building, designed by William Henry Jackson, houses a research library, exhibition galleries, an auditorium, offices, and collections documenting Fairfield's history.

Contents

Acknowledgments

We thank the board of directors, staff, and volunteers of the Fairfield Historical Society for their support of this project. The publication committee that guided the book's development consisted of Richard Durrell, Roberta Hodgson, Bruce Kershner, Marcia Miner, and Paul Siff. We appreciate Robert Berthelson's indispensible work making copy photographs, Stephen Rice's research in the photograph collections of the Connecticut Historical Society, and Cindy Herrington's careful proofreading of the text. Special gratitude is extended to Elizabeth Banks MacRury, who recorded tidbits of Fairfield's history in three books which were used extensively as references.

Most of the photographs are from the collections of the Fairfield Historical Society, unless otherwise noted.

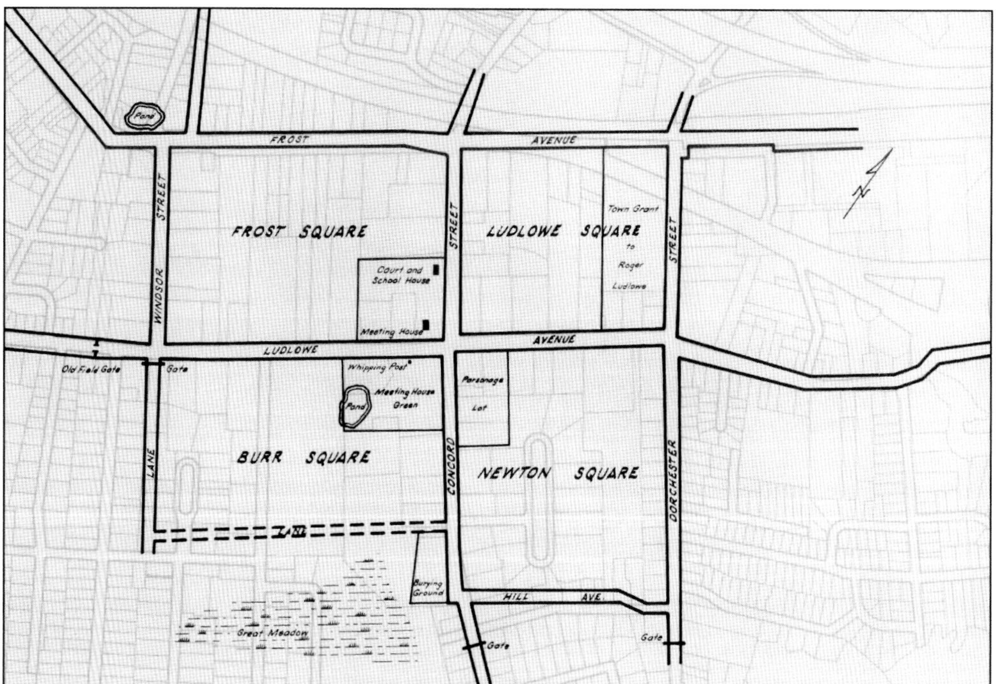

The civic center of Fairfield has always focused on the Town Hall Green, the site where in 1639 founder Roger Ludlow divided the land into four squares; the town court and jail occupied one square, the church another, and residences the other two.

Introduction

Fairfield is the fourth oldest of Connecticut's 169 communities. To many outsiders it is a pleasant, rather affluent shoreline suburb, the sort of place where the most pressing public issues are apt to be the preservation of open space and the size of the annual education budget. Yet both its past and current reality are more interesting and complex. Fairfield was originally a sprawling entity encompassing the coastline between the Pequonnock and Saugatuck Rivers, including most of what is now the town of Westport, and the towns of Weston, Redding, and Easton. It thrived on agriculture and shipping. Later, after having lost its northern and western extremities, its customs house, and its designation as the shire town of Fairfield County, it became home to a significant manufacturing sector and a surprisingly large immigrant population. At the same time Fairfield was favored by a number of the American business elite as the site of their imposing estates, and was something of a summer resort, too. Only in the mid-twentieth century did Fairfield come to share some of the attributes that typically cluster around the term "suburb." The story of Fairfield is one rich in years and variety.

The town, known until 1650 by its Indian name Uncoway (the "place beyond"), owed its existence as a European settlement to Roger Ludlow, an adventuresome and ambitious English Puritan who helped found Massachusetts Bay, only to abandon it in 1635 for fairer fields to the southwest. After the Pequot War of 1637 reduced Native American power in Connecticut, Ludlow purchased a large tract of well-cleared, fertile land from the local Paugussett tribe in 1639 and induced a handful of English families to settle in what centuries later became the town's Old Post Road Historic District. Laying out a group of perpendicular roads, these pioneer Fairfielders created four squares of about 30 acres each, comprising house lots. A town green stood in the center. Although Roger Ludlow left Fairfield in 1654, the physical imprint of his town plan was indelibly fixed upon the local landscape.

A second determinant of Fairfield's layout was the land division of 1671 in which over 50,000 acres of unoccupied territory, located above a 1/2-mile-wide common stretching across the lower part of town, were apportioned into "Long Lots." These lots were each over 13 miles in length, but their width, ranging from 50 feet to nearly 900, depended upon each town proprietor's status and wealth. Today a series of north-south highways in the upper part of Fairfield reflect the general configuration of the Long Lots.

Fairfield survived the perils of the Revolutionary period, including the burning of much of the town by the British in 1779. While Fairfield's population grew slowly into the early nineteenth century, its physical size began to diminish some time earlier, presaging an eventual diminution of population, vigor, and prestige relative to several of its neighbors. Redding, the distant, northernmost section of Fairfield, gained its independence in 1767. Twenty years later the parishes comprising Weston (including what later became the town of Easton), located south of Redding, followed suit. Fairfield was now a fraction of its original dimensions. In 1789 the town had been designated the site of the Fairfield Federal District Customs House, but in 1832, for commercial and political reasons, the customs house was moved across the border to fast-growing Bridgeport. And just three years later Fairfield suffered another blow when its westernmost territory became the town of Westport. Green's Farms, a prime agricultural area, was also lost, being annexed to Westport in 1842. The two crowning blows came in 1853, when the City of Bridgeport wrested away the county courthouse, and in 1870, when Bridgeport annexed Black Rock and its harbor. Fairfield had long been a primarily agricultural community, but that sector, as well as Fairfield's shipping industry, declined by the late 1800s. During the early part of the century, there was a movement to western New York State and the Western Reserve in Ohio, where farmland was more productive and much cheaper than at home. Later, New York City's large and growing port attracted many Fairfield men who became prominent in the shipping industry.

The early twentieth century witnessed manufacturing growth; Fairfield factories turned out a variety of products, including rubber goods, metal products, machine tools, dog food, and underwear. Many of the workers in these plants were either immigrants or offspring of the foreign-born; such people accounted for over half the town's population by 1910, and two-thirds by 1930. At the same time, the construction of trolley lines opened up new areas of Fairfield to development and further differentiated its neighborhoods. Stratfield, bordering Bridgeport, became home to wealthy Bridgeport businessmen, joining the well-established affluent areas of the Old Post Road, Mill Plain, and Greenfield Hill to the north and Southport on the western edge. Eventually the northern reaches of Stratfield would provide single-family dwellings on a more modest scale. On the other hand, Tunxis Hill and Holland Hill, south of Stratfield and close to a number of factories, became the center of Fairfield's working class population. Intensive development here included multifamily housing, often occupied by recent immigrants from eastern and southern Europe. These newcomers brought with them religious as well as ethnic diversity.

Although Fairfield shared in many of the post-Second World War developments that turned the U.S. into a suburban nation, it never became a mere "dormitory community." While the town's population swelled and disruptions were caused by the building of the Connecticut Turnpike, careful planning insured that Fairfield's character would not be swamped by mindless sprawl. Although manufacturing declined, Fairfield continued to nurture a fairly wide variety of enterprises. The largest of these was General Electric Corporation's imposing headquarters complex in northwest Fairfield, which opened in 1974. As the twentieth century drew to a close, the town had become more socio-economically uniform; the great estates, with their huge mansions and armies of servants, had vanished with the 1930s. And though pockets of want might still exist within its borders, by and large the ticket of admission to Fairfield now carries a substantial price tag.

As an old Eastern-European saying has it, "life is with people." Ultimately, it is all the generations and varieties of Fairfielders, at work and at play, in public celebration and private enjoyment, who have given to this community its distinctive flavor.

Paul Siff, Ph.D.
Sacred Heart University

One

All Around the Town

Fairfield, Connecticut, is a town with 53,418 inhabitants in an area of 30.6 square miles. A tour of Fairfield logically begins with its three historic districts. The Old Post Road Historic District centers around the site of the original settlement and the Town Hall Green. The Southport Historic District preserves the grand homes of merchants and sea captains. The Greenfield Hill Historic District encompasses the Congregational church, a green, and the surrounding homes. Other areas recorded here, while they bear no formal designation, also reflect Fairfield and its history. Among these are Fairfield Beach, the Post Road commercial area, and, on the town's eastern edge, Stratfield and Tunxis Hill. Each neighborhood has its own identity and a core of steadfast residents.

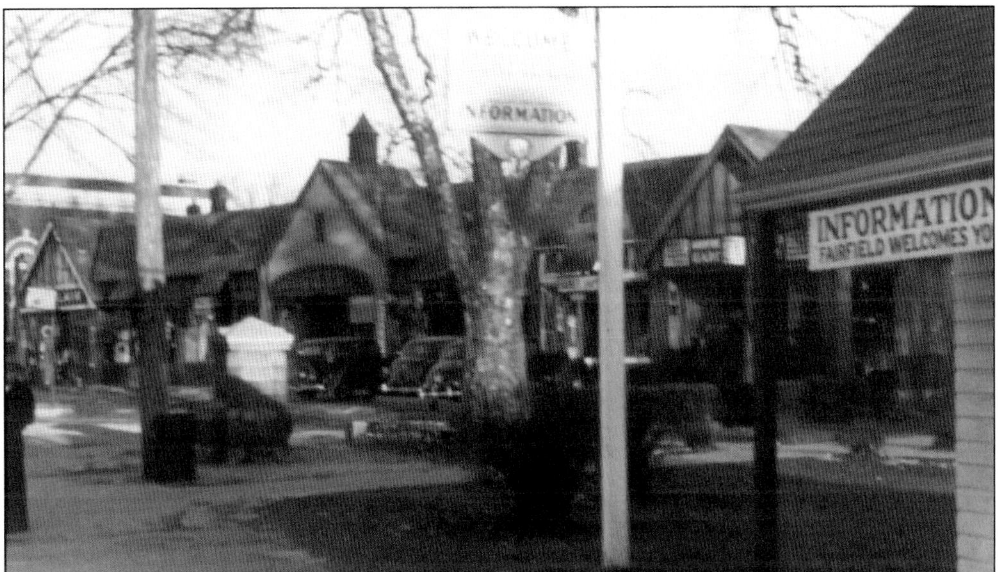

Fairfield was founded in 1639 by a group of eight to ten families led by Roger Ludlow, and it was one of the earliest settlements on the historic Post Road between Boston and Philadelphia. This view of the Post Road in the center of Fairfield was taken three hundred years later, when the town population had grown to about 20,500.

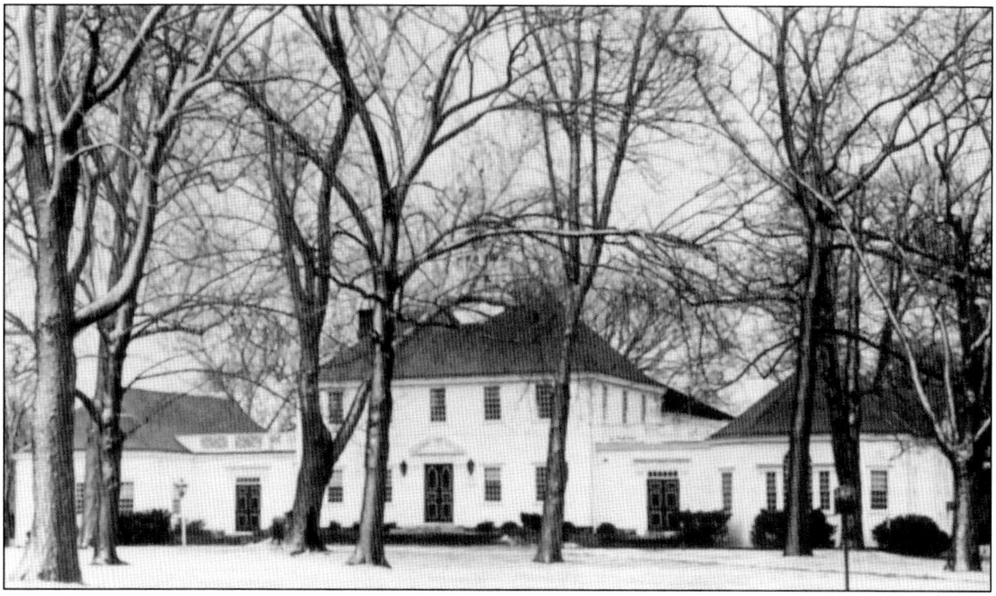

The Town Hall is shown as it has looked since its 1939 remodeling from the Victorian style. The renovations were completed in time for the town's tercentenary celebration and were funded by Annie B. Jennings, one of Fairfield's benefactors. A second town administration building, Independence Hall, was constructed nearby in 1979.

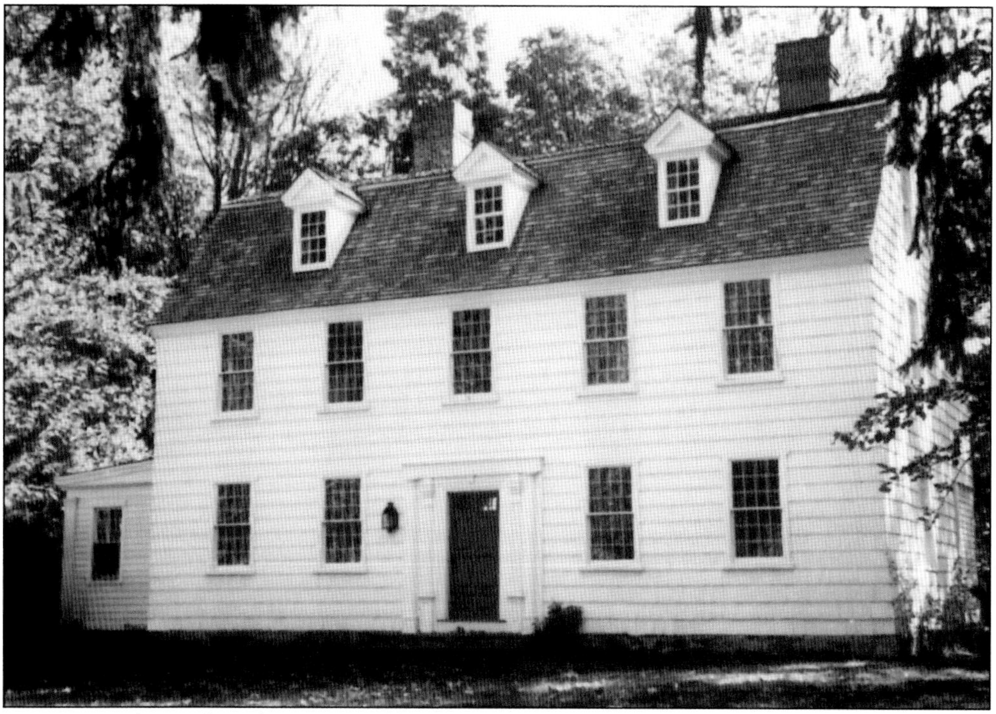

Sun Tavern, located on the Town Hall Green, was one of several taverns in Fairfield during the eighteenth century. The Sun Tavern provided accommodation to "politicians" attending county court. George Washington stayed here the night of October 13, 1789, on his presidential tour of New England.

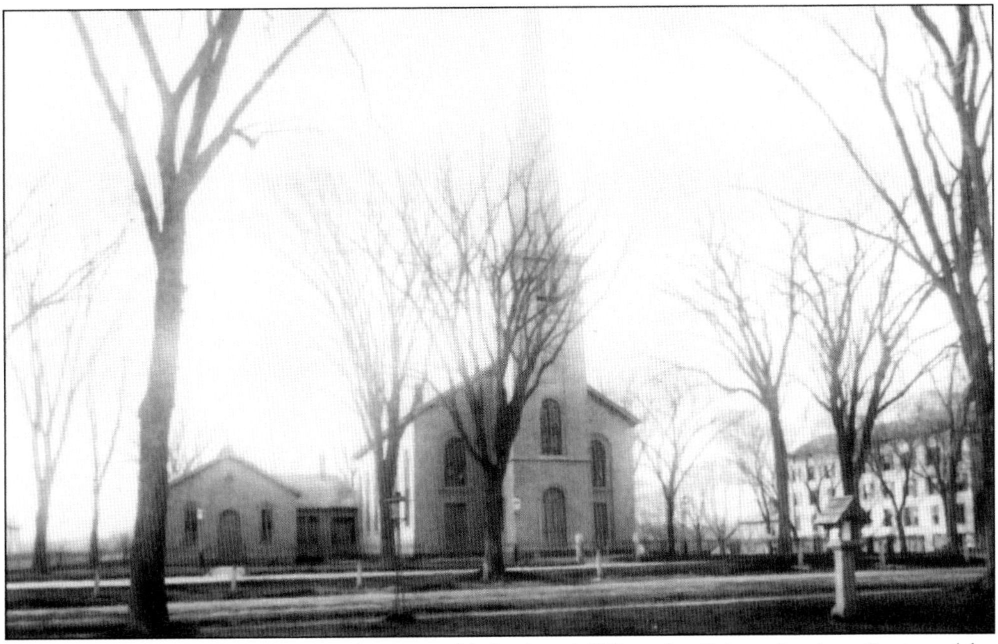

The First Church Congregational was established in 1639 as the Prime Ancient Society (the business arm of the church) and the Church of Christ (its spiritual arm). The Church of Christ was the established religious body in colonial Connecticut and thus earned a place of honor in the town's planning—facing the Town Hall Green. This structure, the fifth built on the original site, burned to the ground May 30, 1890.

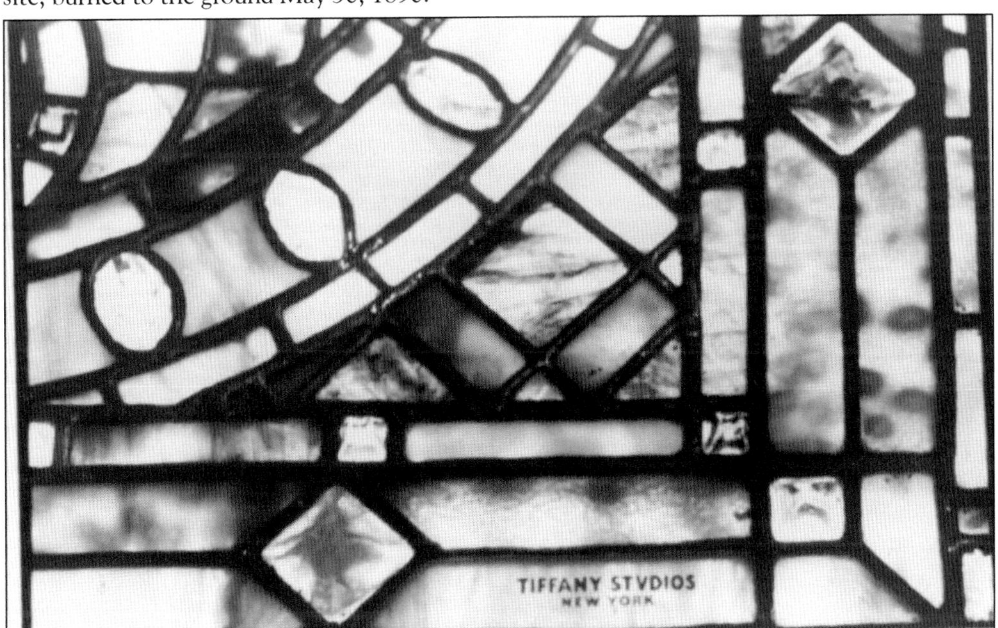

Eighteen Tiffany windows grace the present First Church building. The six windows flanking the sanctuary were installed in memory of the church's colonial ministers. The windows behind the pulpit were given in 1908 in memory of Oliver B. and Esther Jennings. (*Fairfield Citizen-News*, Michaud photograph, 1989.)

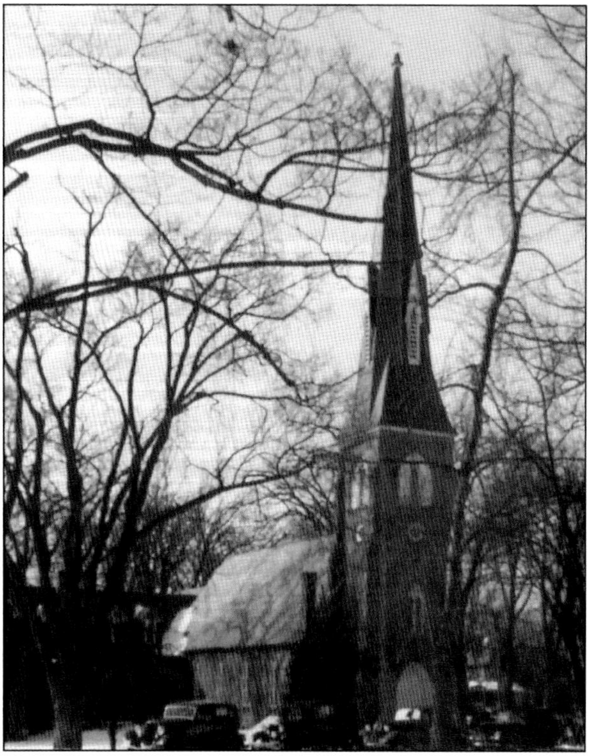

St. Paul's Episcopal Church, pictured in 1940, also faces Town Hall Green. The parish was formed in 1853 by people who did not want to travel to Southport to attend Trinity Episcopal Church. The building occupies land that was once the site of the county jail.

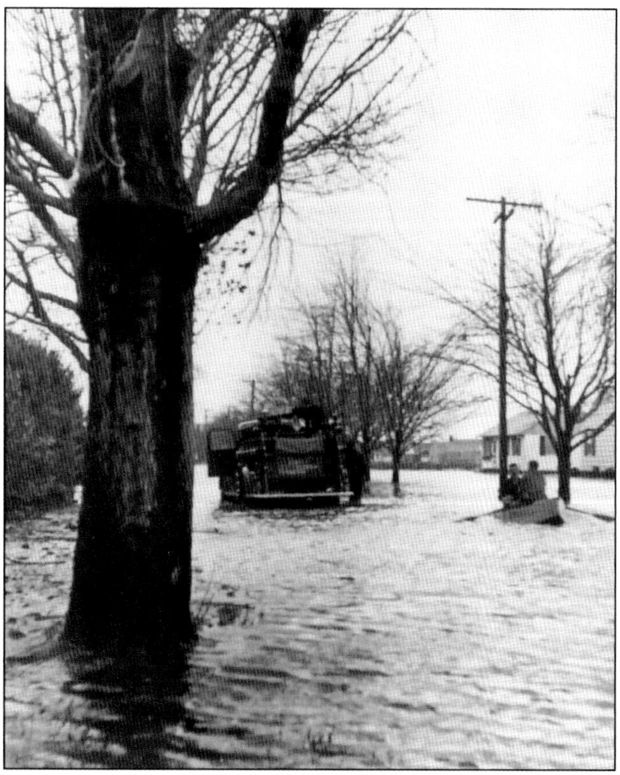

This November 1953 photograph was taken on Beach Road, nearly a quarter of a mile from the water. Flooding and storms are still a fact of life for those who live along the beach.

The Old Post Road takes a ninety-degree turn where it meets Oldfield Road. This photograph, taken around 1900 when elms still lined the street, looks north toward the Post Road at this turn. The Andrew Rowland house on the right was built before 1769. Rowland was a judge of probate, state's attorney, and Fairfield's town clerk.

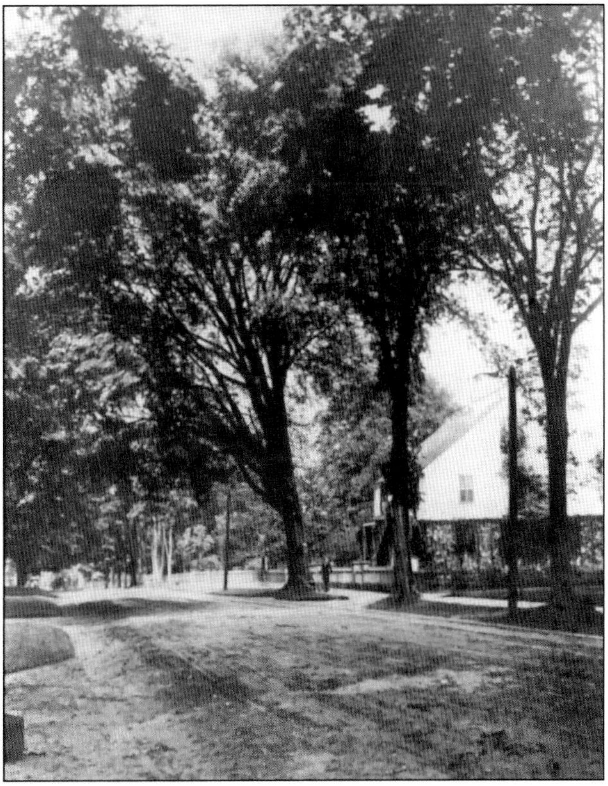

Judge Roger Minott Sherman built this elegant home on the Old Post Road in 1808, just a few steps from Town Hall. He bequeathed the house to the First Church for a parsonage, a use which continued until 1951. It is now a private residence, one of many buildings within the Old Post Road Historic District.

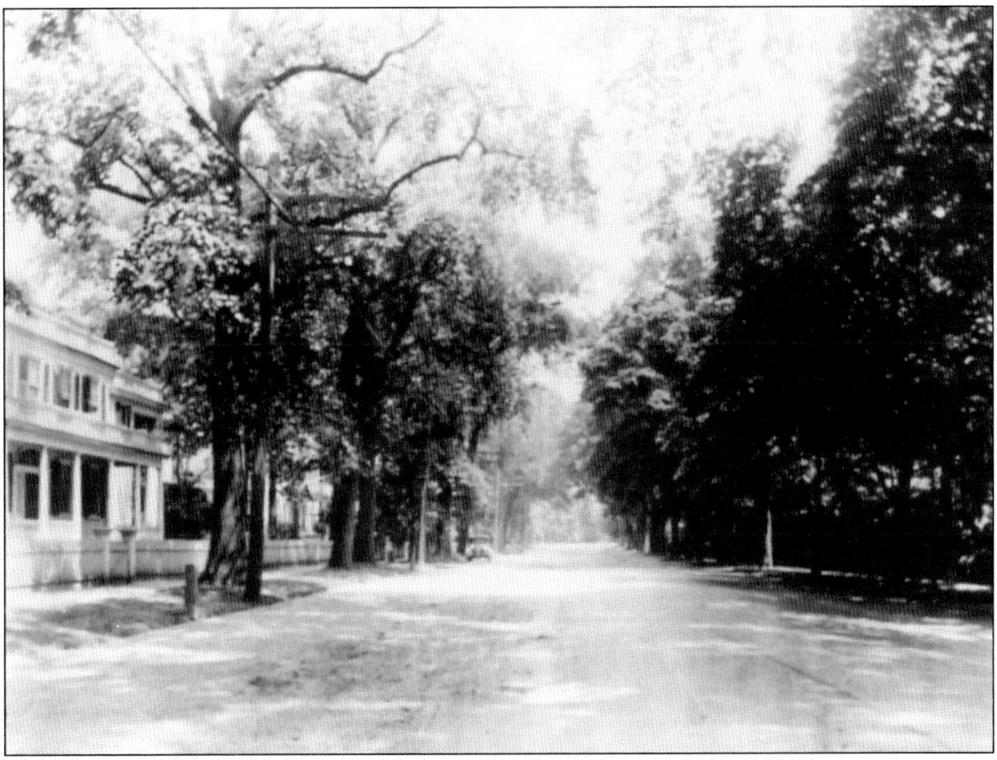

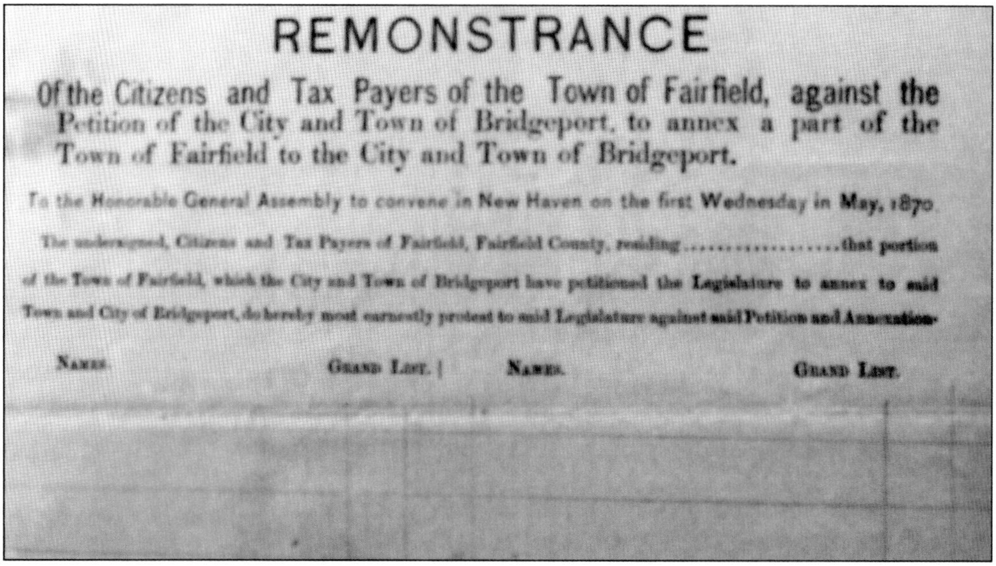

REMONSTRANCE

Of the Citizens and Tax Payers of the Town of Fairfield, against the Petition of the City and Town of Bridgeport, to annex a part of the Town of Fairfield to the City and Town of Bridgeport.

To the Honorable General Assembly to convene in New Haven on the first Wednesday in May, 1870.

The undersigned, Citizens and Tax Payers of Fairfield, Fairfield County, residing .... that portion of the Town of Fairfield, which the City and Town of Bridgeport have petitioned the Legislature to annex to said Town and City of Bridgeport, do hereby most earnestly protest to said Legislature against said Petition and Annexation.

Names.	Grand List.	Names.	Grand List.

When initially settled, Fairfield encompassed lands from Stratford to Norwalk. After the Civil War, many residents of the area called Black Rock, bordering Bridgeport, felt Fairfield was ignoring their needs. They wanted city amenities such as sidewalks, sewers, and gaslights and believed that joining Bridgeport would solve the situation and lower their taxes. In 1870, despite protests such as this petition to the Connecticut General Assembly, residents voted 7 to 1 for annexation. Phineas T. Barnum, mayor of Bridgeport, was one of the ardent supporters of the move.

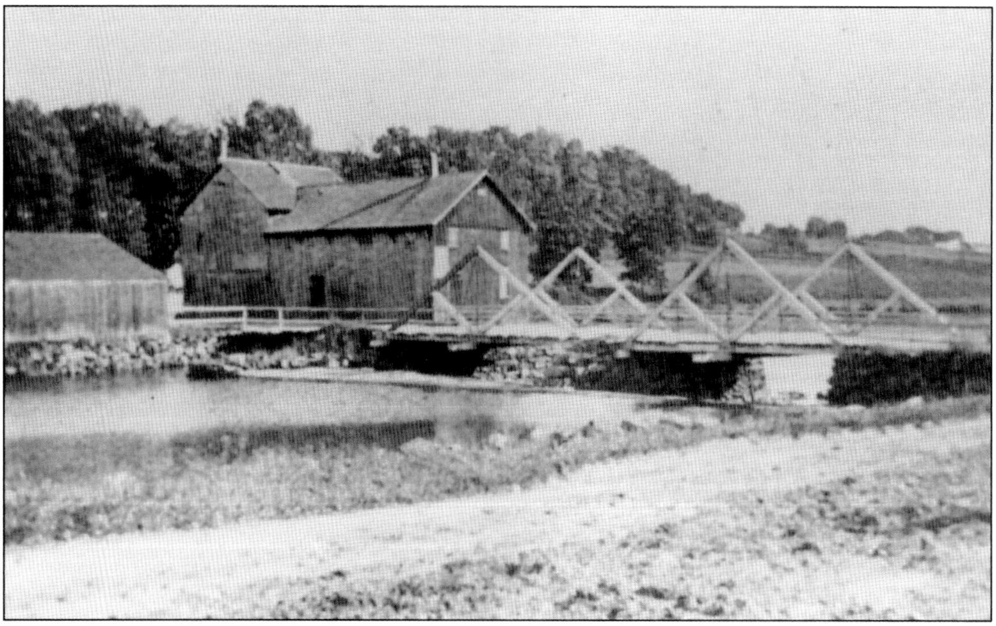

The bridge at the Tide Mill spans the Mill River between Southport and Sasco Hill. In 1697 Thomas Bedient received the Town's permission to erect a gristmill at this site. He was the first of many millers who used the tide to power his mill wheel. The building, photographed about 1910, has been adapted to a number of uses over the years; it housed several restaurants, and more recently it has been used as office space.

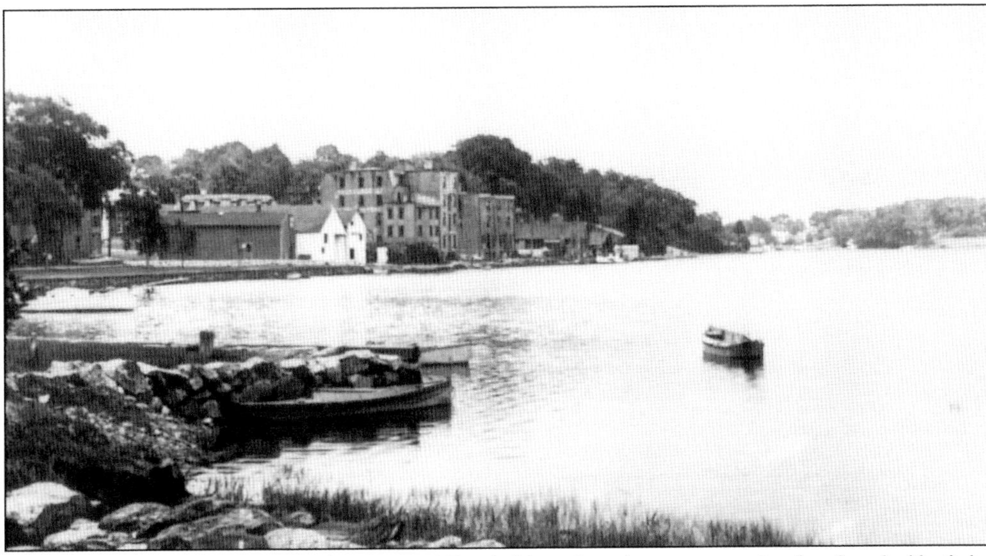

Southport was the commercial center of Fairfield and its busiest port in the first half of the nineteenth century. A postcard scene of the harbor around 1900 shows the wharves and warehouses along the shore, remnants of Southport's earlier coastal trade. The photographer stood at the mouth of the Mill River looking north into the harbor.

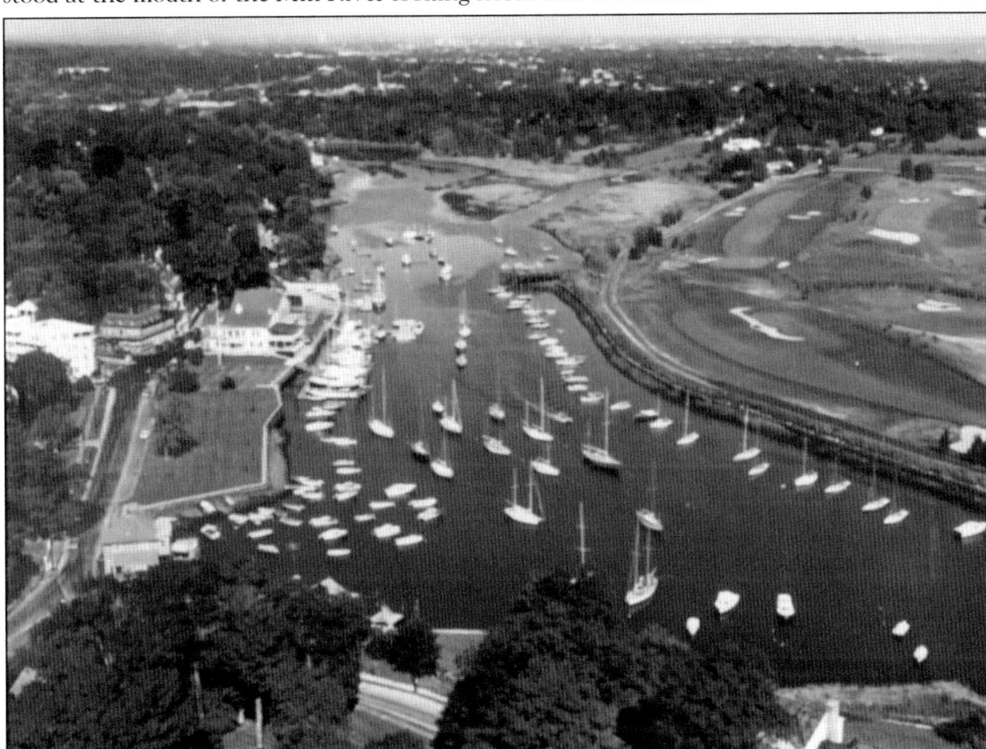

In this 1969 aerial view of Southport Harbor, the commercial structures have been replaced by the Pequot Yacht Club (left), and merchant vessels, by private yachts and pleasure craft. The Country Club of Fairfield golf course is visible on the right, with Bridgeport's skyline on the horizon.

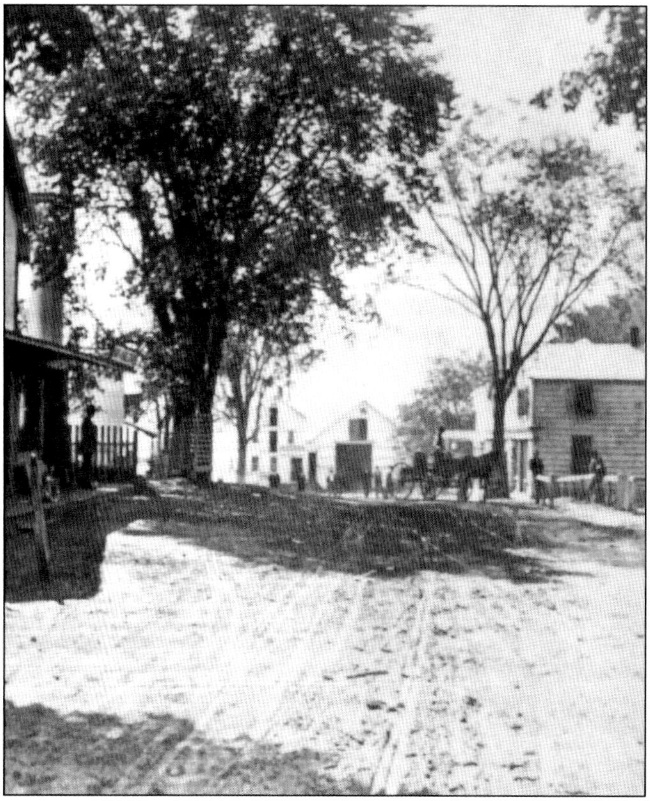

Looking south on Main Street in this *c.* 1874 photograph, you can see the Jennings & Son warehouses and store in the background. Jennings & Son shipped produce and general merchandise by coastal schooner from Southport to New York City.

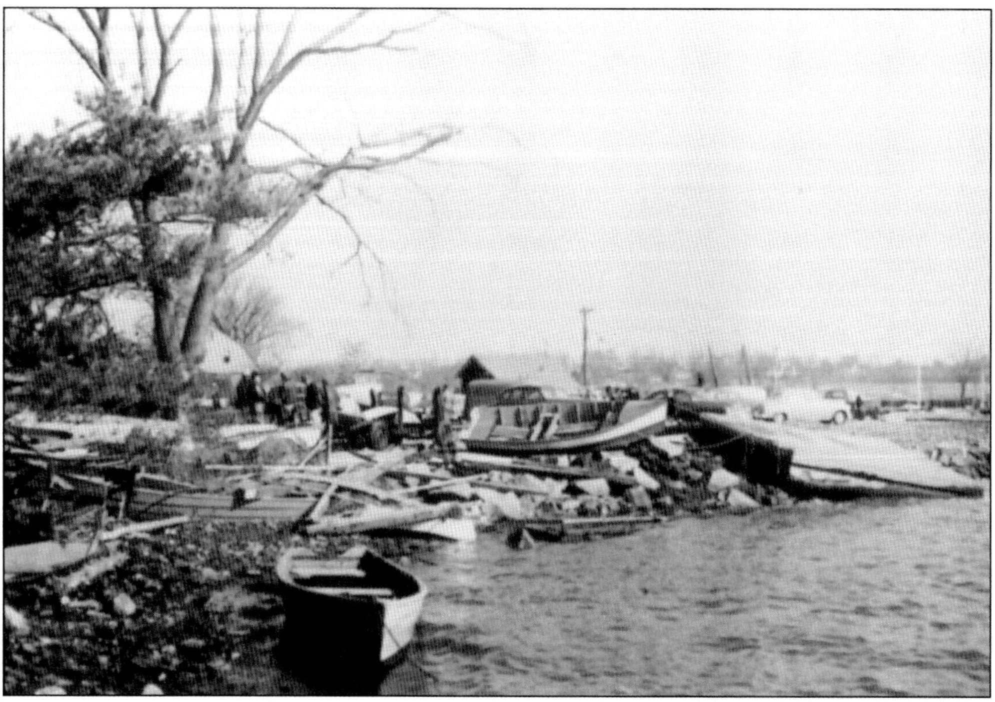

A winter storm in November 1953 damaged boats and docks in Southport Harbor.

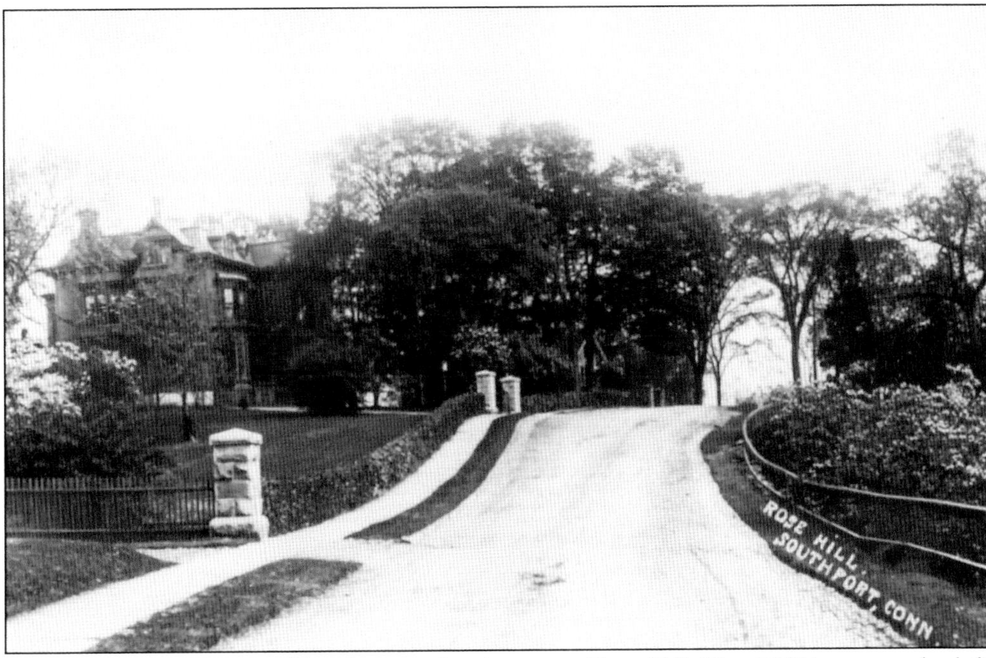

The rise along Harbor Road heading north is known as Rose Hill. The 1867 house on the left, the home of Zalmon Wakeman, was designed by Bridgeport architects Lambert & Bunnell.

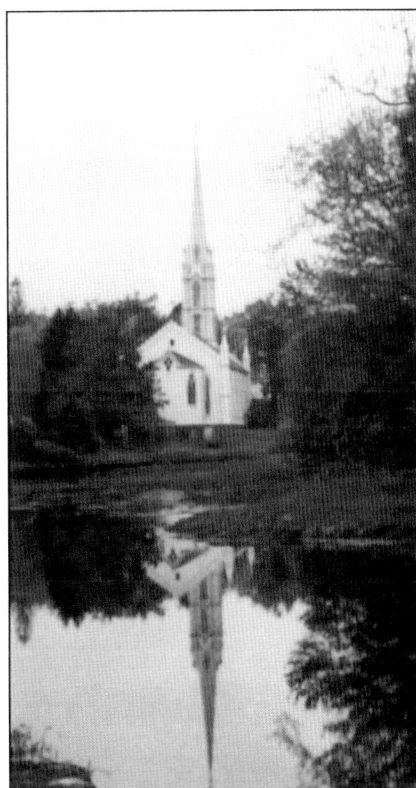

Fairfield's Trinity Episcopal parish was organized in 1724; its first church was on Mill Plain Green. In 1835 the parish moved to its Rose Hill location in Southport. The current building, shown in this 1940 photograph by realtor and photographer Charles J. Walsh, is situated on Pequot Avenue, a short distance from the Congregational church.

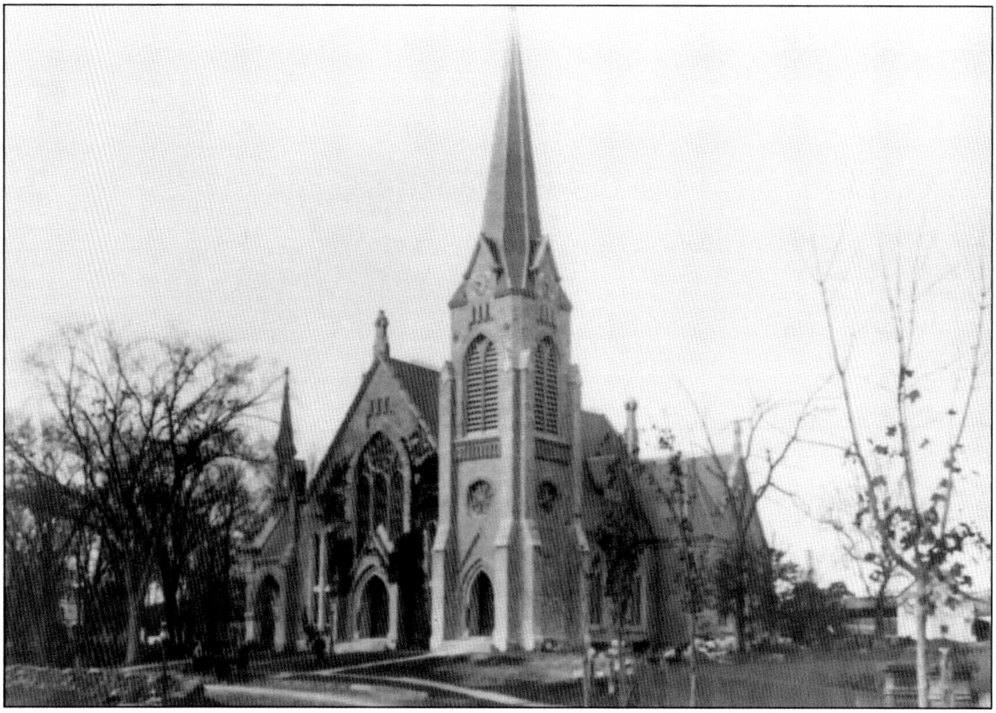

The Southport Congregational Church was officially organized and dedicated in 1843. Pews were sold to provide income for the "new" building, a practice that continued to 1946. The current structure, a high Victorian Gothic style, was dedicated in 1876. This photograph dates from about 1890.

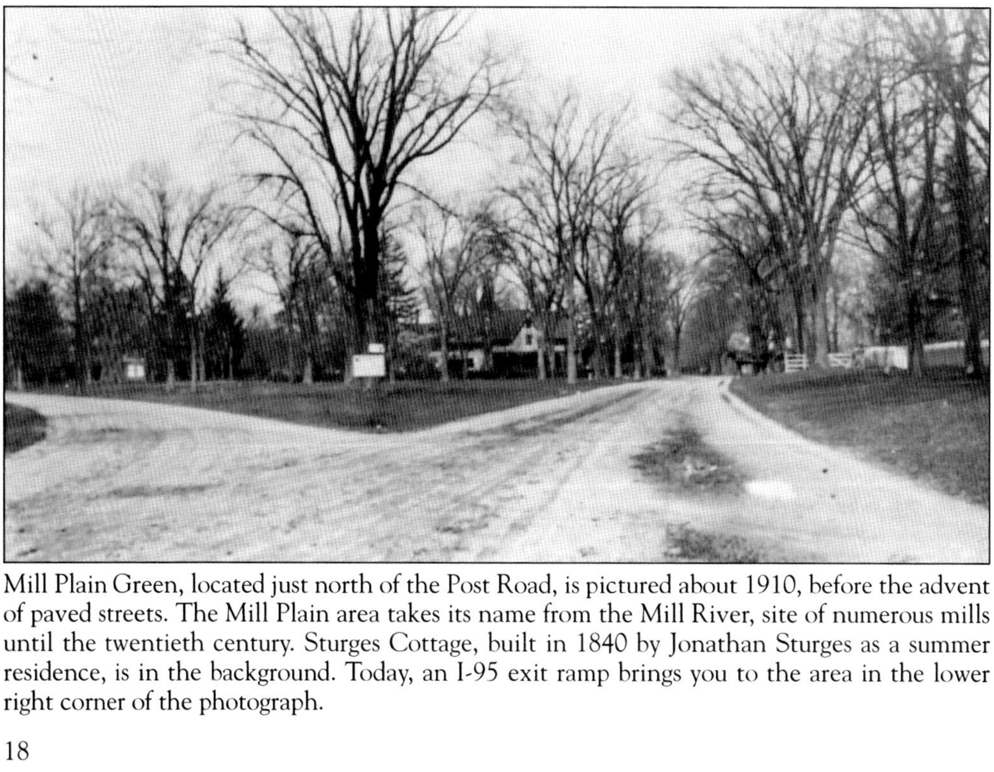

Mill Plain Green, located just north of the Post Road, is pictured about 1910, before the advent of paved streets. The Mill Plain area takes its name from the Mill River, site of numerous mills until the twentieth century. Sturges Cottage, built in 1840 by Jonathan Sturges as a summer residence, is in the background. Today, an I-95 exit ramp brings you to the area in the lower right corner of the photograph.

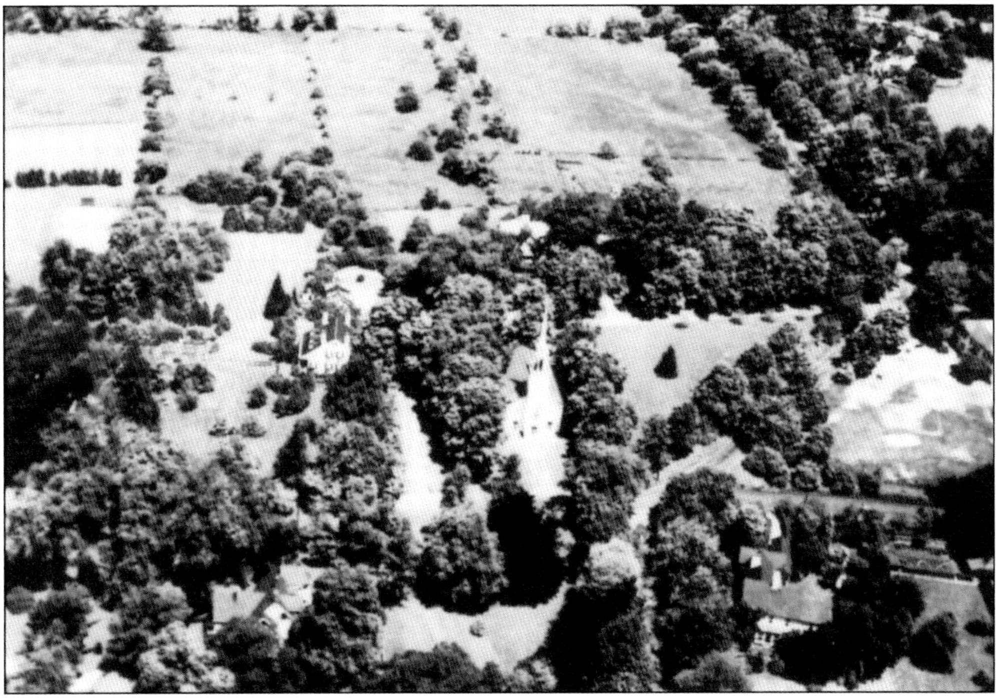

The left fork at Mill Plain Green is the most direct route to the heart of Greenfield Hill. This aerial photograph shows the Greenfield Hill Congregational Church, the Dwight School, and the open land beyond, around 1946.

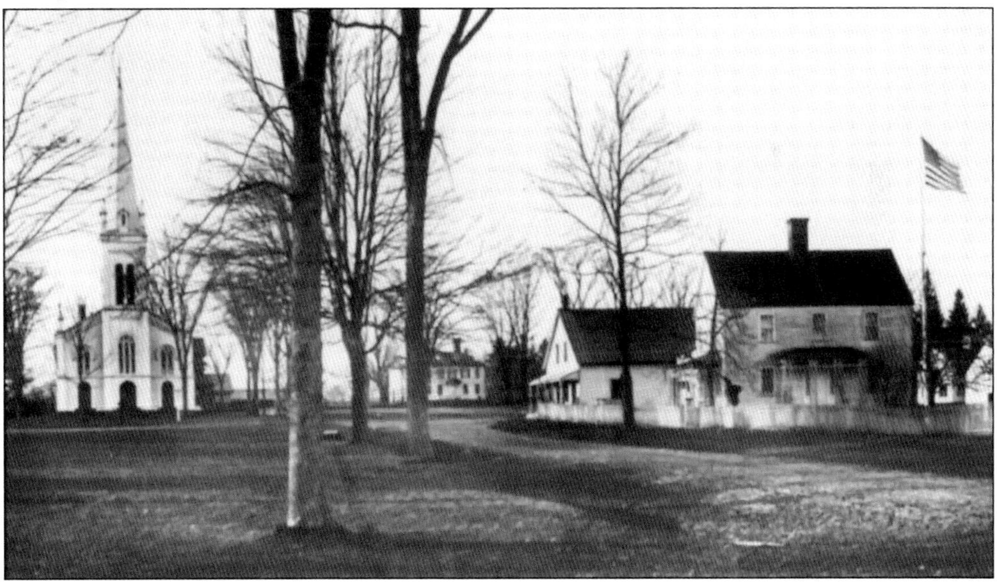

The Greenfield Hill Congregational Church was established in 1724 by worshippers who did not want to travel the 5 miles to the First Church. This, the fourth structure, was erected in 1854 and underwent extensive renovations following a 1944 hurricane. In the foreground of this c. 1895 photograph is the home of Fairfield Customs Collector Samuel Smedley. Immediately beyond is Banks' store, the only commercial enterprise in the neighborhood. It provided dry goods and a place to meet friends and pick up mail.

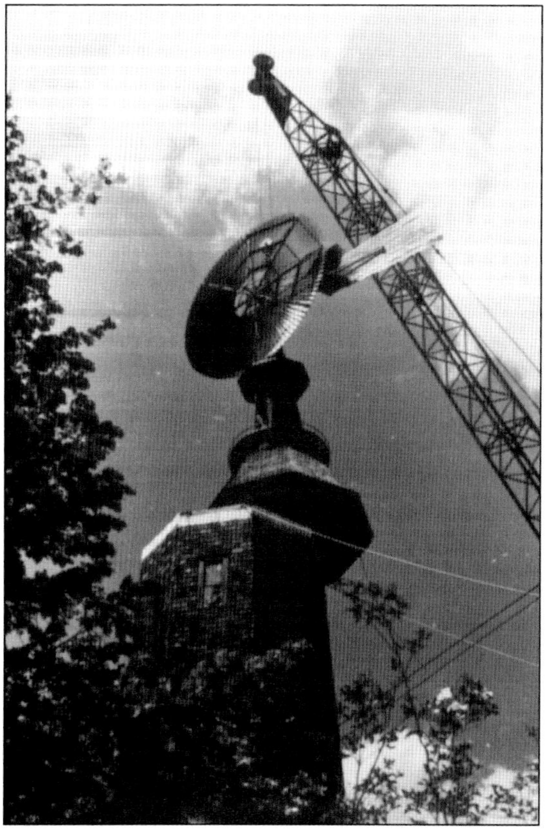

The Bronson Windmill, a landmark on Greenfield Hill, was built in 1894 for Frederic Bronson at Verna, his estate on Bronson Road. The windmill provided water to the main house and to the nearby greenhouses. Used until the 1930s, the mill fell into disrepair. Four Greenfield Hills residents led efforts to restore the landmark structure. In this photograph, McClinch Crane, Inc. of Fairfield caps off the 1980 restoration.

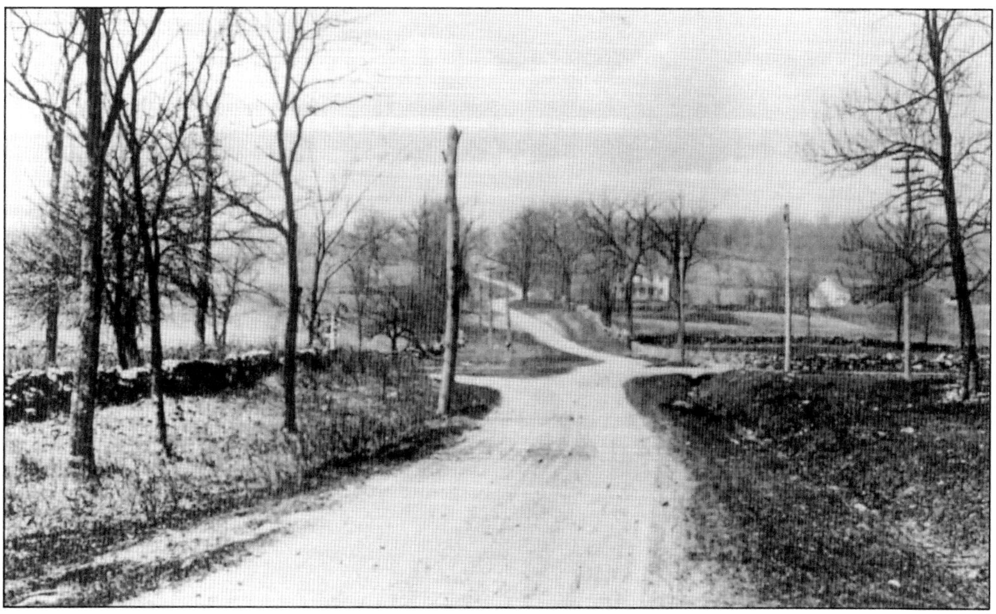

Snake Hill Road (now Burr Street), depicted in a 1910 postcard, was the site of an automobile road-climbing contest that same year and was used regularly by recreational drivers to test their new cars.

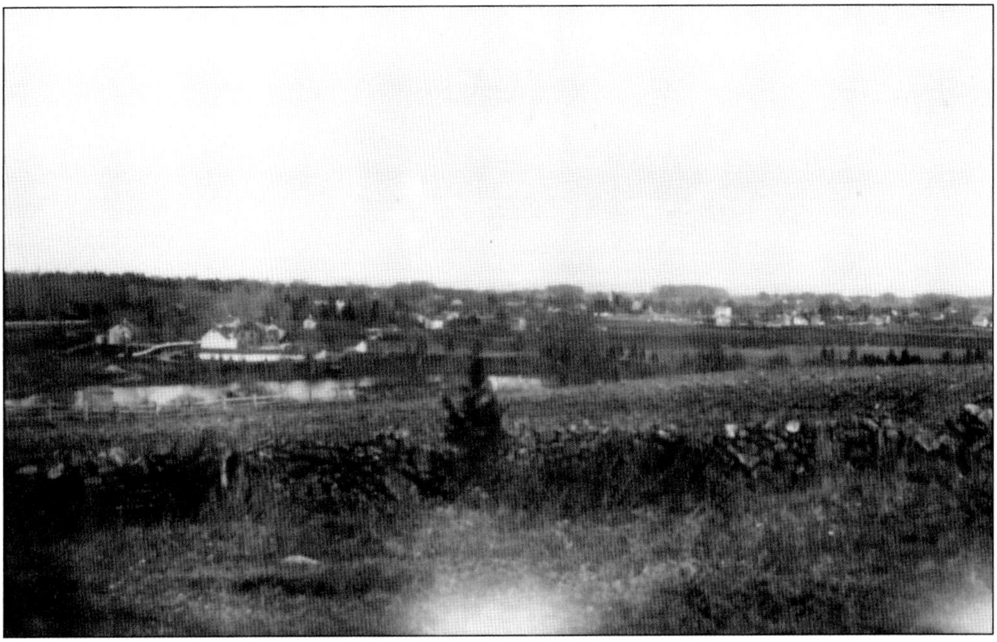

Fairfield was largely a farm community until the mid-twentieth century. This panorama from Mill Hill, with Long Island Sound in the background, was taken in 1889. The stones of St. Thomas Parish Cemetery can be seen just to the right of center.

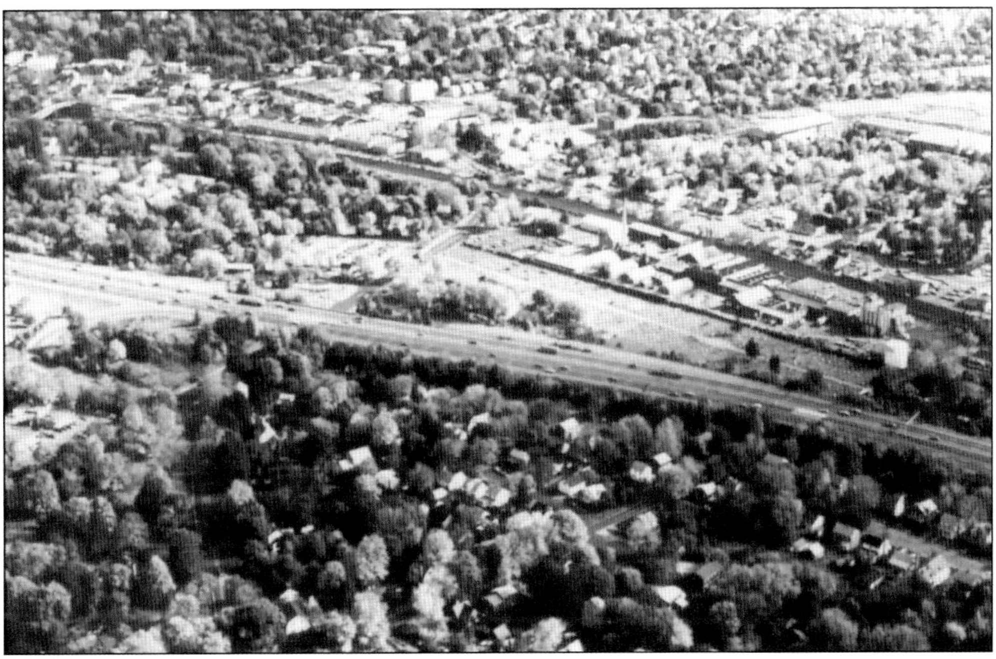

A 1980 aerial view closes in on one area shown in the previous photograph. The Connecticut Turnpike (now I-95), Metro North tracks, and Post Road are in close proximity here. Trees and houses have filled in the open land. St. Thomas Parish Cemetery again appears in the center of the picture.

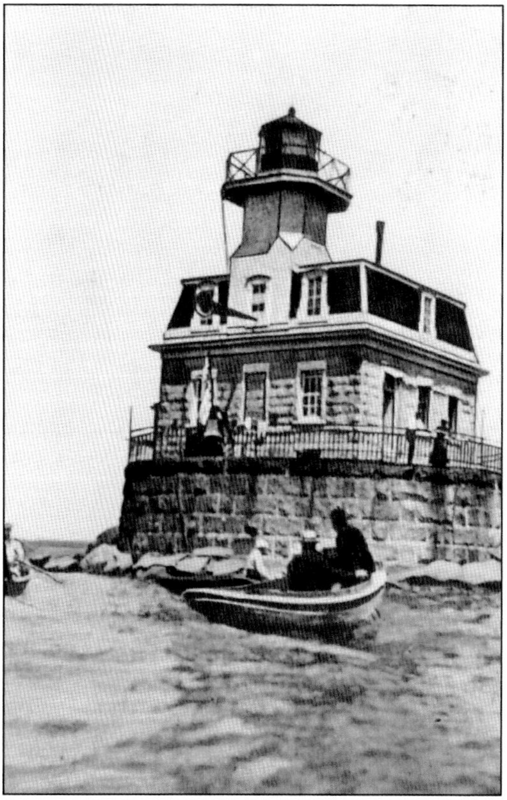

Penfield Light, shown on a c. 1910 postcard, was built in 1874, one mile south of Fairfield's shore line. It marks the end of the hazardous Penfield Reef and sandbar which are exposed at low tide. It represents one of the most popular lighthouse designs from the 1860s and 1870s, with its masonry dwelling, mansard roof, and wooden tower. The lighthouse was manned until 1971 when the light was automated.

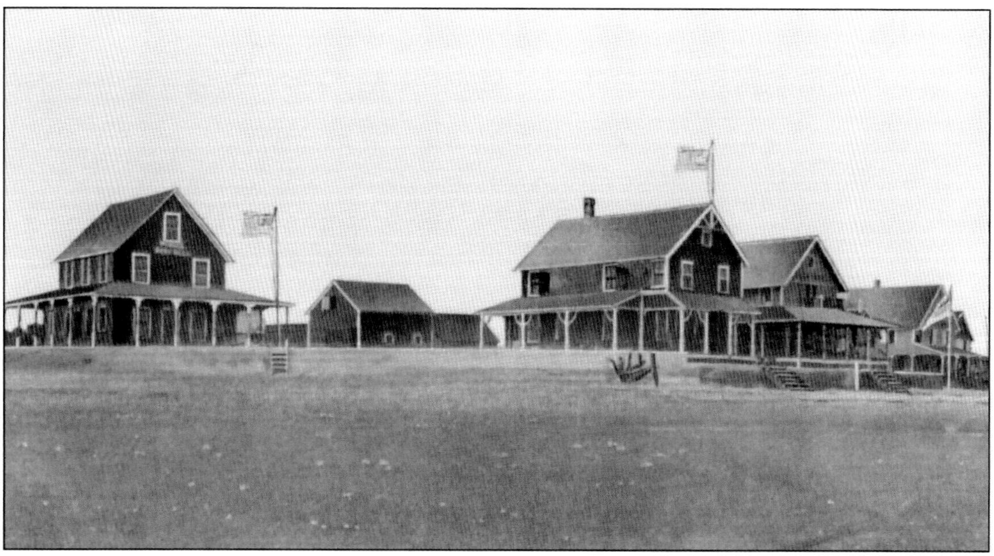

Little Danbury was the name given to a group of cottages along Fairfield Beach, so called because a number of Danbury residents summered there. This image is from a c. 1900 postcard.

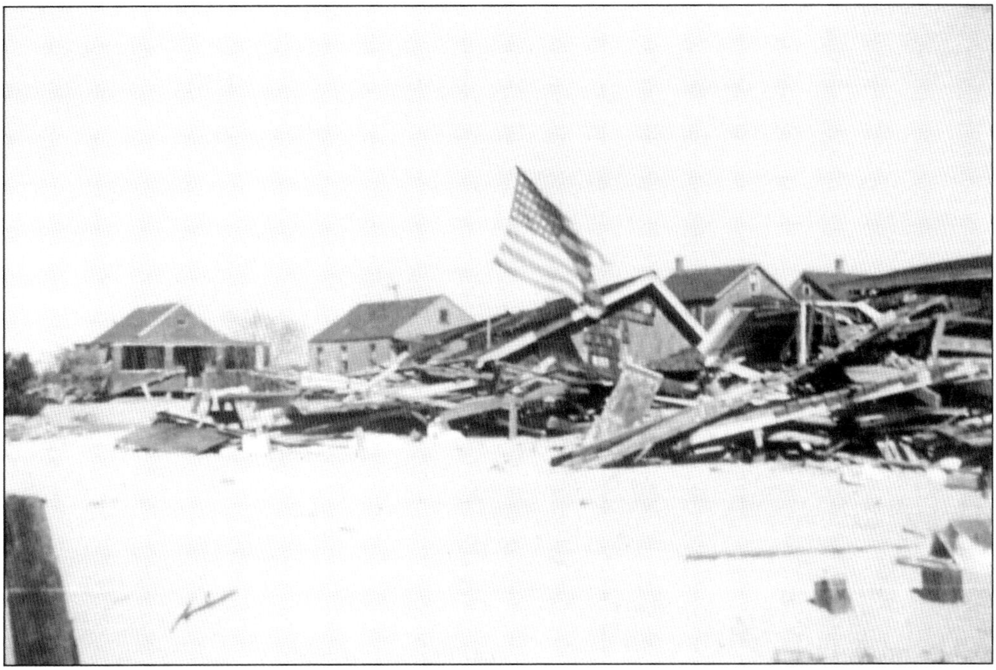

The worst storm in the town's history, called the Great New England Hurricane, toppled trees and buildings from Long Island to Massachusetts on September 21, 1938. Twenty-five cottages at Fairfield Beach were destroyed or washed away, and twenty-three homes suffered damage. The railroad needed six days to reestablish freight service and thirteen days to restore passenger service between New York City and New England.

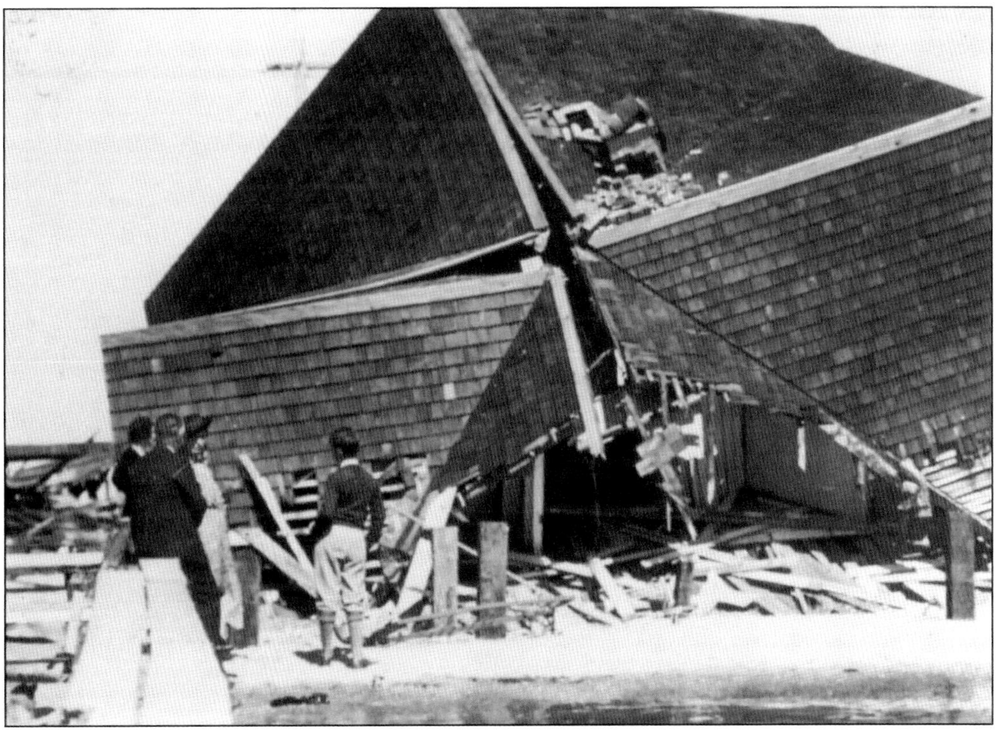

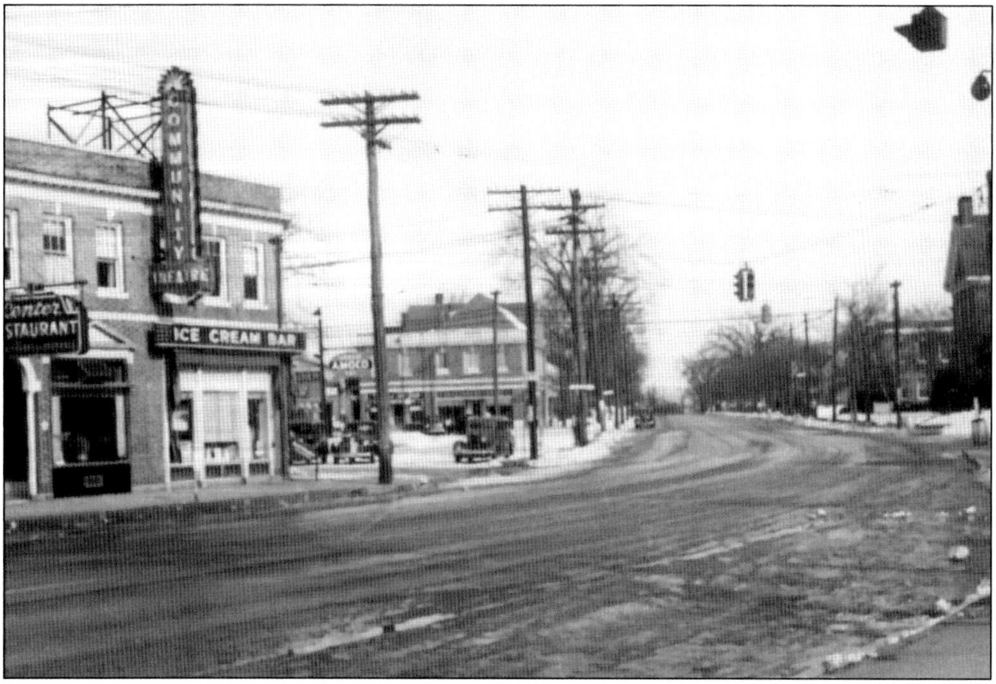

The Post Road developed as the commercial center of Fairfield after 1850, when the railroad came through town. This image, taken in 1939, looks east from the information center near the present Sherman Green.

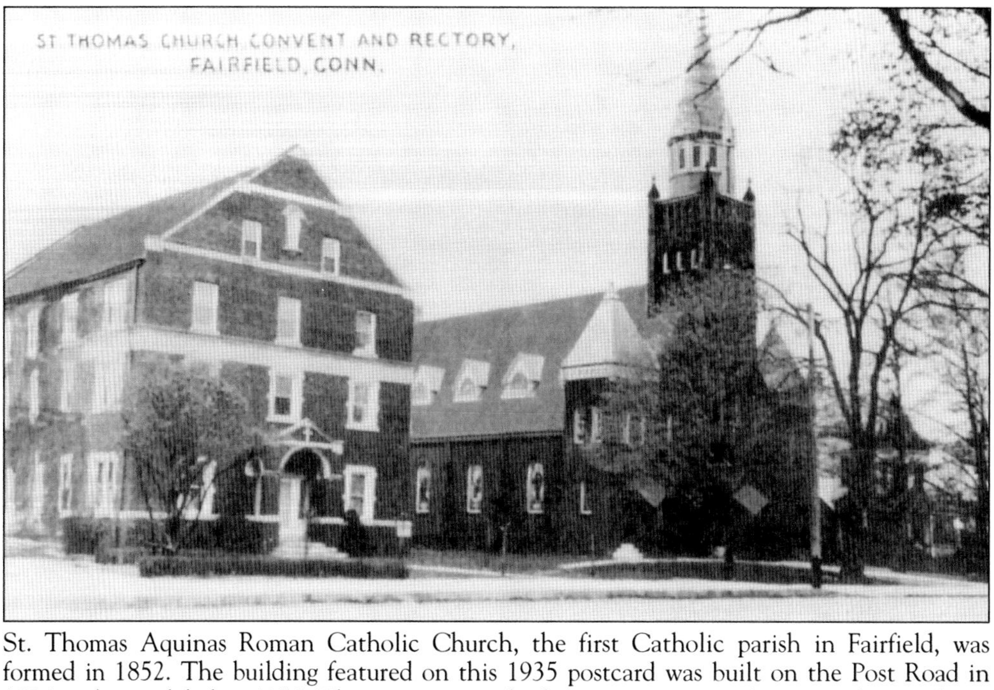

St. Thomas Aquinas Roman Catholic Church, the first Catholic parish in Fairfield, was formed in 1852. The building featured on this 1935 postcard was built on the Post Road in 1894 and remodeled in 1956. The structure to the left was a convent for nuns who taught in the parish school. In the 1980s the convent was converted to Bishop Curtis Homes, apartments for senior citizens.

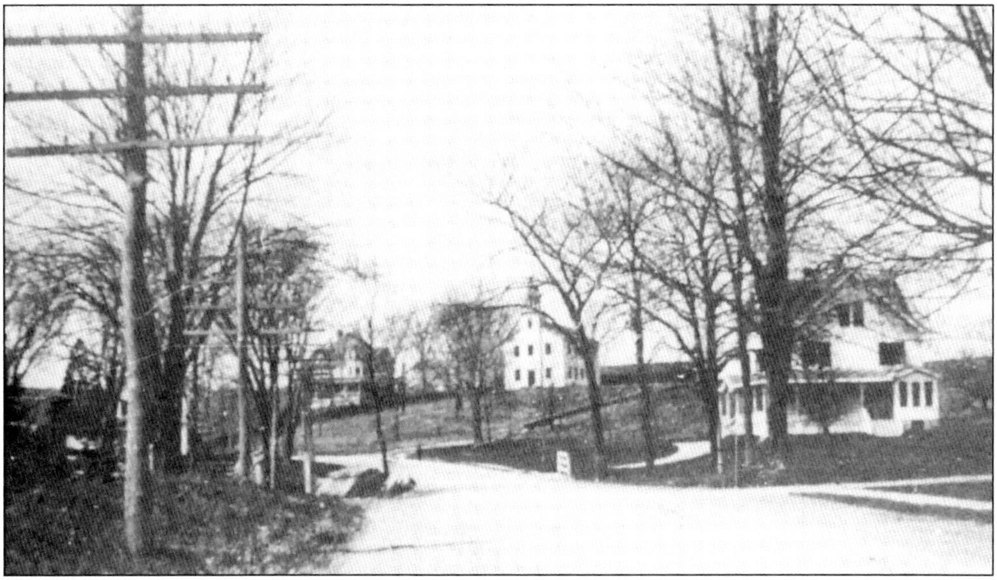

The Stratfield Baptist Church, built in 1814, is the oldest continuously used church building in Connecticut. This 1890 picture looks north along today's Stratfield Road. The Stratfield neighborhood, formed from the east parish of Fairfield and the west parish of Stratford, was named by the colonial assembly in 1701. In the eighteenth and nineteenth centuries, it grew as one of four distinct districts within Fairfield's borders, with its own surveyors, assessors, school board, and tax collectors.

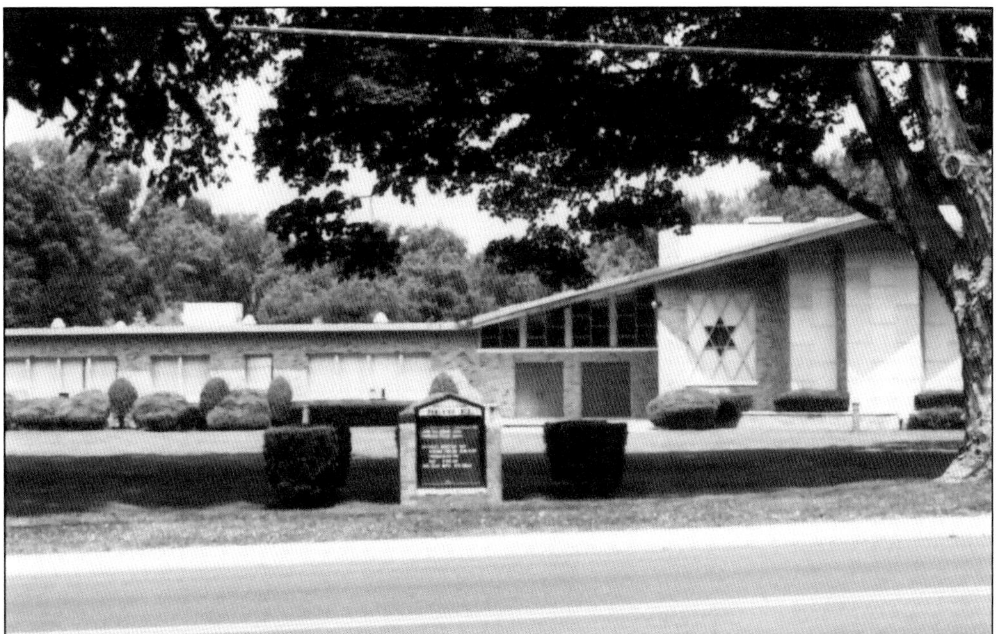

Congregation Beth El, on Fairfield Woods Road, is a Conservative congregation and one of two temples in Fairfield. The cornerstone for their synagogue, laid in 1961, came from Jerusalem. The Orthodox Congregation Ahavath Achim is located on Stratfield Road. (Rob Wallace photograph, 1997.)

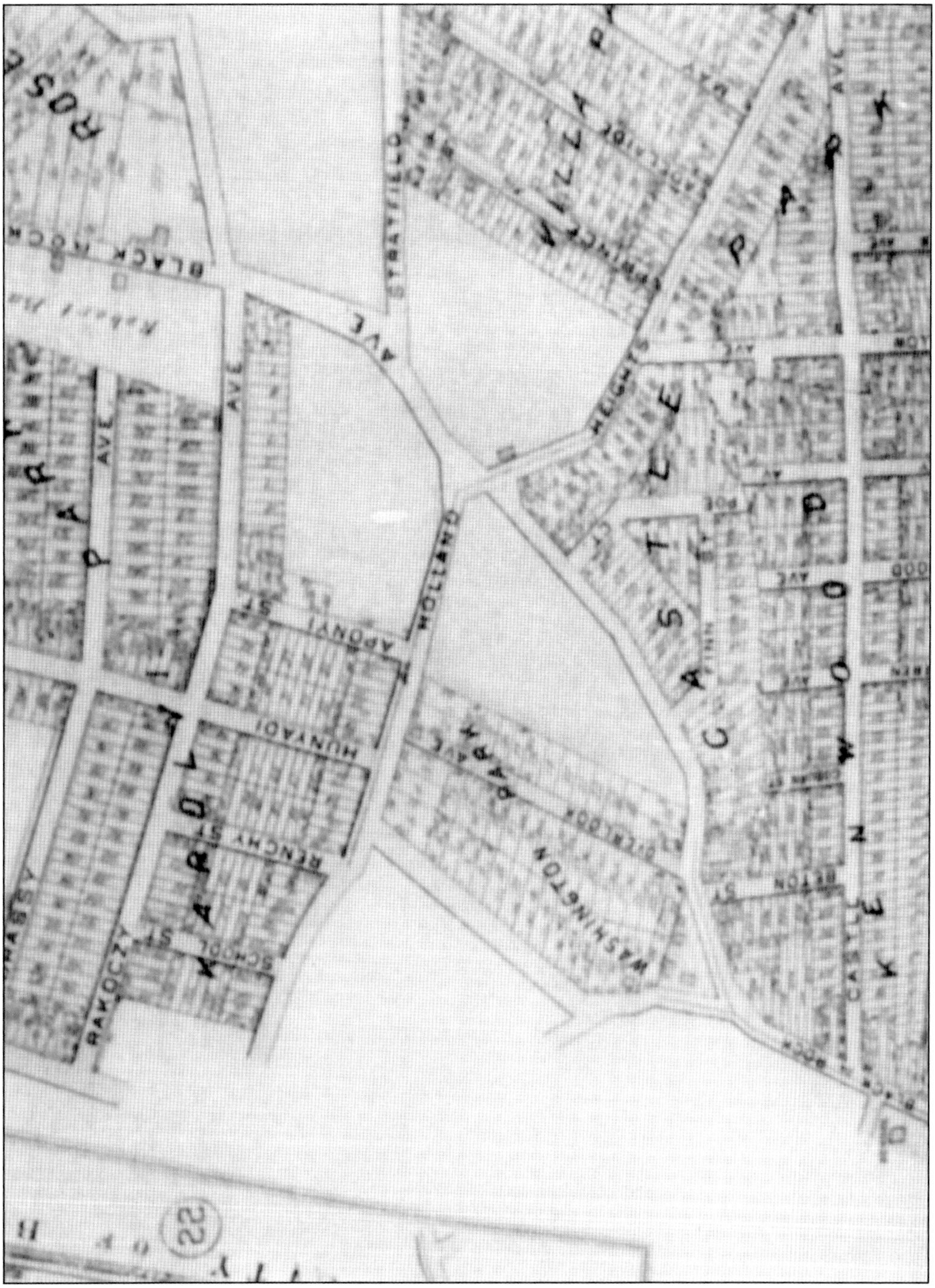

The plan for Karolyi Park near the intersection of Black Rock Turnpike and Jennings Road in Fairfield was created about 1914 by John Dezso, Samuel Greenbaum, and John Renchy, members of Bridgeport's Hungarian community. Streets were named for Hungarian military heroes such as Count Julius Andrassy and Prince Francis Rakoczi II of Transylvania. Land was divided into small lots and sold to workers in Bridgeport so they could enjoy the country air and plant a garden. Eventually, land owners built houses and moved permanently to Fairfield.

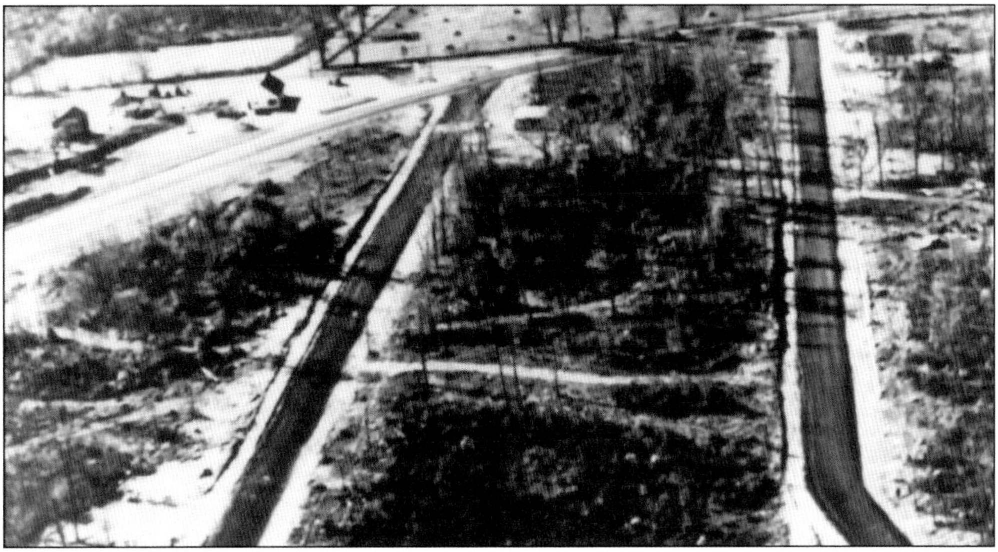

Farms dominated the landscape where Black Rock Turnpike and Tunxis Hill Cutoff are located today. In 1946 developers constructed Whitewood Road (left) and Candlewood Road (right) in preparation for what was to become a post-war building boom in Fairfield. This photograph was taken looking west toward Black Rock Turnpike. Industries in Bridgeport attracted a large number of workers who needed housing, and Fairfield developers were ready to answer the need. In 1954 more than three-quarters of the residents of the Stratfield area worked in Bridgeport.

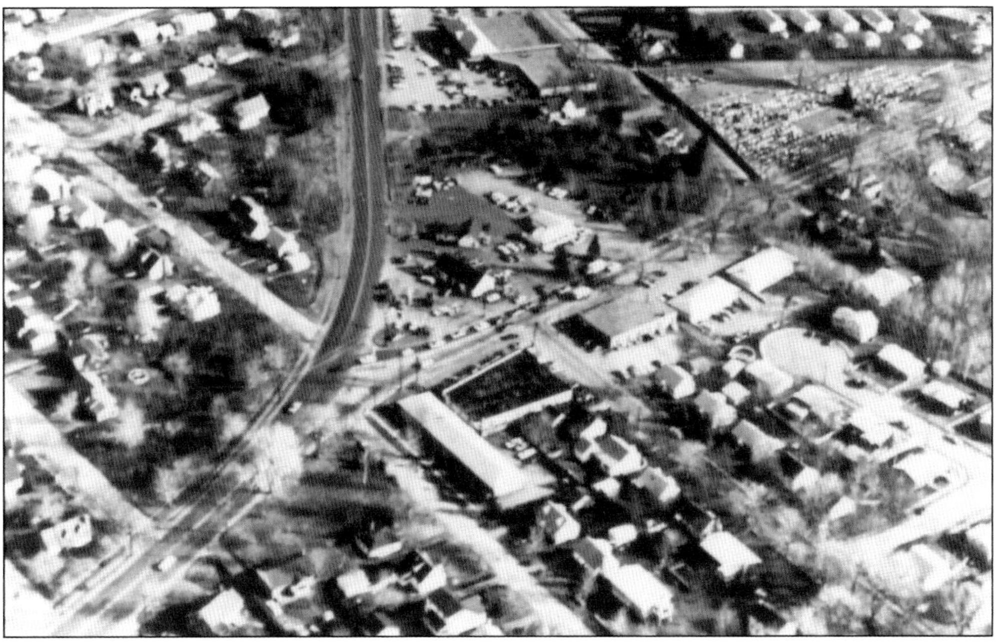

Twenty years later, Whitewood and Candlewood Roads (left center) are lined with single-family houses, making the transformation from farm to suburb nearly complete. This 1969 photograph is taken from almost the opposite perspective of the previous one. The intersection of Black Rock Turnpike and Tunxis Hill Road is commonly called Kuhn's Corner in reference to the Kuhn-Rady hot dog stand that once stood here.

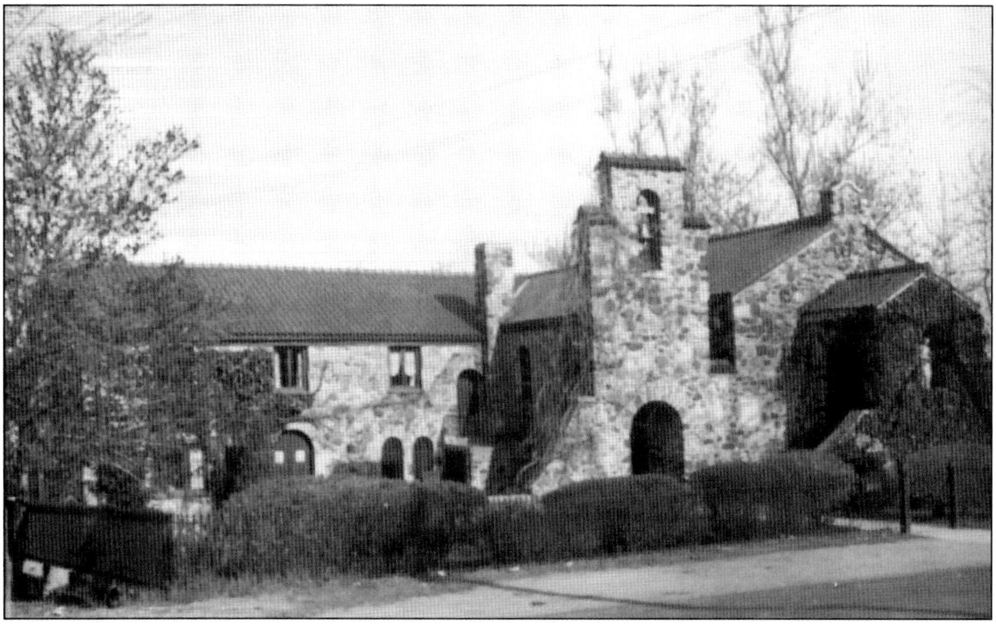

Trinity-St. Michael's Parish, an Episcopal church on Tunxis Hill Road, was established in 1922 as a mission of Trinity Episcopal Church in Bridgeport to minister to Italian immigrants in the area. This picture was taken in 1941 before the building was expanded.

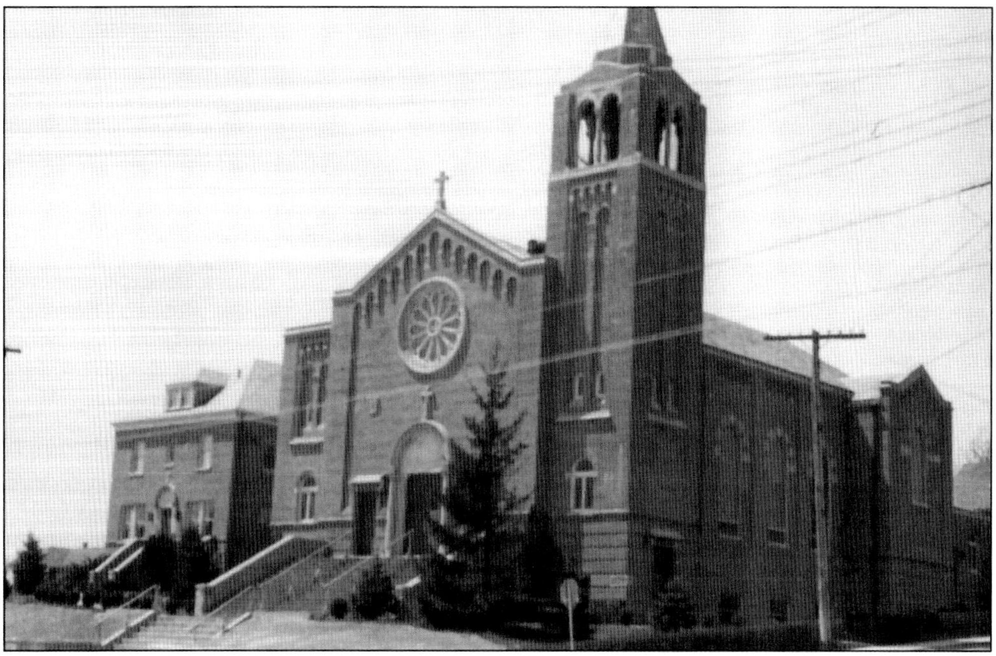

St. Emery's Roman Catholic Church is a landmark in the Tunxis Hill-Kings Highway area. The church, built in 1932 and depicted in 1941, still offers one Mass in Hungarian and Saturday Hungarian language classes for its children. Other parishes in Fairfield with Eastern European roots include St. Anthony's Roman Catholic Church on South Pine Creek (Polish), Calvin United Church on Kings Highway (Hungarian), and Holy Cross Church on Tahmore Drive, the only Slovenian church in New England.

Two

Friends and Neighbors

A place is its people. Friends and neighbors have been and are those who live next door, who offer security, who contribute to the community, and who, together, make Fairfield a place to call home.

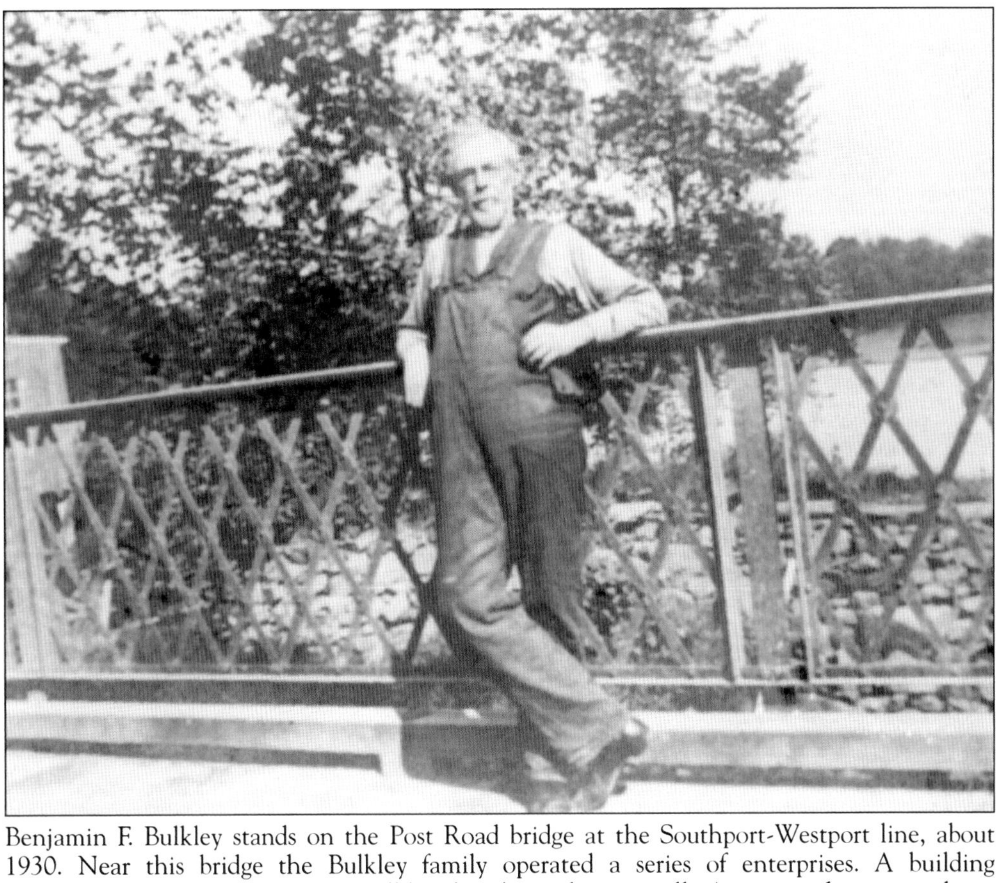

Benjamin F. Bulkley stands on the Post Road bridge at the Southport-Westport line, about 1930. Near this bridge the Bulkley family operated a series of enterprises. A building constructed in 1874 by Francis Bulkley first housed a sawmill. A wagon shop came later, and with the advent of the automobile, a garage. The Bulkley Mill, still standing, contains retail shops.

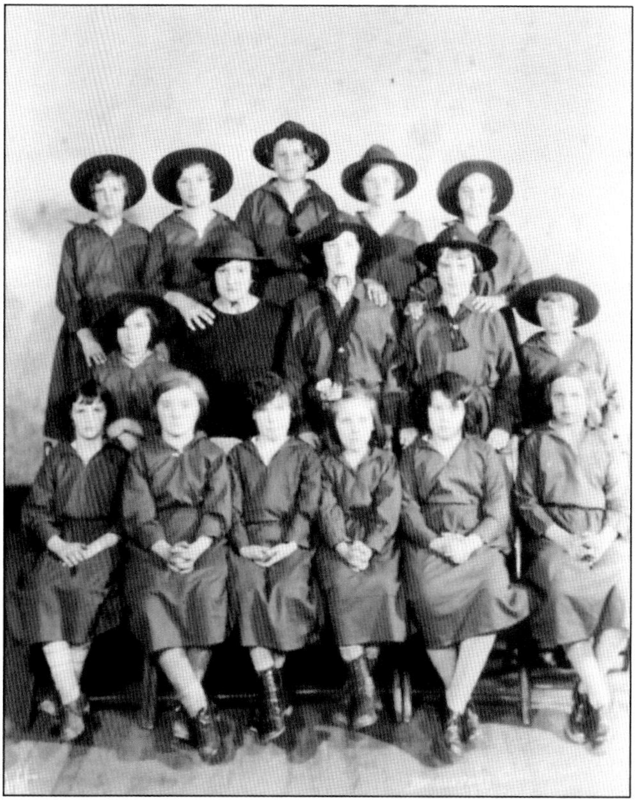

The Greenfield Hill Girl Scout Troop from Dwight School represented the town of Fairfield at the 1929 Bridgeport Girl Scout Festival. (The Corbit Studio photograph, Bridgeport.)

Neighborhood newsboys rode their bicycles to deliver the *Times-Star*. Joseph Simmons, kneeling in the center of the front row, donated this photograph, which was taken about 1935. Although this Bridgeport paper cost 12¢ a week, Joe confided that he tried to get 15¢ so he would have a tip. Fairfield depended on the larger papers in Bridgeport for its daily news.

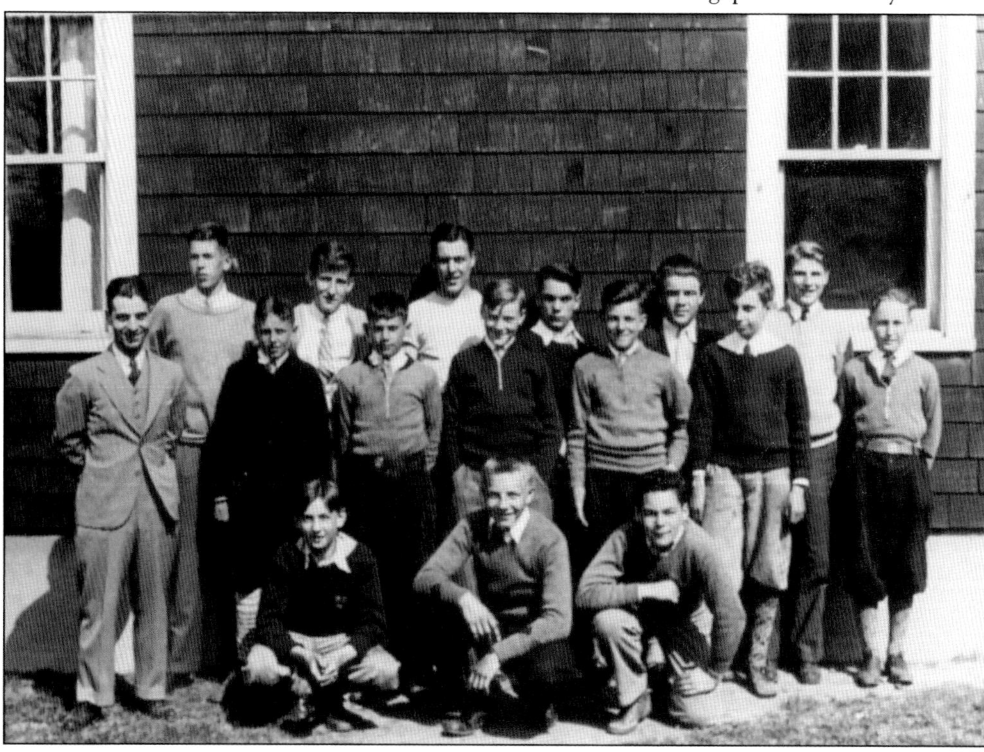

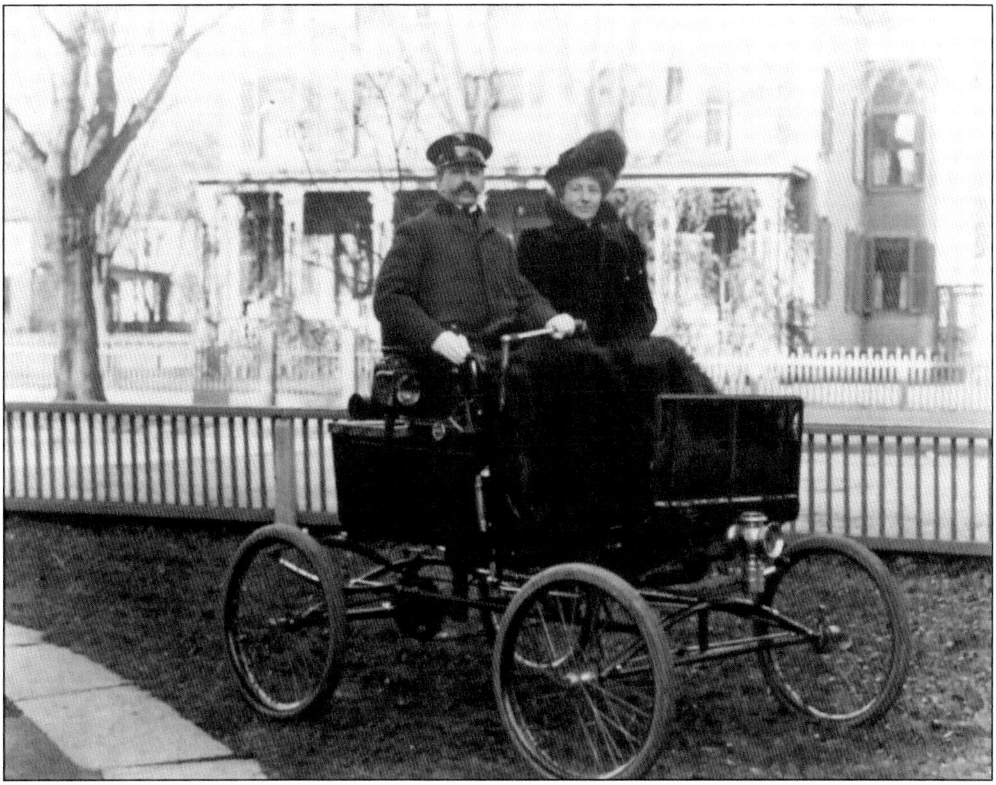

Andrew and Edith Riker pose in their fashionable automobile about 1900. Andrew Riker, designer of the Locomobile, was a pioneer in the U.S. automotive industry. At the age of twenty-eight, he established the Riker Automobile Company in New Jersey. He then made his way to Bridgeport with his gasoline-powered designs to work for Locomobile, which was making steam-powered vehicles. Riker chaired the committee that developed the first town plan for Fairfield.

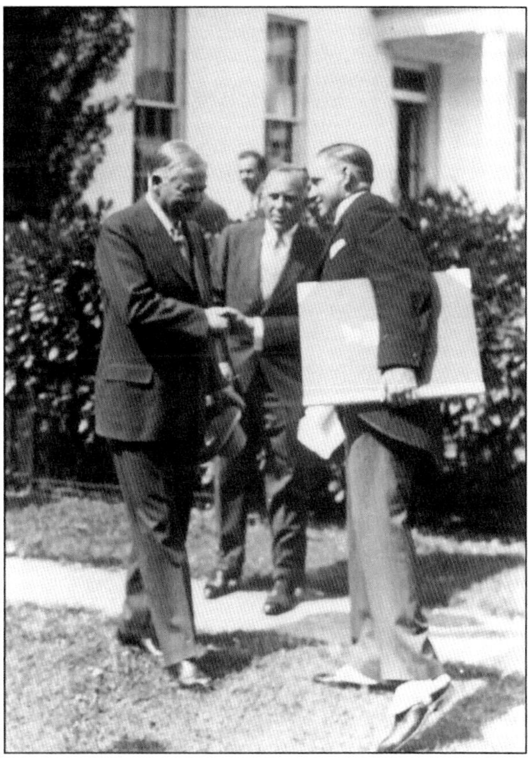

John Taylor Arms (right), noted Fairfield artist and president of the Society of American Etchers, presented President Herbert C. Hoover with a set of twenty etchings on September 15, 1932. The etchings, depicting scenes in the life of George Washington, were created by members of the society.

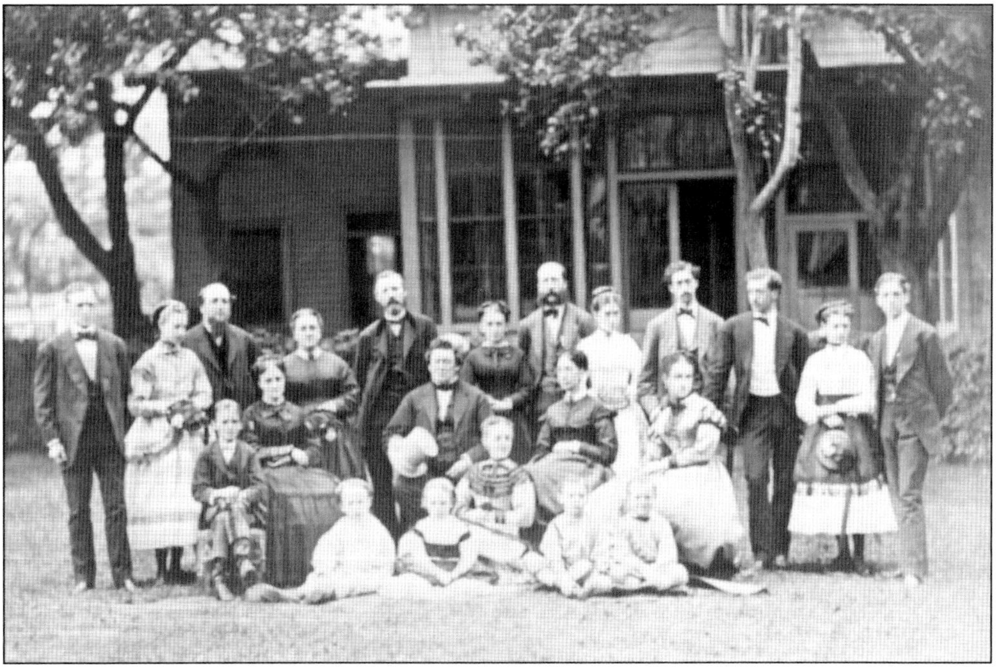

The Shelton family gathered for a group portrait in the 1870s. Philo Shelton was the rector of Trinity Episcopal Church when it was located on Mill Plain Green. His son and successor, William, started monthly services in Southport village, where the church later relocated. Regretfully, we have no identification for these family members.

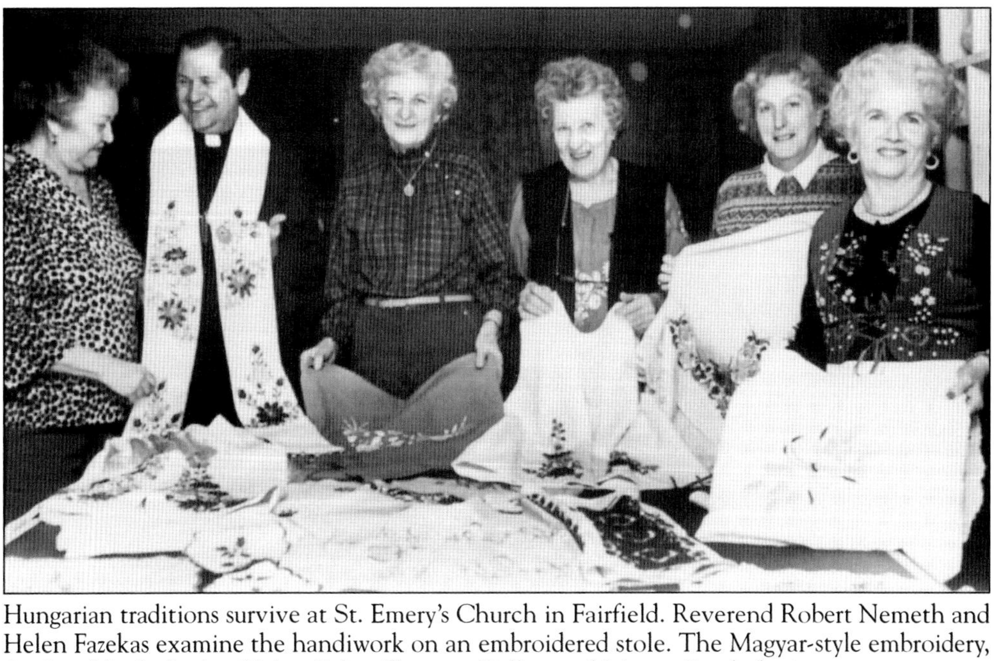

Hungarian traditions survive at St. Emery's Church in Fairfield. Reverend Robert Nemeth and Helen Fazekas examine the handiwork on an embroidered stole. The Magyar-style embroidery, displayed by Jo Lasko, Helen Sabo, Florence Ballas, and Marge Gaydosh, is very exacting—a single rose can take three hours to complete. (*Fairfield Citizen-News* photograph, 1984.)

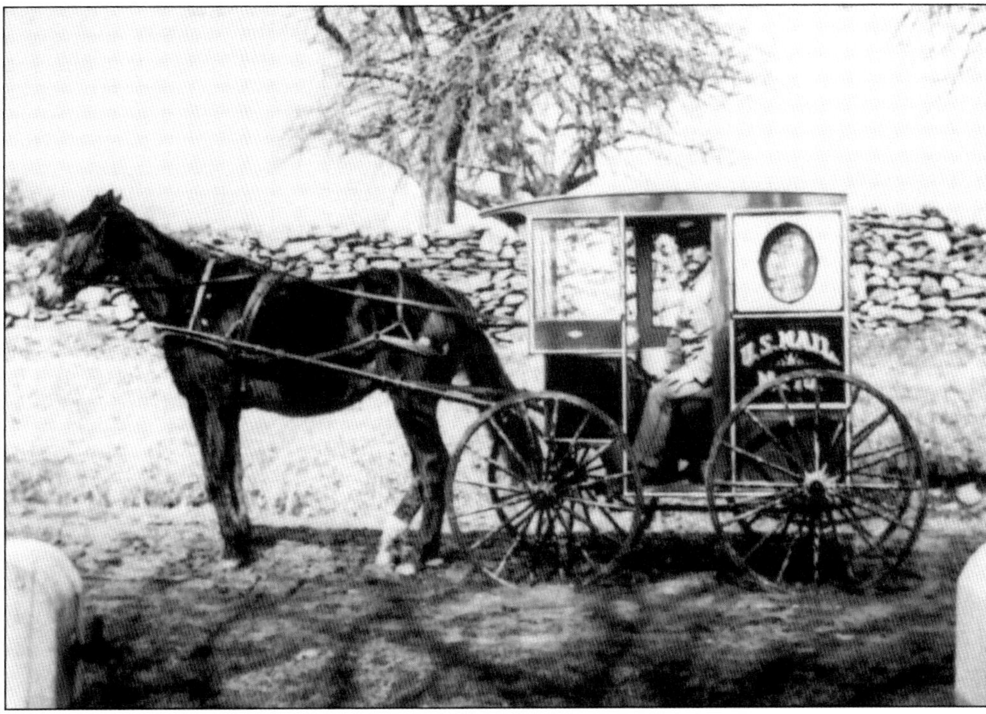

Christopher Columbus Wells became Fairfield's first rural free delivery mail carrier about 1896. Mail boxes such as this one made from a leather traveling case appeared with the advent of the new service.

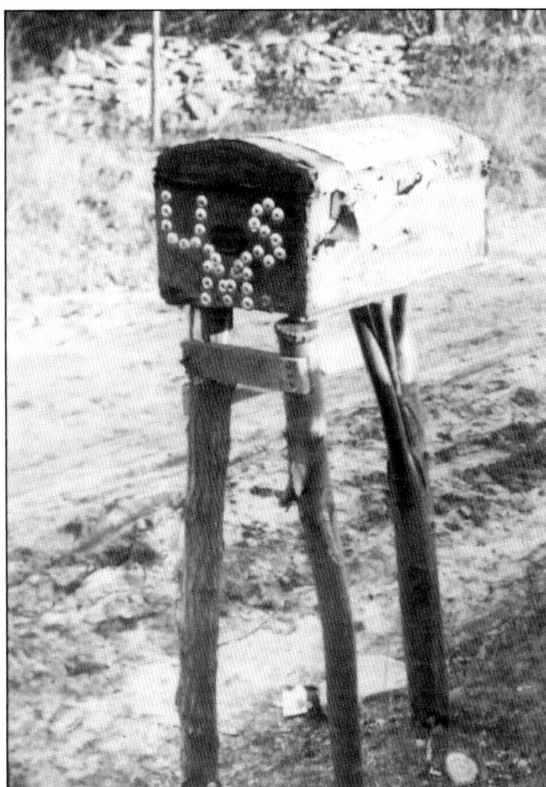

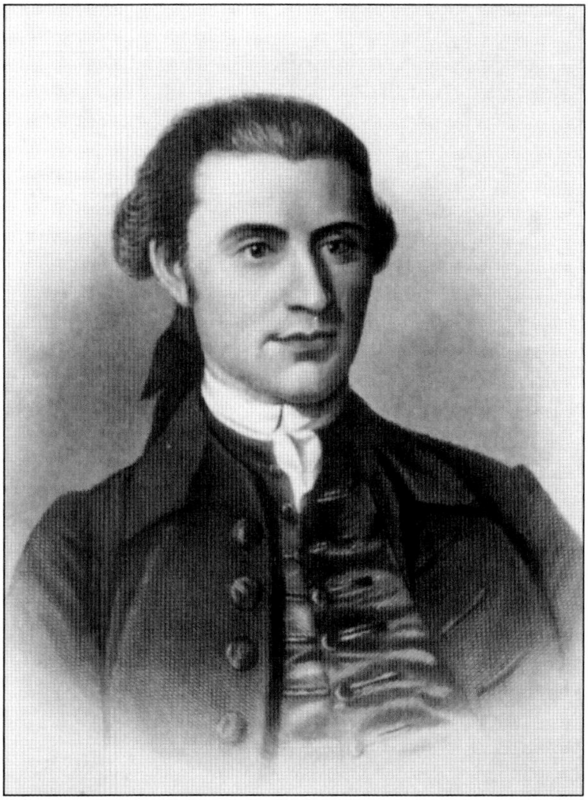

Thaddeus Burr, a cousin of Aaron Burr, owned the Burr Homestead on the Old Post Road. Thaddeus served as Fairfield's deputy to the General Court and as a member of the Council of Safety during the Revolutionary War. His home was described by a local historian as "the center of vigorous patriotic propaganda for the Independence of the Colonies." (E.C. Betts, photograph of an engraving.)

The Burr family holds a reunion at their Fairfield Beach cottage, the Quiet, on July 13, 1906. Members of the Burr family owned at least six beach cottages at the turn of the century, including Sand Reef, Wohsuppee, and the Racket.

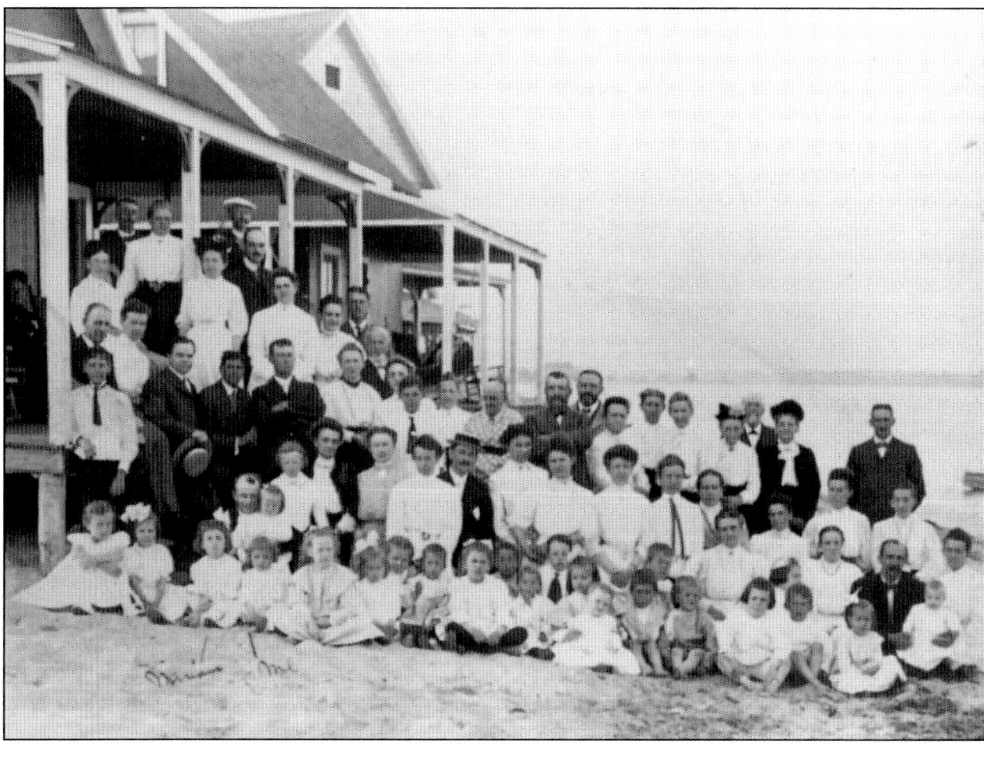

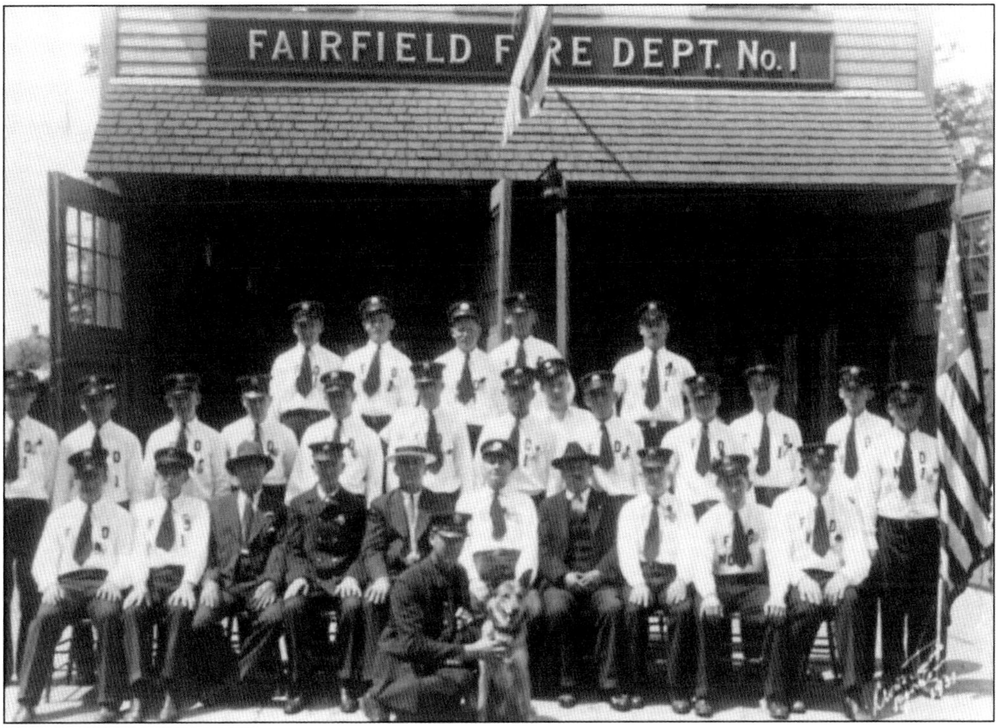

Fairfield's first fire company was established September 11, 1893, when thirteen men met at Otto Jacoby's barbershop. In 1928 the Town formed a fire commission to establish standards of operation in each of the fire districts. Each company was led by a volunteer chief; the first town-wide fire chief, Joseph Stopa, was hired in 1957. This view of Fairfield Fire Station No. 1 on Reef Road was taken in 1933. A replacement for the first structure, this station consisted of part of the original Sherman School and is now the Firehouse Deli.

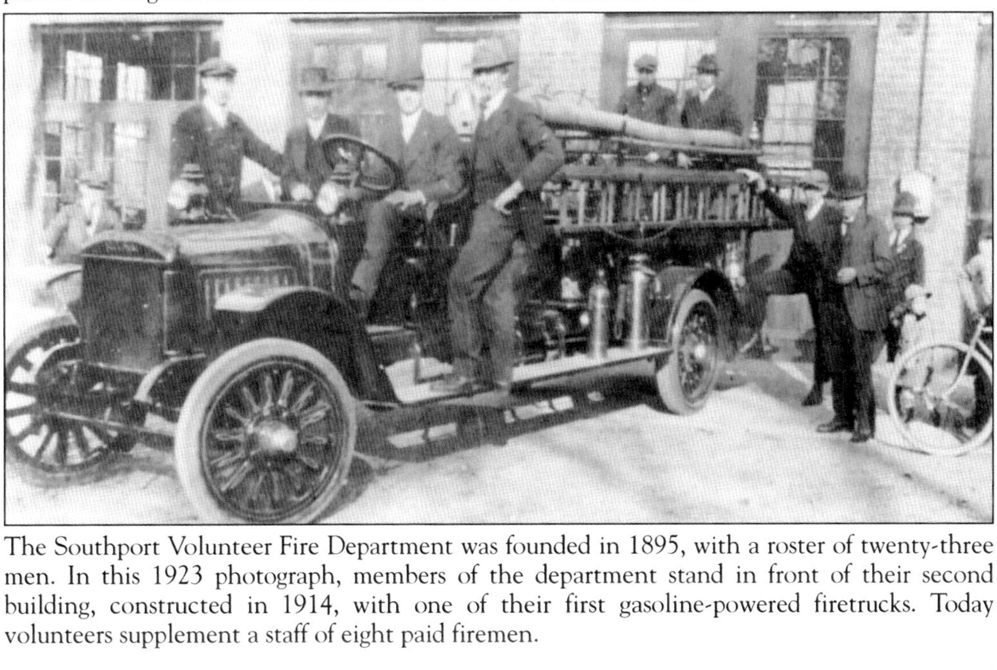

The Southport Volunteer Fire Department was founded in 1895, with a roster of twenty-three men. In this 1923 photograph, members of the department stand in front of their second building, constructed in 1914, with one of their first gasoline-powered firetrucks. Today volunteers supplement a staff of eight paid firemen.

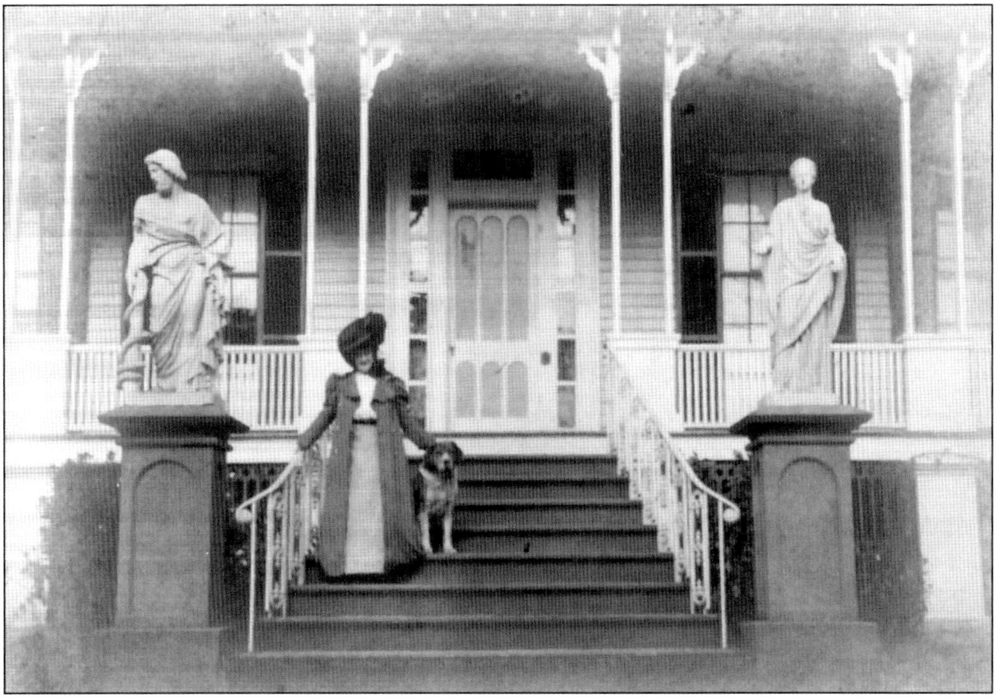

Pearl Richards visits the Browns at 200 Unquowa Road in 1907. This residence became Fairfield's first high school in 1916 and is now the site of the Tomlinson Middle School, a building dating from 1924. Annie B. Jennings gave the house to the Town so students would no longer have to take the trolley to Bridgeport.

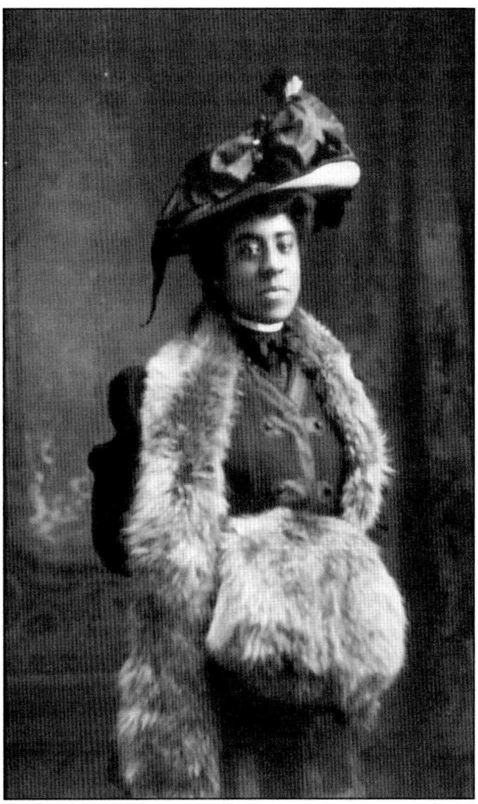

May F. Price gave her photographed portrait to her neighbors, Ida and William Miller. May died in 1929 at the age of forty-eight. She lived on Round Hill Road in a neighborhood with a number of African-American families, many of whom were related. (Charles Cochran photograph, *c.* 1900.)

Colonel Paul Daly (right) stands with his son, Captain Michael Daly, who won the Congressional Medal of Honor at the age of twenty for his service in World War II. Colonel Daly, who served in both World Wars I and II, was decorated by the United States, France, and Italy.

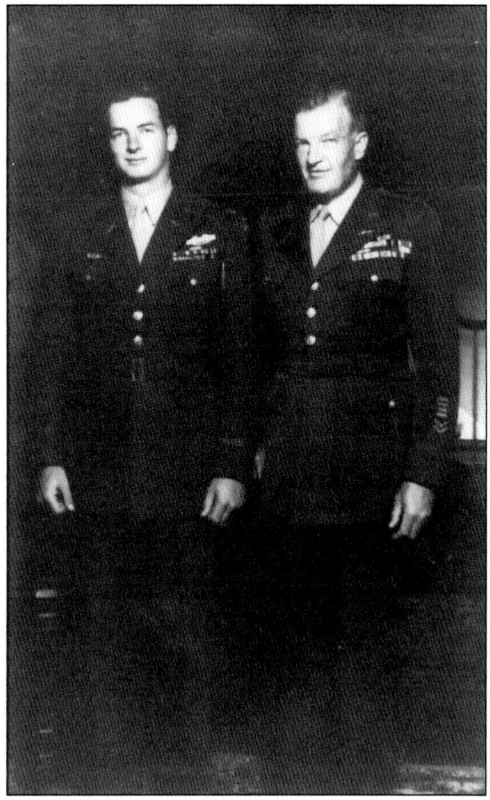

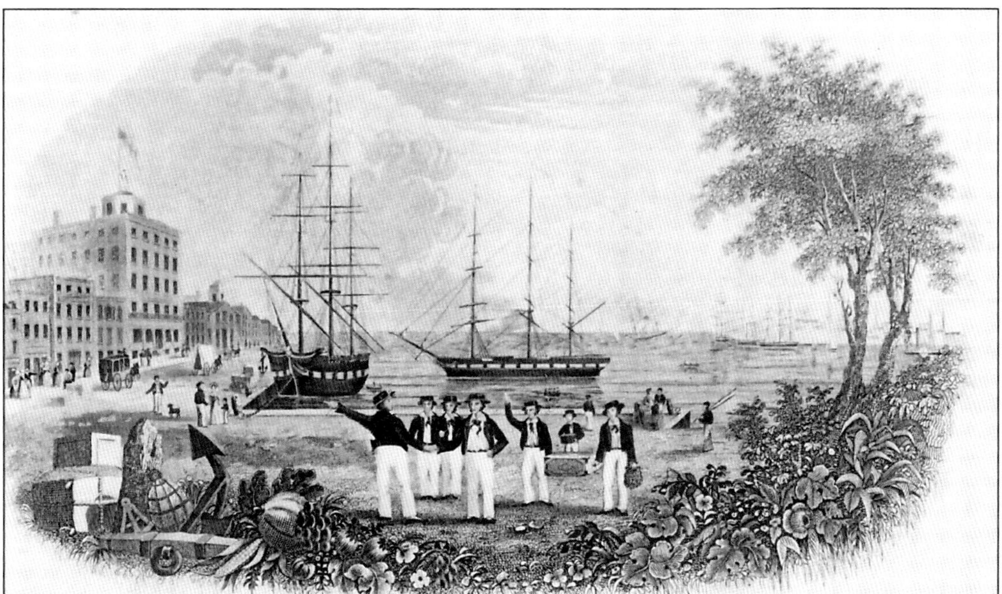

William H. Burr's mother made the donation for his life membership in the American Seamen's Friend Society on April 21, 1859. (Membership certificate.)

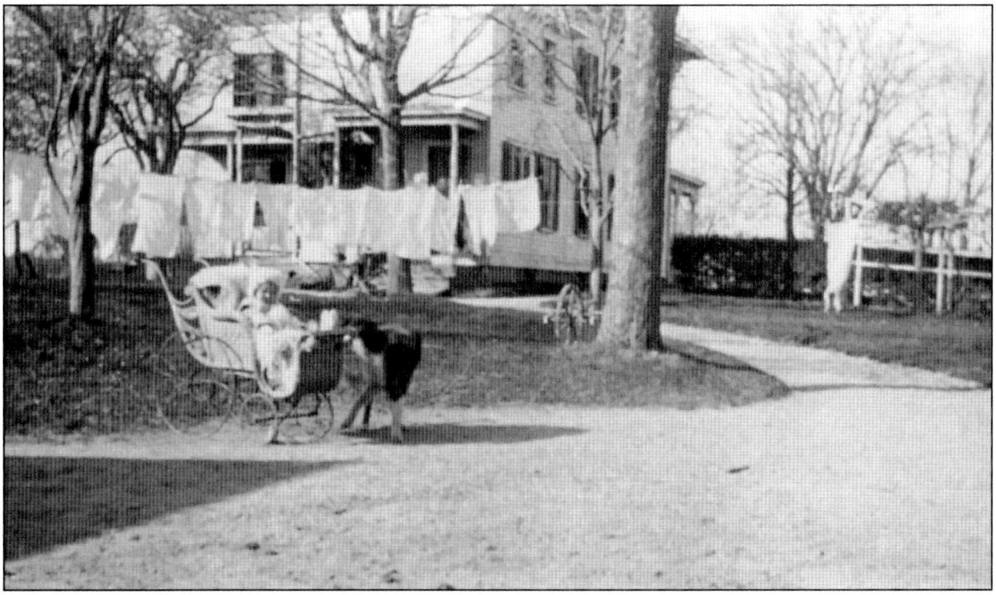

Rhoda Turney Sharps peers from her carriage in front of the Turney homestead on the Old Post Road, under the supervision of the family dog. The progenitor of the family, Benjamin Turney, settled in Fairfield in 1644. The Turney name has been given to a creek and to a road at the east end of Fairfield where the family established their homes. (Cyanotype, *c.* 1902.)

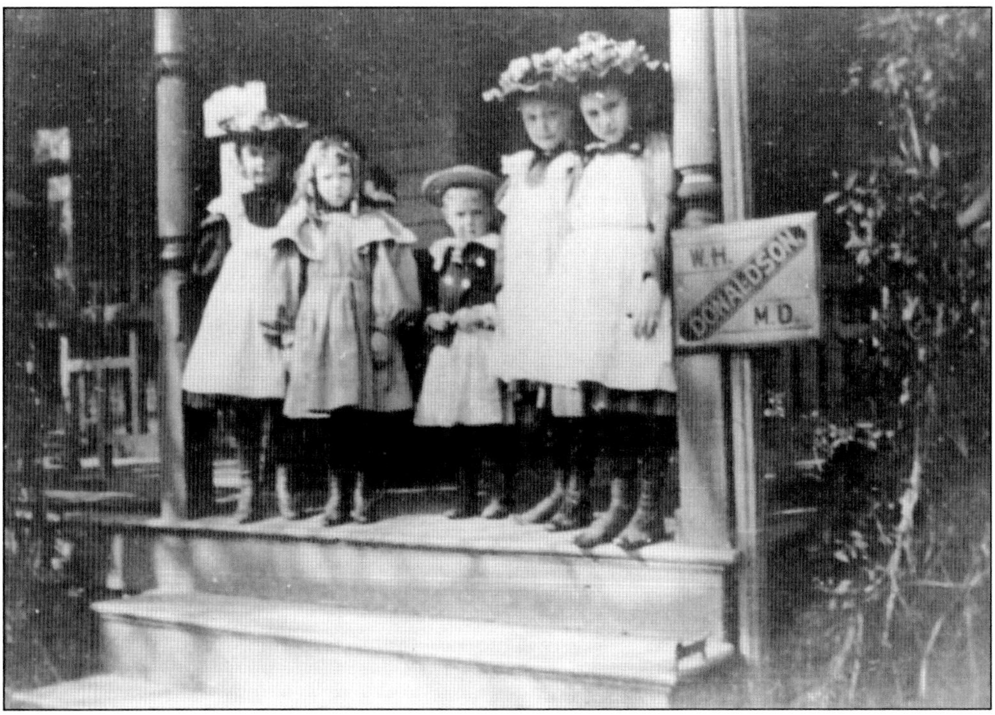

Five friends gather on Dr. William H. Donaldson's front porch, May 1897. They are Mabel, Ethel, John, Rachel, and Marian. Dr. Donaldson lived on the Old Post Road across from the library. He was an active participant in town meetings and in the early twentieth century served as the town health officer.

Ida Miller, wife of farmer William H. Miller, lived at 368 Round Hill Road and baked the communion bread for her church, the First Church Congregational. This 1870s cabinet card was made at Montignani Photo Studio, Bridgeport.

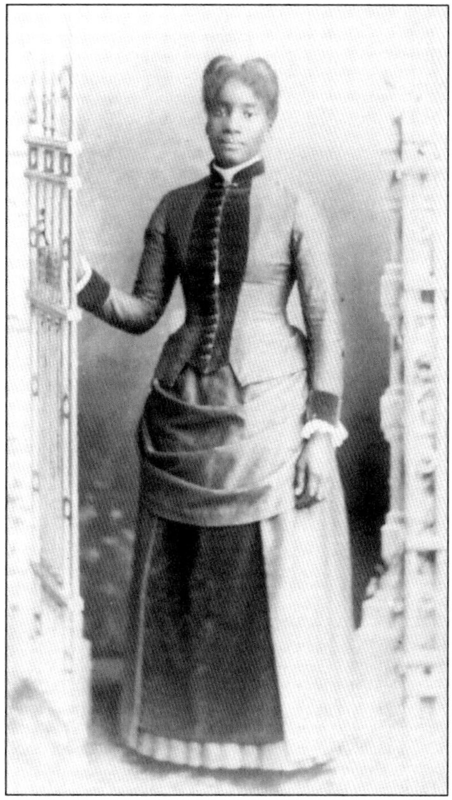

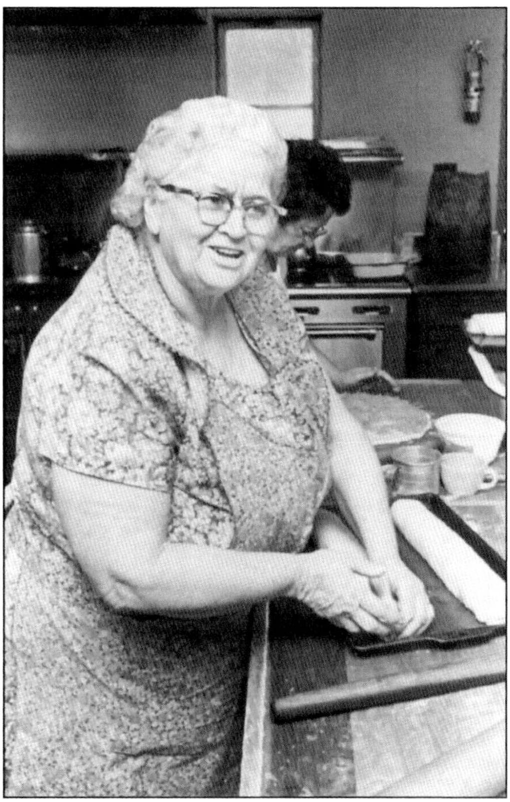

Helen Racz shapes poppy seed rolls for a parish dinner at St. Emery's Church. Poppy seeds are traditionally used in Hungarian baked goods at Christmas and Easter. (*Fairfield Citizen-News* photograph, c. 1980.)

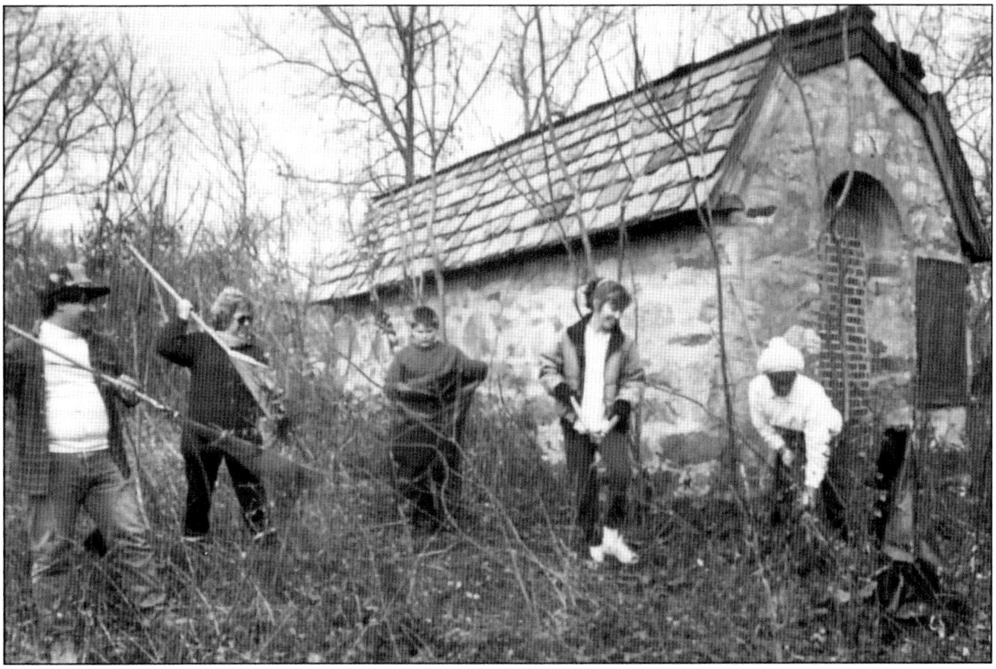

The volunteer clean-up crew of Brian and Elaine Kaufman, Aaron Radder, and Janice and Doris Koehler (from left to right) came from the members of the Children of the American Revolution and Boy Scout Troop 82. Fairfield residents built the Powder House, seen in the background, in response to the War of 1812 when they feared another invasion by the British.

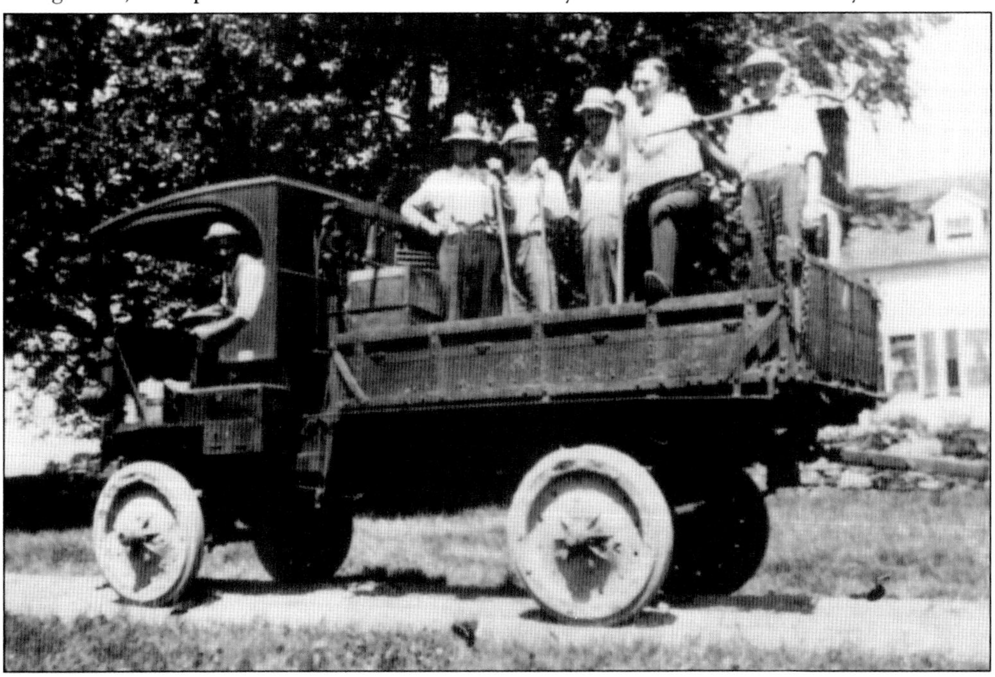

John Horn, pictured in 1925, was a farmer who later became a landscape gardener. His change in profession illustrates the transition from agricultural use of the land to domestic landscaping—from using the land to decorating it.

George Washington, a.k.a. Sam Morehouse, poses for a postcard about 1908. Fairfield's colonial history has captured the imagination of the town's residents for generations.

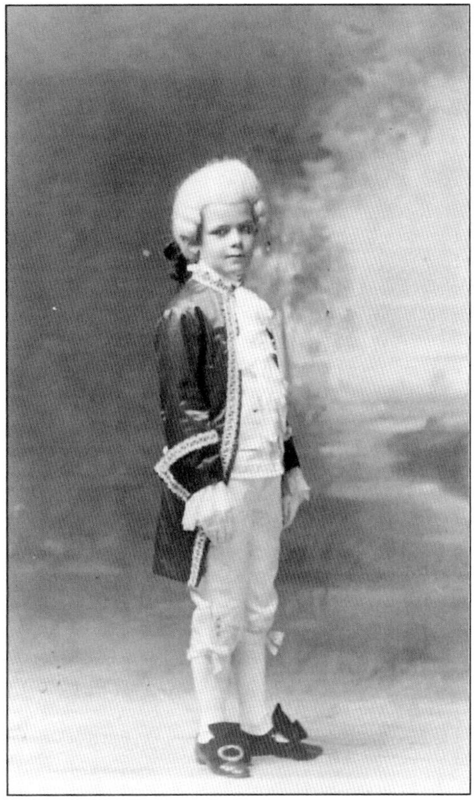

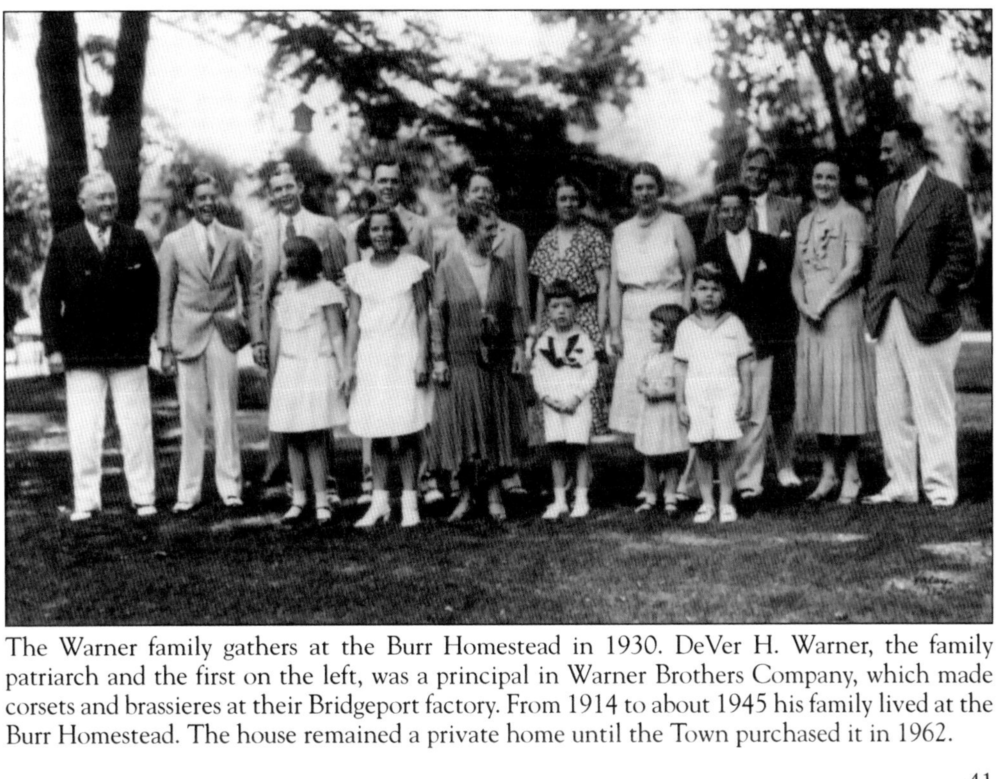

The Warner family gathers at the Burr Homestead in 1930. DeVer H. Warner, the family patriarch and the first on the left, was a principal in Warner Brothers Company, which made corsets and brassieres at their Bridgeport factory. From 1914 to about 1945 his family lived at the Burr Homestead. The house remained a private home until the Town purchased it in 1962.

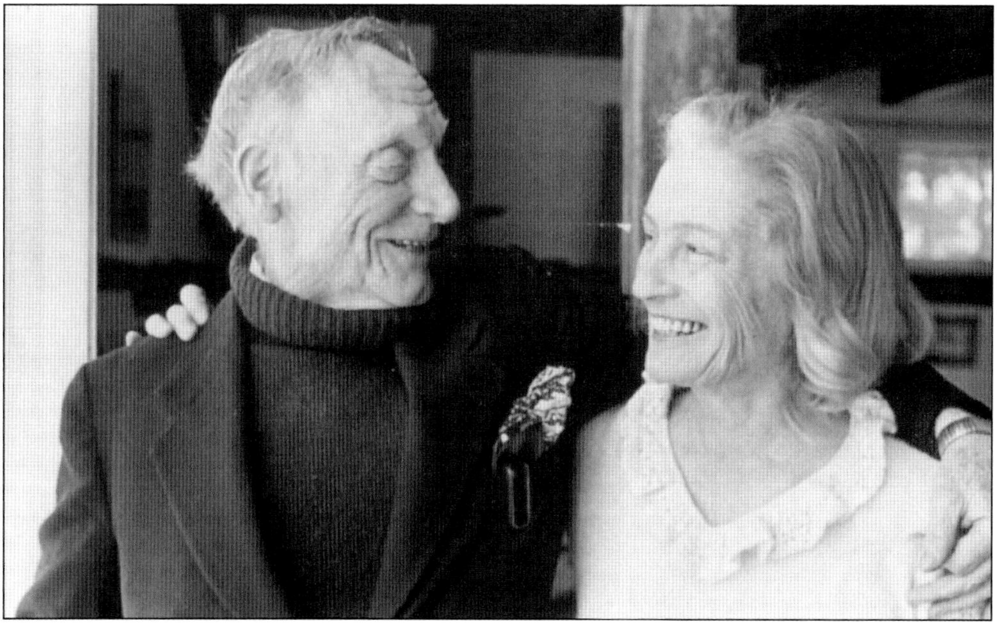

Noted authors Robert Penn Warren and Eleanor Clark made their home on Redding Road in Fairfield. Warren won numerous prizes, including the Guggenheim Fellowship and the Pulitzer Prize for fiction for *All the King's Men* (1947). Clark was also a Guggenheim Fellow and received the National Book Award in 1965 for *The Oysters of Lacmariaquer*.

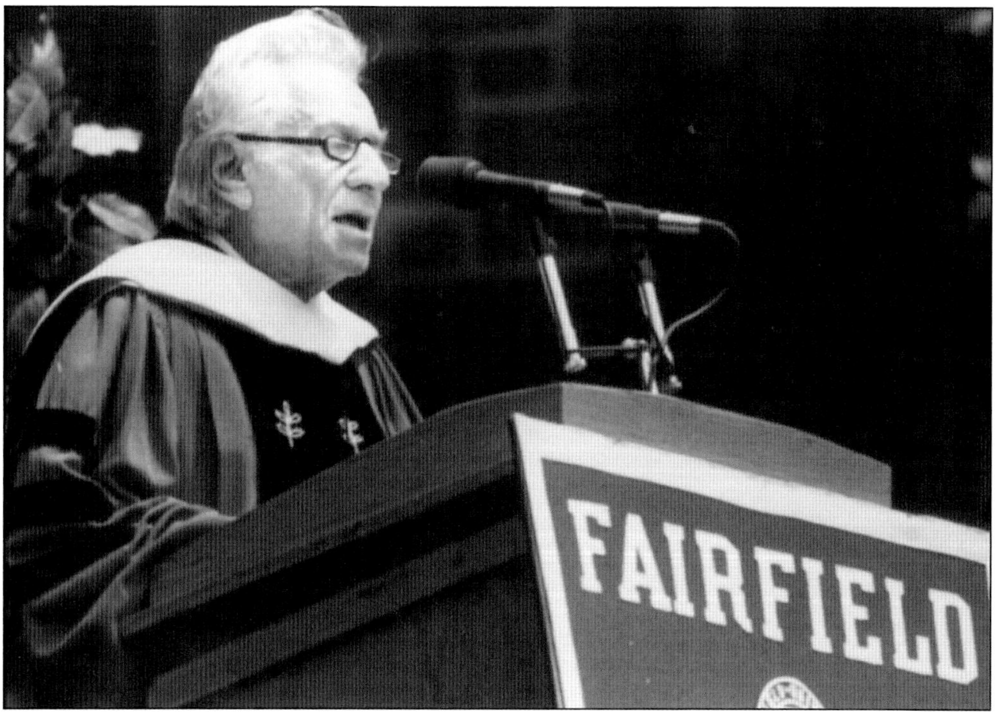

The late composer and conductor Leonard Bernstein, a longtime Fairfield resident, was awarded an honorary degree at Fairfield University's 1989 commencement. (*Fairfield Citizen-News* photograph.)

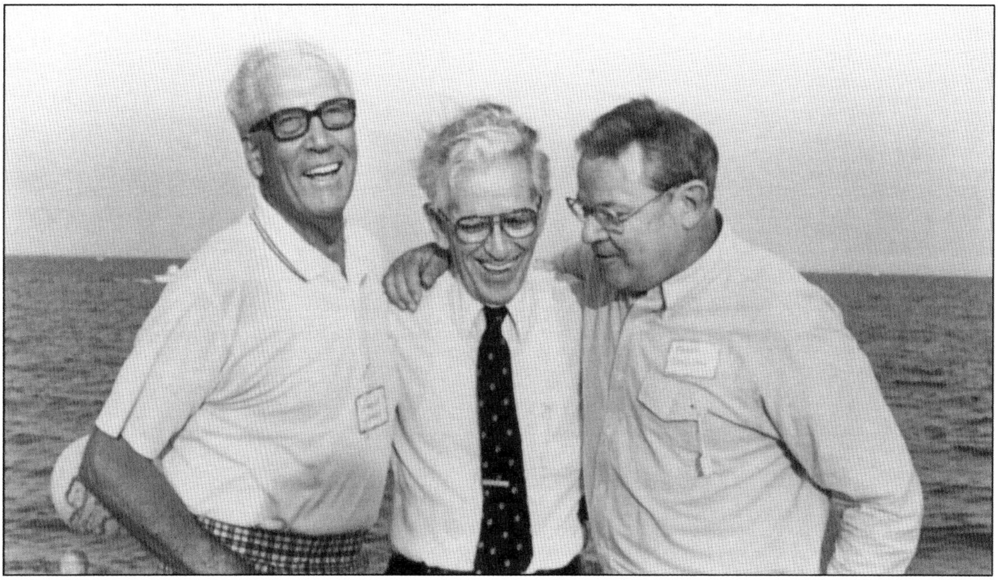

John J. Sullivan (center) shares a moment of levity at a 1983 Fairfield Chamber of Commerce clambake. On the left is Harold Harris, executive director of the Chamber, and on the right is Frank Donovan of General Electric Co. Sullivan, a Democrat, was Fairfield's first selectman for twenty-four years (twelve terms). (*Fairfield Citizen-News* photograph.)

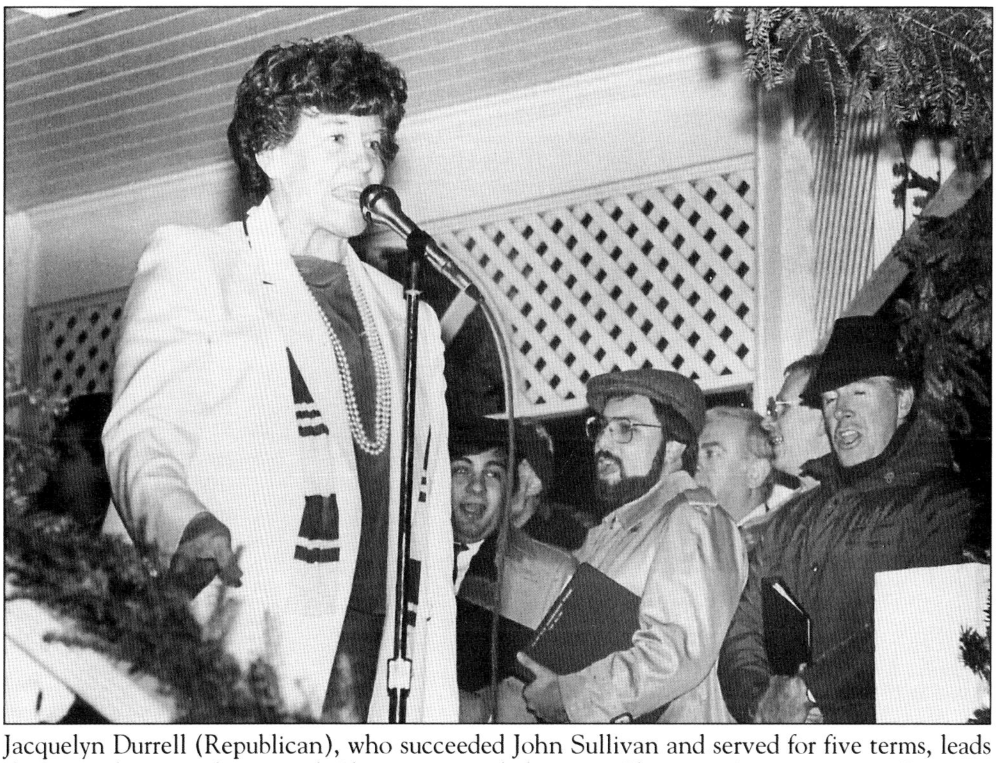

Jacquelyn Durrell (Republican), who succeeded John Sullivan and served for five terms, leads the countdown to the annual Christmas tree lighting at Sherman Green in 1990. Between them, Sullivan and Durrell administered the town of Fairfield for more than a third of a century. (*Fairfield Citizen-News* photograph.)

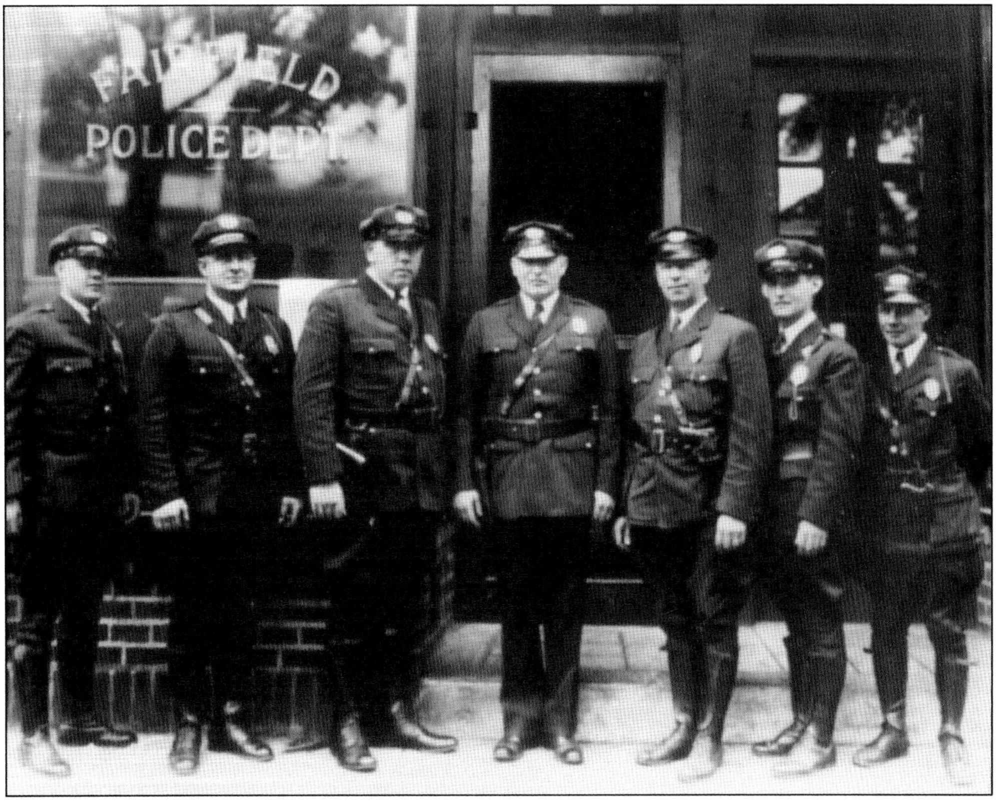

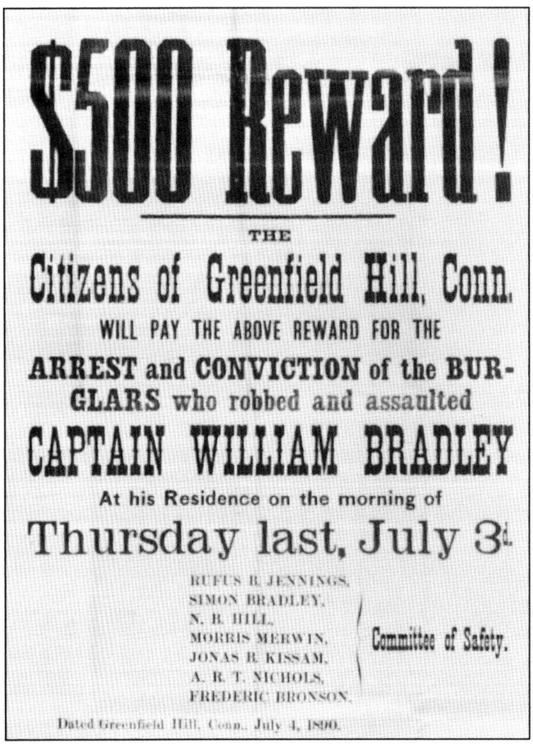

$500 Reward!

THE

Citizens of Greenfield Hill, Conn.

WILL PAY THE ABOVE REWARD FOR THE

ARREST and CONVICTION of the BURGLARS who robbed and assaulted

CAPTAIN WILLIAM BRADLEY

At his Residence on the morning of

Thursday last, July 3d.

RUFUS B. JENNINGS,
SIMON BRADLEY,
N. B. HILL,
MORRIS MERWIN,
JONAS B. KISSAM,
A. B. T. NICHOLS,
FREDERIC BRONSON,
Committee of Safety.

Dated Greenfield Hill, Conn., July 4, 1890.

The first Fairfield Police Department, with headquarters at 633 Post Road, was organized September 1, 1930. The initial force was composed of (from left to right) Christian Schick, Eugene Burns, Thomas Shaughnessy, Chief Arthur Bennett, Charles Gandorf, Thomas Murphy, and William T. Burr. Constables maintained the law prior to the creation of a police force.

Not all policing was left to the authorities. This broadside offers a reward for the arrest and conviction of Greenfield Hill burglars. The offer is made by an extra-legal "citizen police force" in 1890.

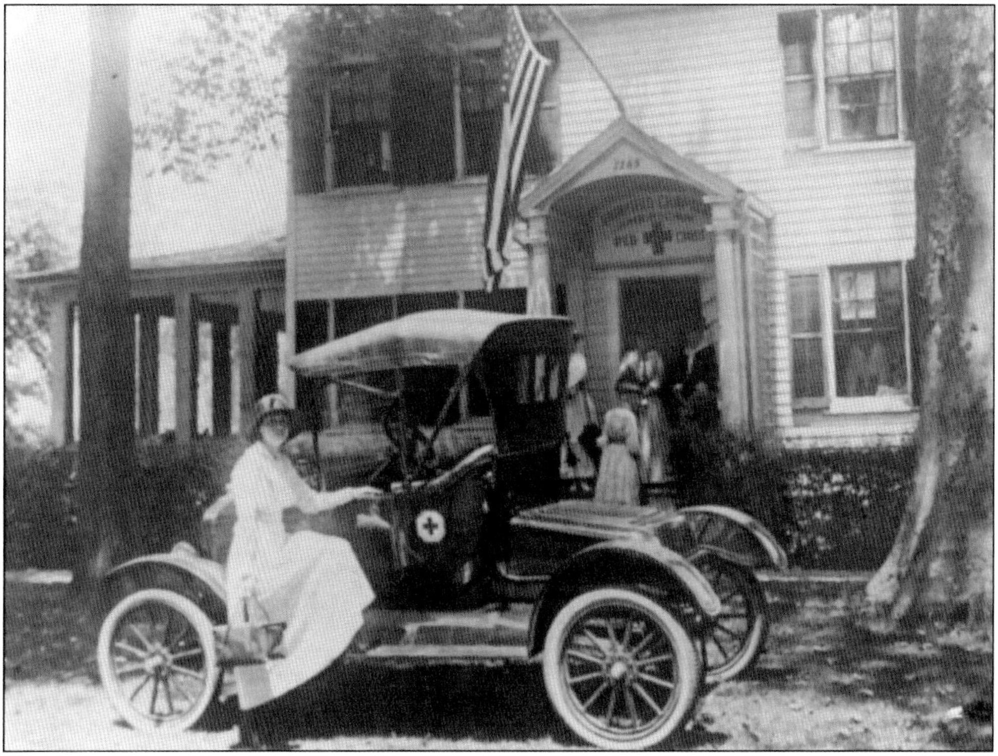

During World War I, members of the Fairfield Chapter of the American Red Cross made surgical dressings and hospital garments at their headquarters in the Justin Hobart house on Beach Road. Annie B. Jennings, who owned the house, lent it to the Red Cross for its war relief work.

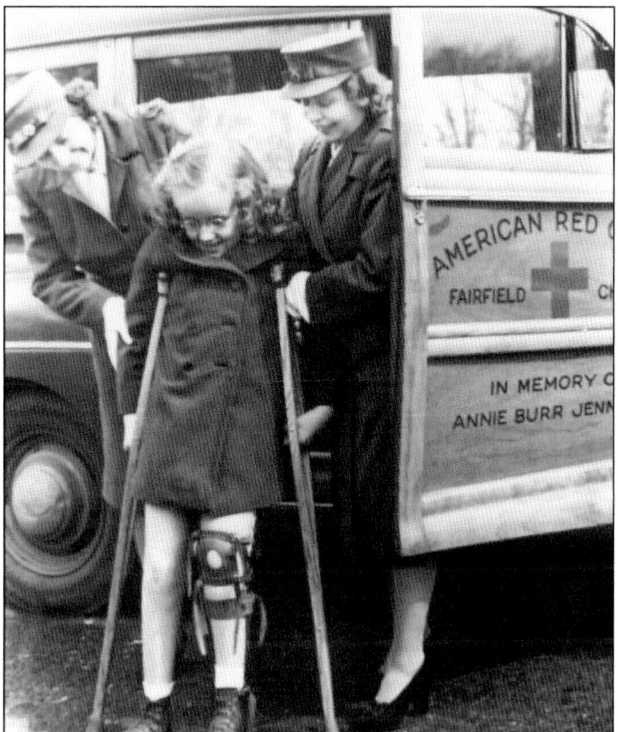

Captain Ruth Gallup (left) and Private Olga Kilborn (right) of the Red Cross Motor Corps assist Mary Jane Swanson. Among the services provided by the Motor Corps during World War II was the transportation of handicapped children on outings and for treatment. Fairfield's chapter was fortunate to have its own vehicle, donated by Annie B. Jennings. (George Weising photograph, *c.* 1945.)

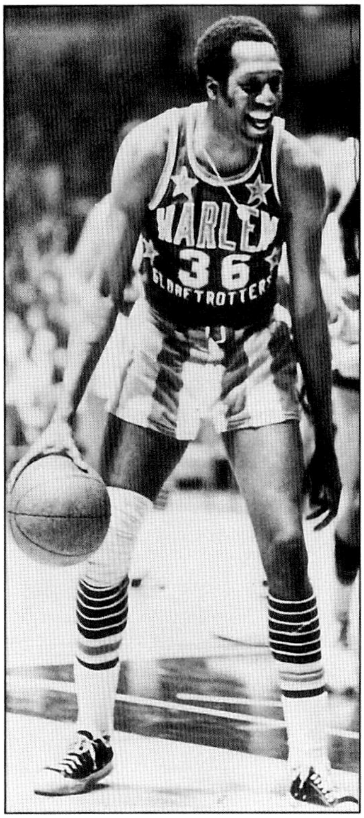

Meadowlark Lemon, "clown prince" of basketball and Fairfield resident, entertained millions as the captain of the Harlem Globetrotters from 1954 to 1978. (*Fairfield Citizen-News* photograph.)

September 8, 1952, was proclaimed Julius Boros Day in Fairfield in honor of the 1952 winner of the U.S. Open and the Tam O'Shanter golf championships. This scene is the testimonial dinner at Brooklawn Country Club. Boros is the third person from the right. (Courtesy of Brooklawn Country Club.)

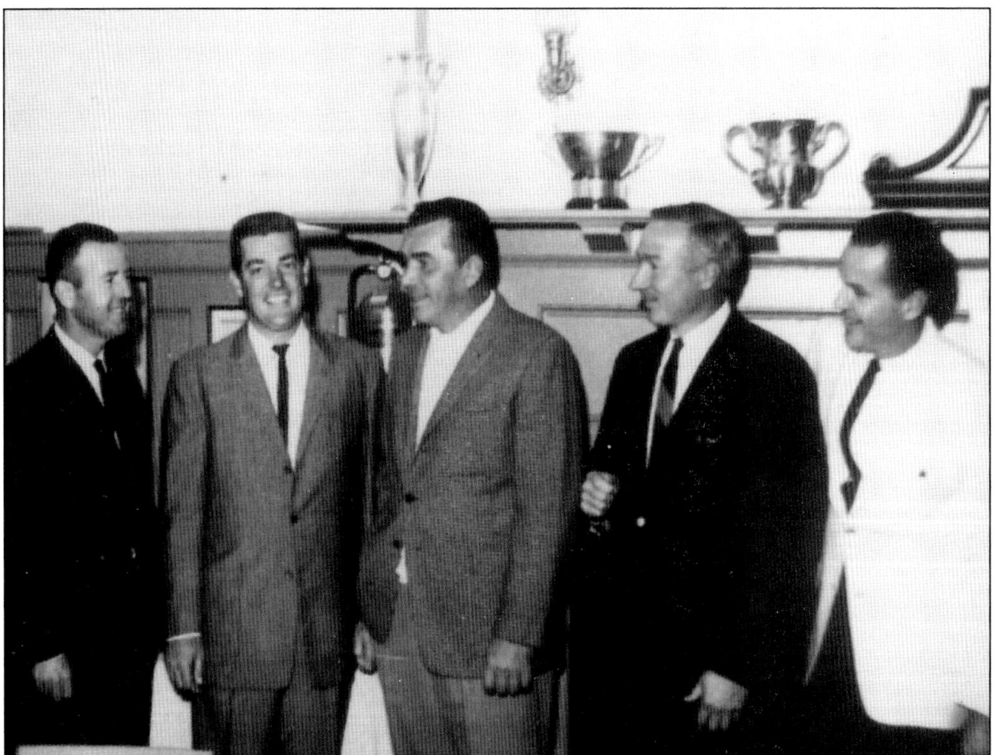

Charles Nagy, a graduate of Fairfield High School, is one of five starting pitchers for the Cleveland Indians. He played for the 1988 U.S. Olympic team that won the gold medal, was the number one pick of Cleveland in the 1988 June draft, and has pitched in two All-Star games and a World Series. (Mark Conrad photograph, 1997; courtesy of *Fairfield Citizen-News*.)

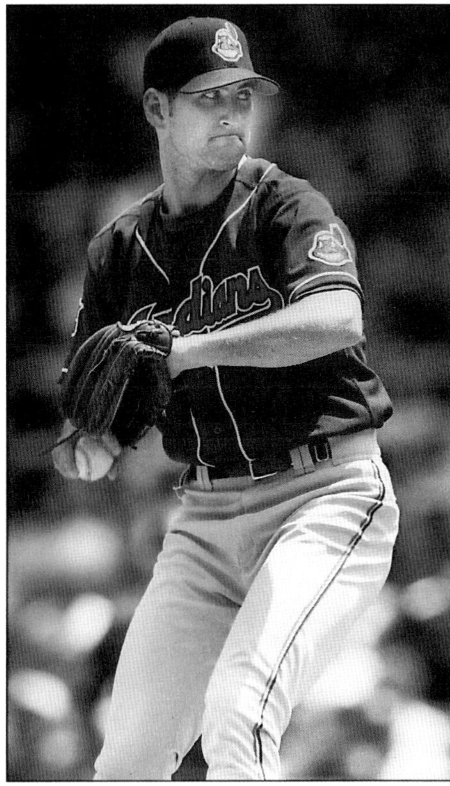

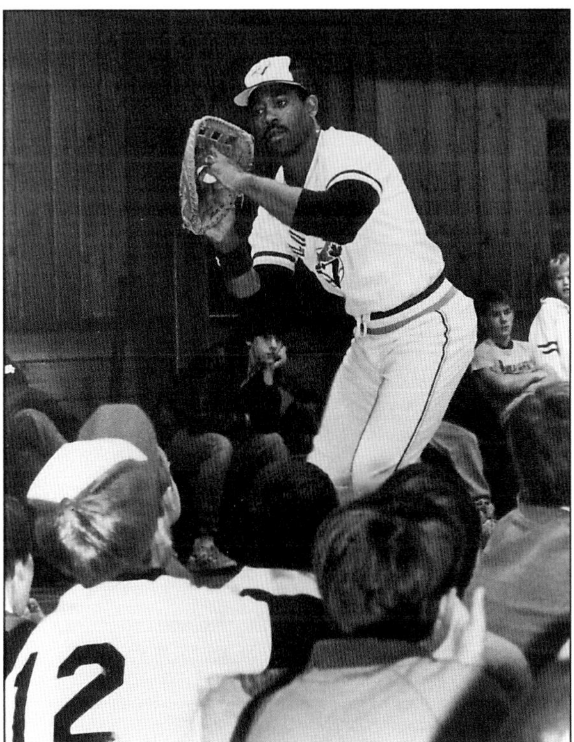

Fairfield resident Willy Upshaw, in his Toronto Blue Jays home uniform, demonstrates the proper way to catch a ball at a 1988 workshop. Upshaw is now the hitting coach for the Blue Jays. (*Fairfield Citizen-News*, Kat G. Ward photograph.)

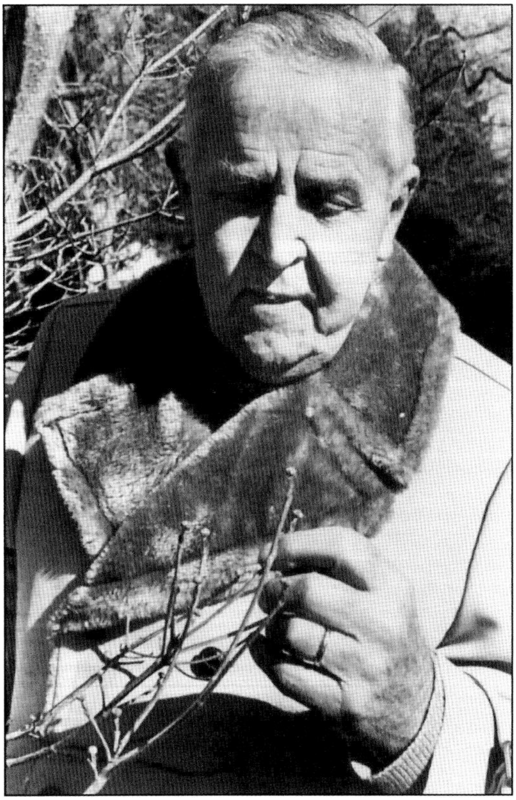

Lloyd Godfrey examines dogwood buds. Lloyd nurtured the Greenfield Hill dogwoods for decades so they would be at their best for the annual Dogwood Festival. He maintained a garden shop on the Post Road and ran a landscape gardening business. (*Fairfield Citizen-News* photograph, c. 1977.)

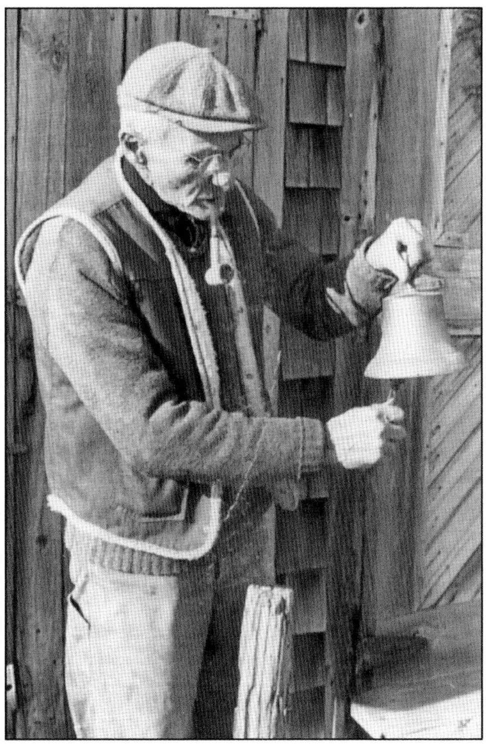

For more than sixty years Howard Burr greeted visitors to Ye Yacht Yard, the town marina in Southport. He hauled and launched boats, took care of moorings, installed a gasoline tank, and generally kept things going at the boatyard. Characterized as a "feisty Yankee," Howard was known for his corncob pipe and his love of children. (*Fairfield Citizen-News* photograph, c. 1987.)

Three

Home Fair Home

Fairfield is noted for its historic homes. Although they constitute a minority of the houses, they are a major contributor to the vision of Fairfield as a colonial town. In reality, Fairfield, as other New England communities, is a showcase of architectural styles from the seventeenth-century saltbox to the Gothic cottage, and from World War II housing to today's version of the Colonial Revival.

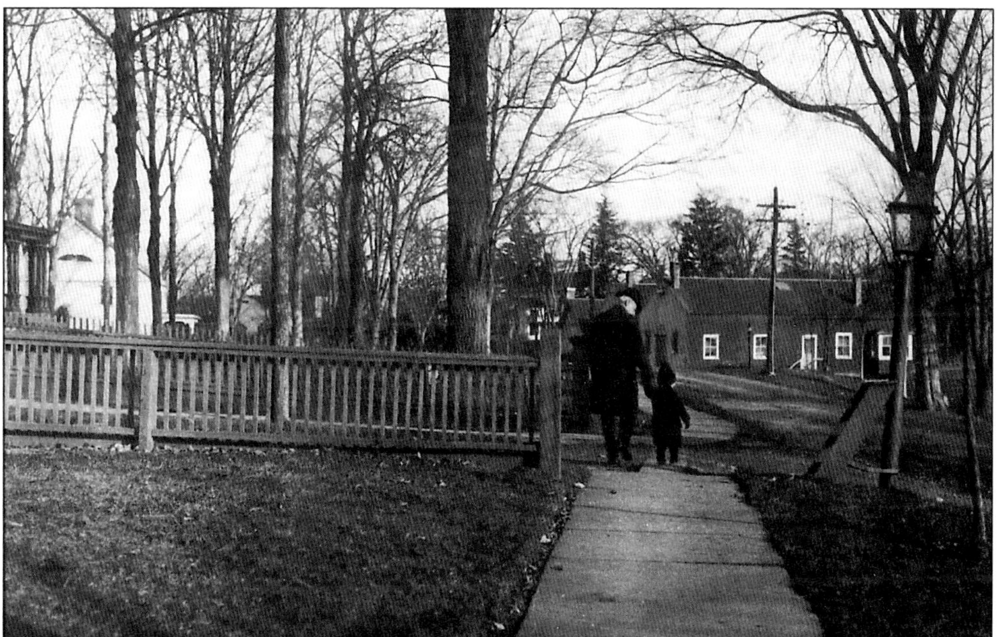

A man and child stroll along Harbor Road in Southport where many historic homes still stand. This view was taken about 1890 at the corner of Harbor Road and Old South Road.

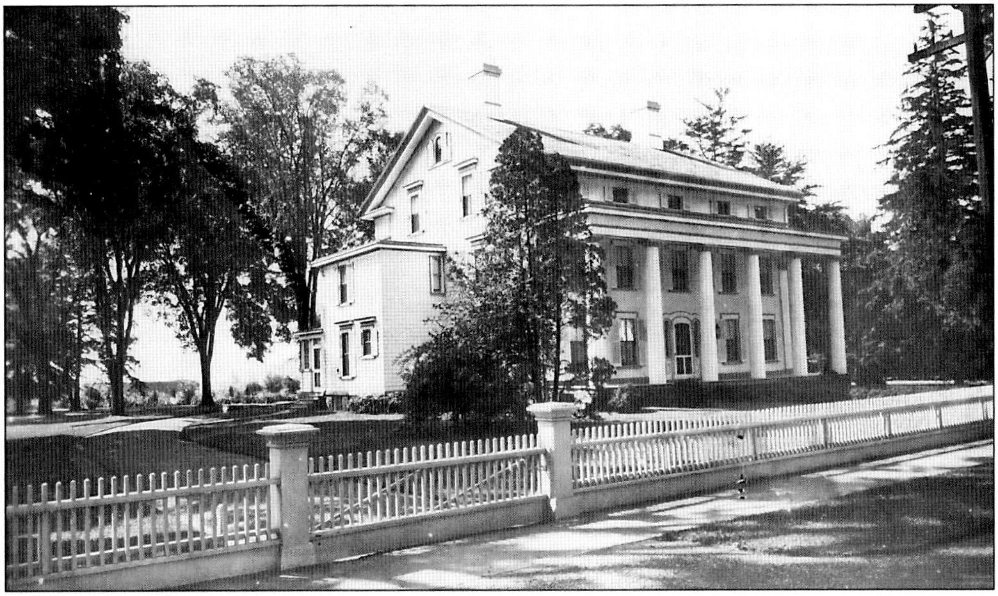

The original Burr Homestead was the site of the August 1775 wedding of Miss Dorothy Quincy and John Hancock, president of the Continental Congress. She had been sent from Boston to the home of Thaddeus Burr for safety. The Burr Homestead was one of the houses destroyed by the British and was rebuilt in 1792. The house, now owned by the Town, is managed by the Fairfield Historical Society and used for exhibitions, receptions, and other private and public functions.

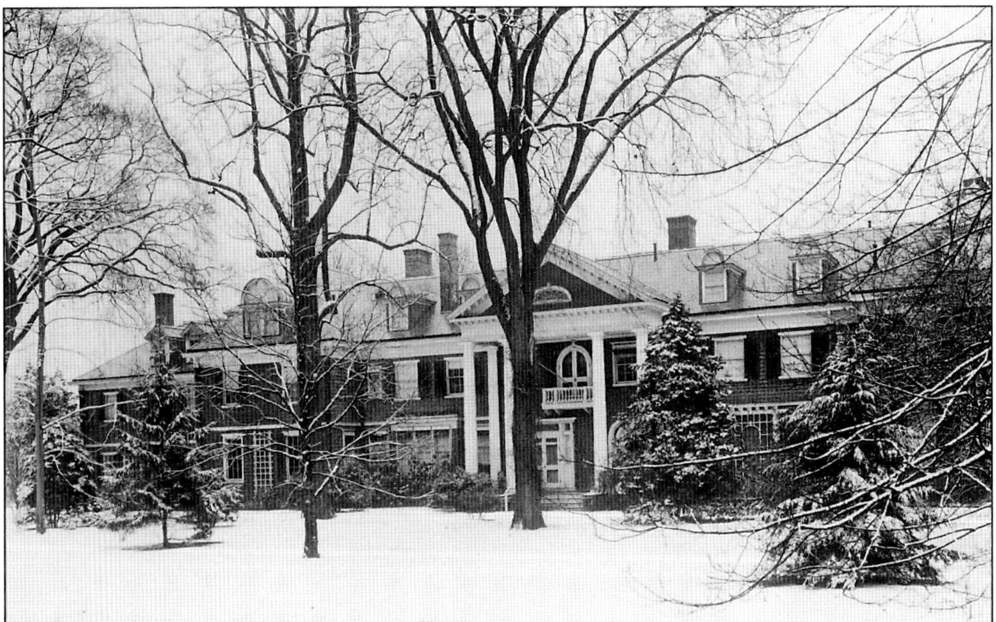

Annie Burr Jennings, daughter of Oliver B. Jennings of Standard Oil fame, inherited her wealth, which she generously shared with the town of Fairfield. Annie B., as she was known, was active in cultural and civic affairs and chaired Fairfield's celebration of the Connecticut Tercentenary in 1935.

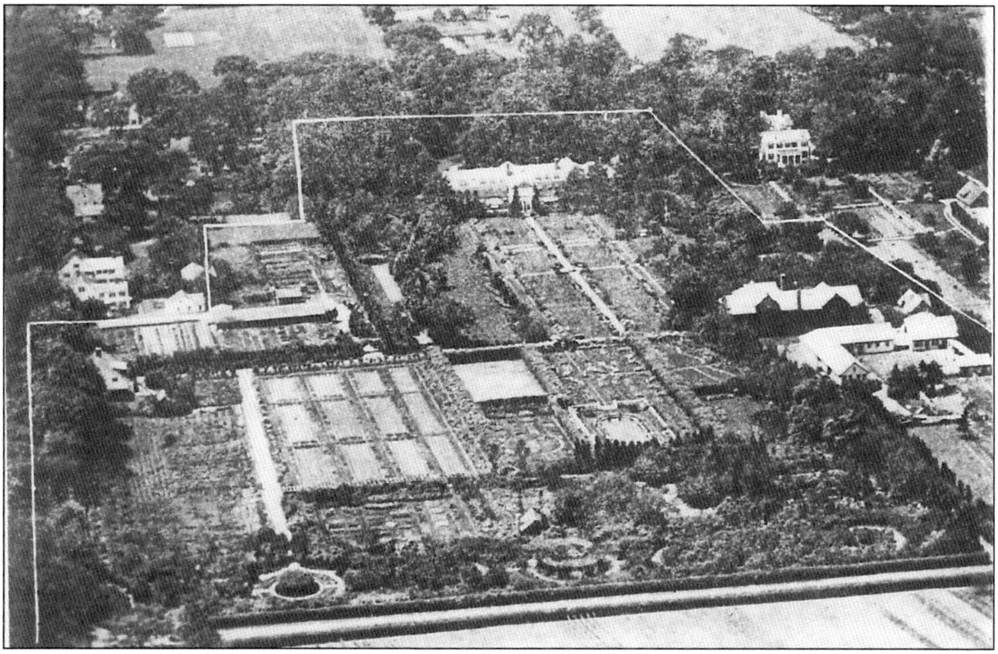

Annie B. Jennings's estate on the Old Post Road, called Sunnie-Holme and outlined in white in this image, encompassed extensive gardens which she frequently opened to the public.

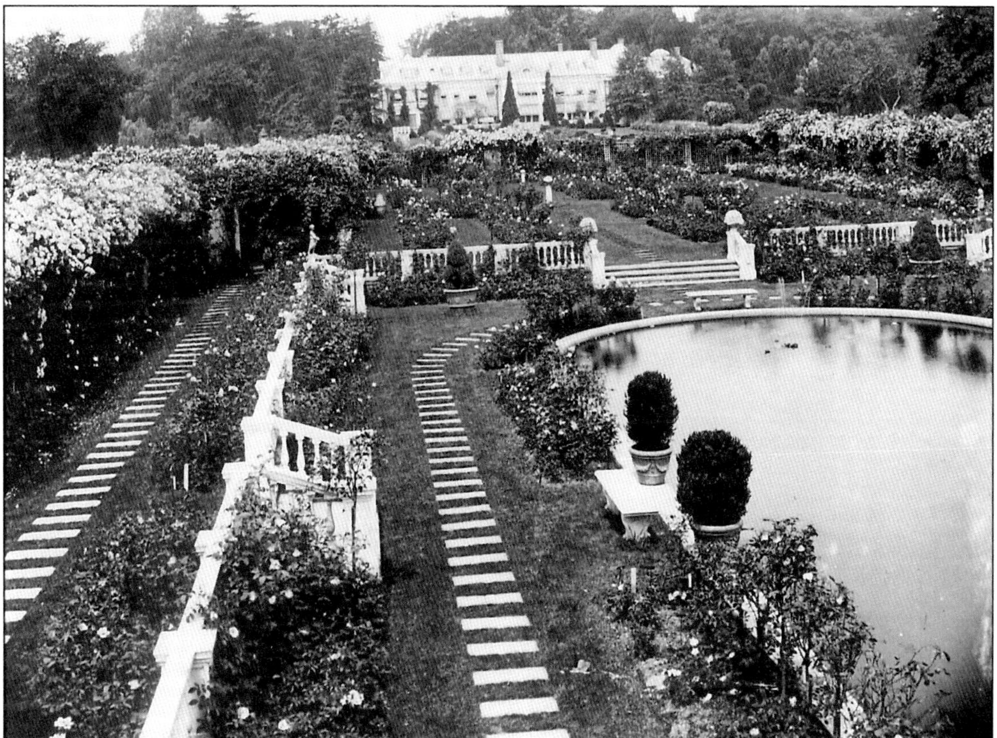

After Annie's death in 1939, in accordance with her will, Sunnie-Holme was torn down. A shadow of her elegant rose garden remains in the design of Sunnie-Holme Drive.

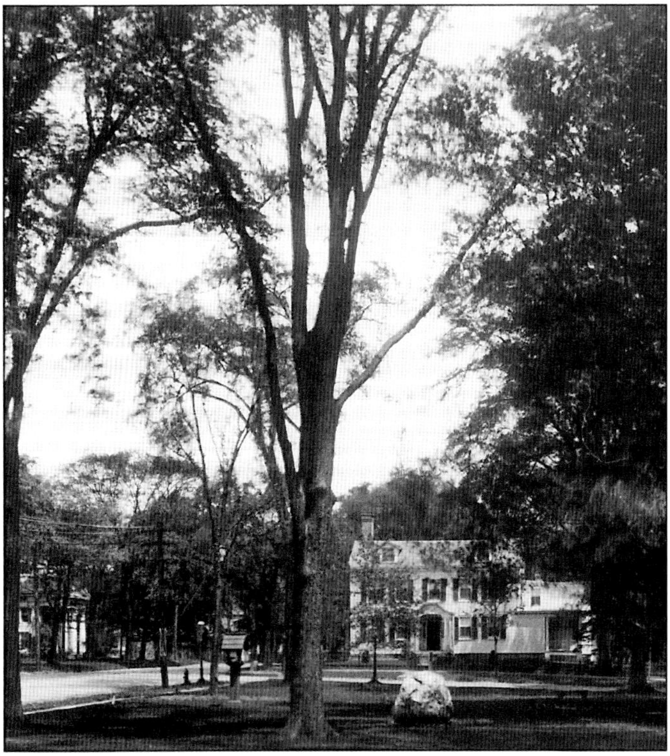

The Fowler house at 205 Beach Road, seen here across the Town Hall Green, dates from 1783. The original structure was partially destroyed when the British invaded and burned Fairfield in 1779. It is located in the Old Post Road Historic District.

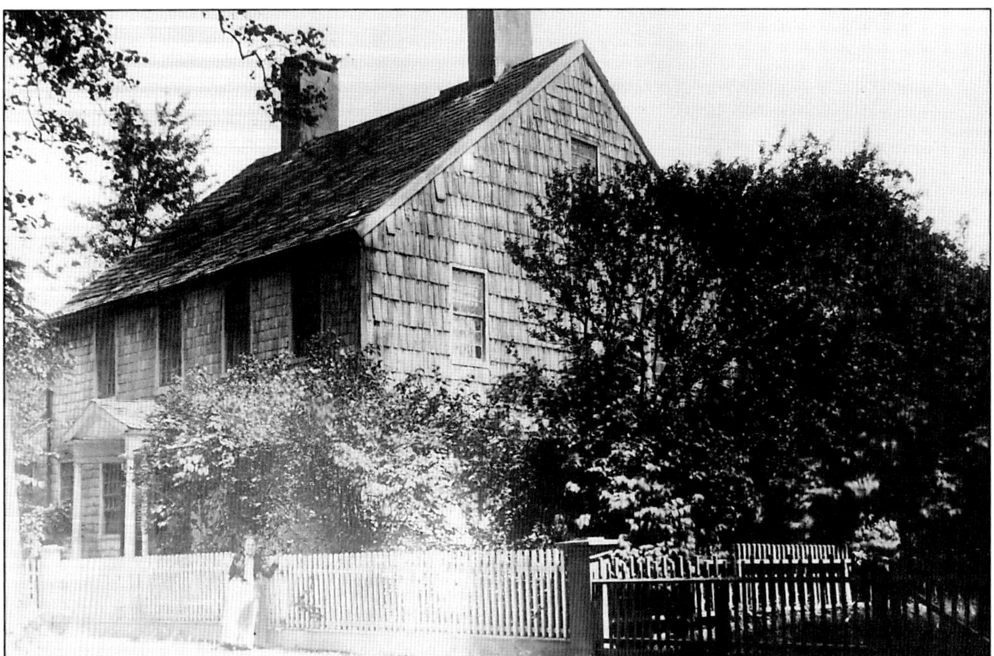

Hannah Hobart stands in front of the family home at 289 Beach Road. The house, built in 1765 by her grandfather, cabinetmaker Justin Hobart, is one of the few structures that survived the British attack. It later was used as the headquarters of the Fairfield Chapter of the American Red Cross.

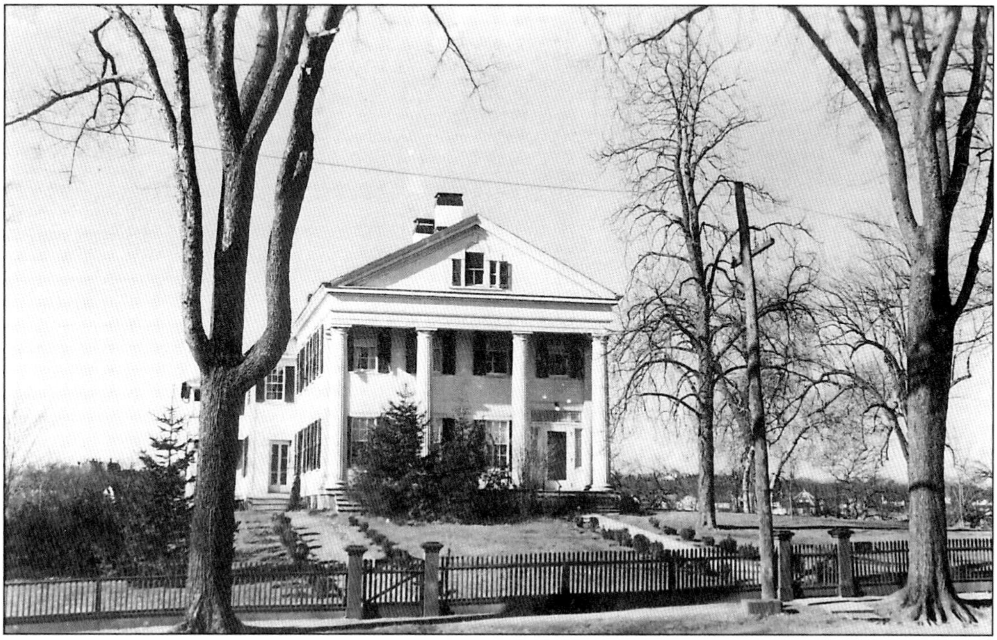

Captain John Gould built this house in 1840 on the Old Post Road. It was the family residence until 1910, when Captain Gould's daughter Elizabeth, through her will, created the Gould Summer Home for Women. It provided a free vacation home to working women of Fairfield until 1955, when the building was taken down to make way for a supermarket.

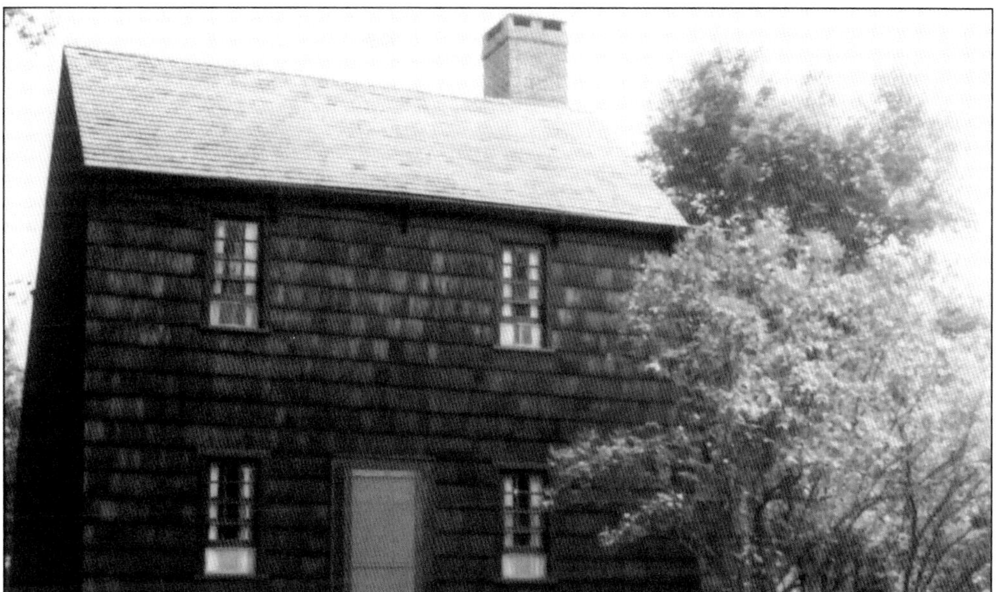

One of Fairfield's earliest extant houses, shown in this 1970 photograph, was built in 1690 by Sergeant John Smith in the area of town called Hull's Farms. The house retains its original salt-box roof line.

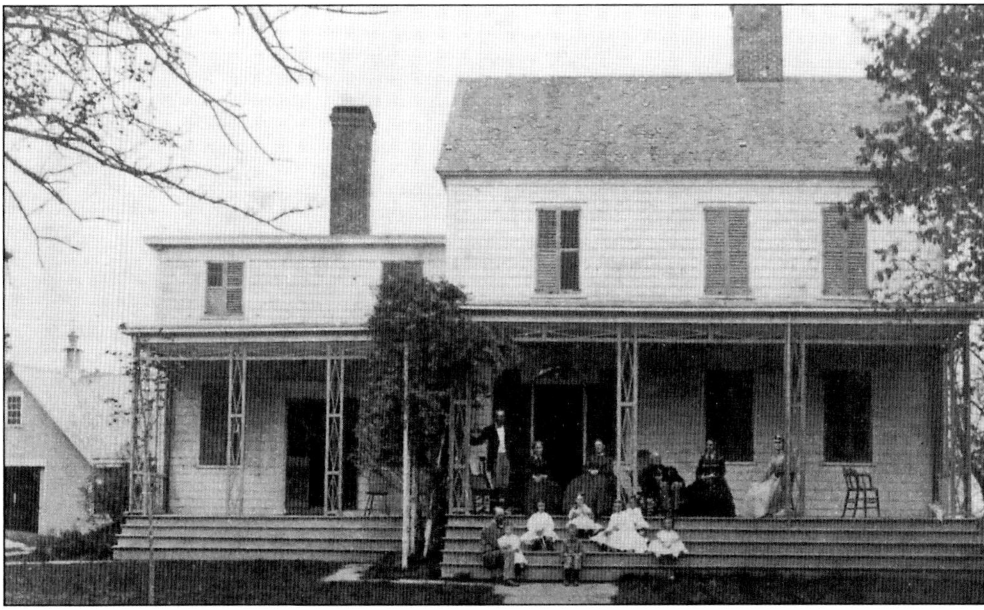

The Moses Bulkley family lived on Main Street in Southport in 1868 when this photograph was taken. The Southport newspaper, the *Chronicle*, reported that "Messrs. Wilson & Davis enjoyed the other day in photography of the residence of Capt. Moses Bulkley. The still fall weather is just the time for having outdoor pictures taken."

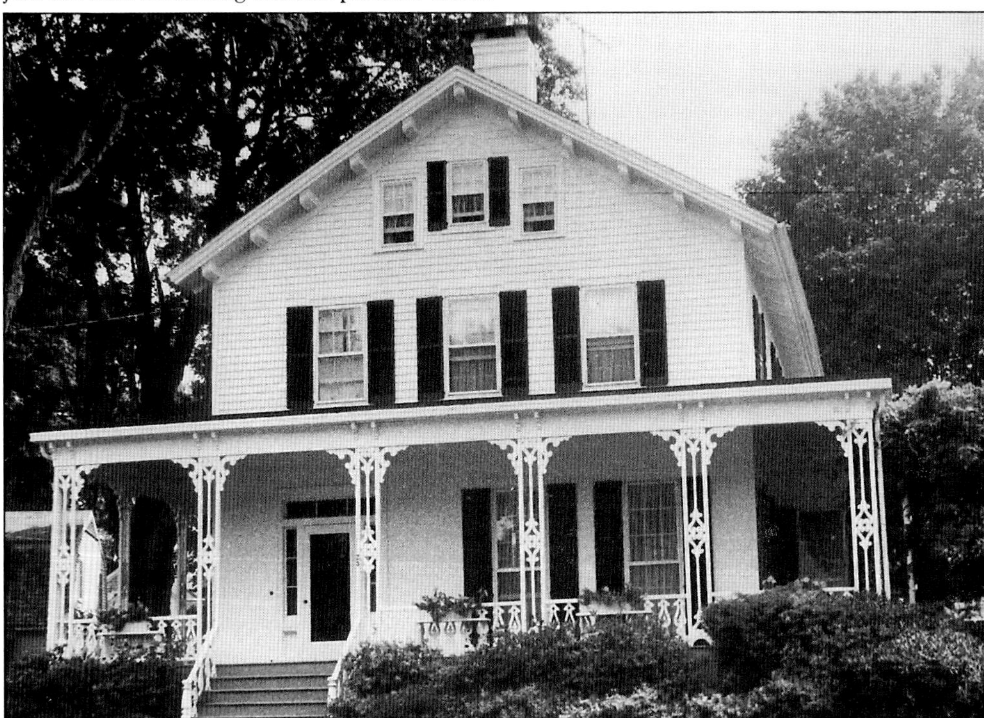

Wakeman Meeker built this house at 24 Westway Road in Southport for his son, Wakeman Jr., upon his marriage in 1856. It is a typical mid-nineteenth-century village home with wraparound porch, long ground-floor windows, and gingerbread trim. (Felix photograph, 1977.)

The Oak Lawn Cemetery Association was organized in 1865. John Abel Alvord, who served as superintendent from 1865 to 1868, was the first person to live in this cottage, which was built on land acquired from Timothy Bulkley. The cottage served as the superintendent's residence until it was demolished about 1934.

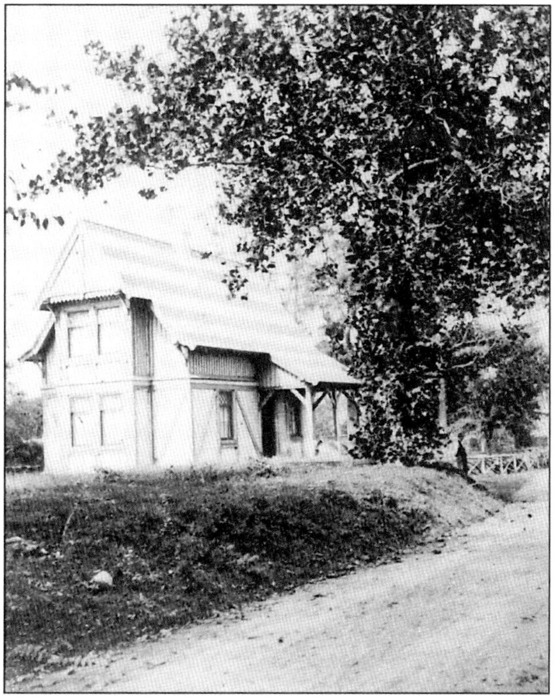

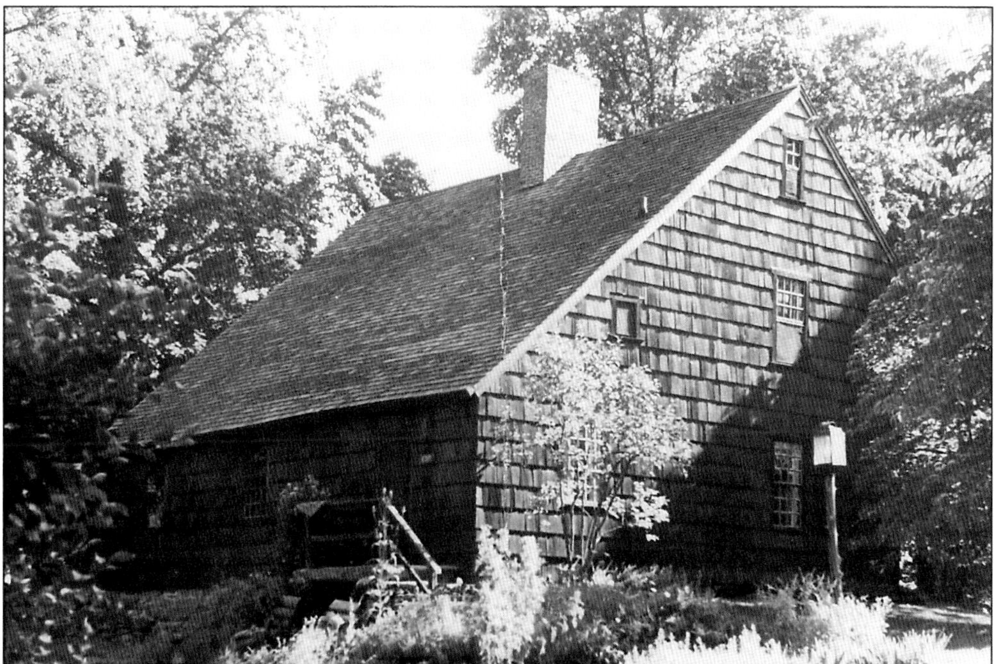

The Ogden House, a 1750s farmhouse built by David Ogden, is owned and operated by the Fairfield Historical Society as a historic house museum. Here the society sponsors special events, tours, and archaeology and education programs. The Garden Club of Fairfield maintains the period gardens. The house is located on Bronson Road, near the entrance to Oak Lawn Cemetery.

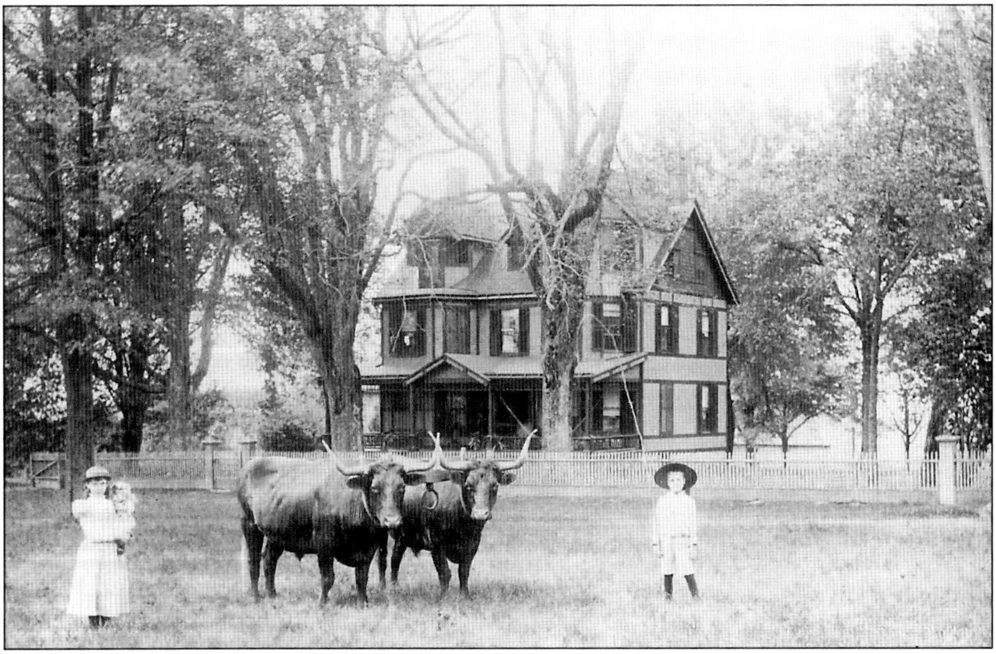

The Milbank House, at the corner of Bronson and Old Academy Roads, faces the Greenfield Hill Green. The house was built in 1887 and looked as it does in this *c.* 1890 photograph, until it was remodeled in 1949 after its purchase by the Greenfield Hill Congregational Church. The residence and outbuildings were adapted for use as a church school and for adult education and youth activities.

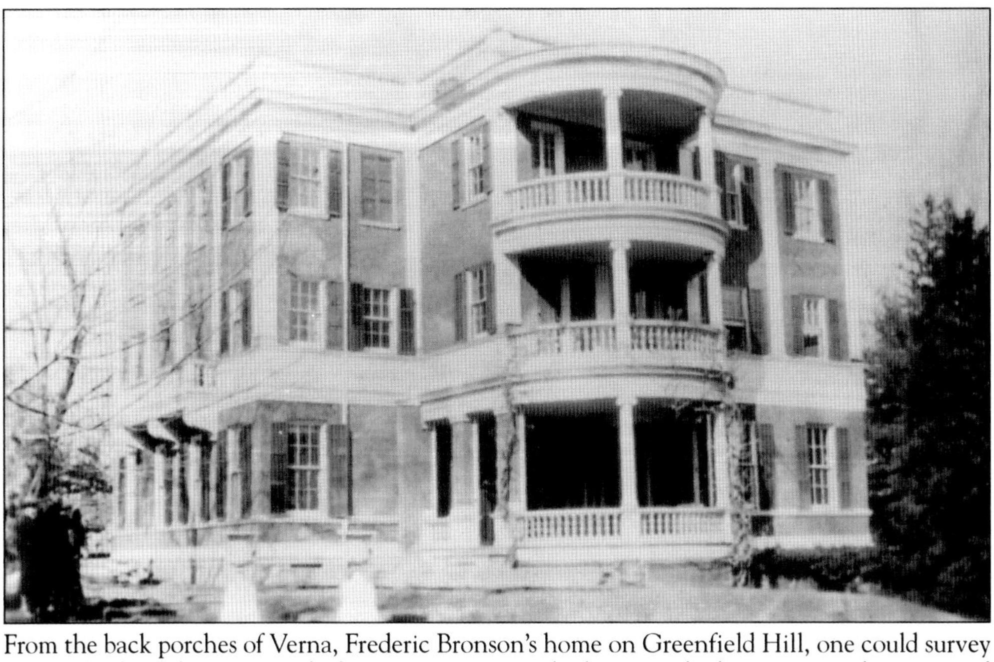

From the back porches of Verna, Frederic Bronson's home on Greenfield Hill, one could survey the model farm that consisted of 200 to 300 acres. The house and adjacent grounds are owned by Fairfield Country Day School.

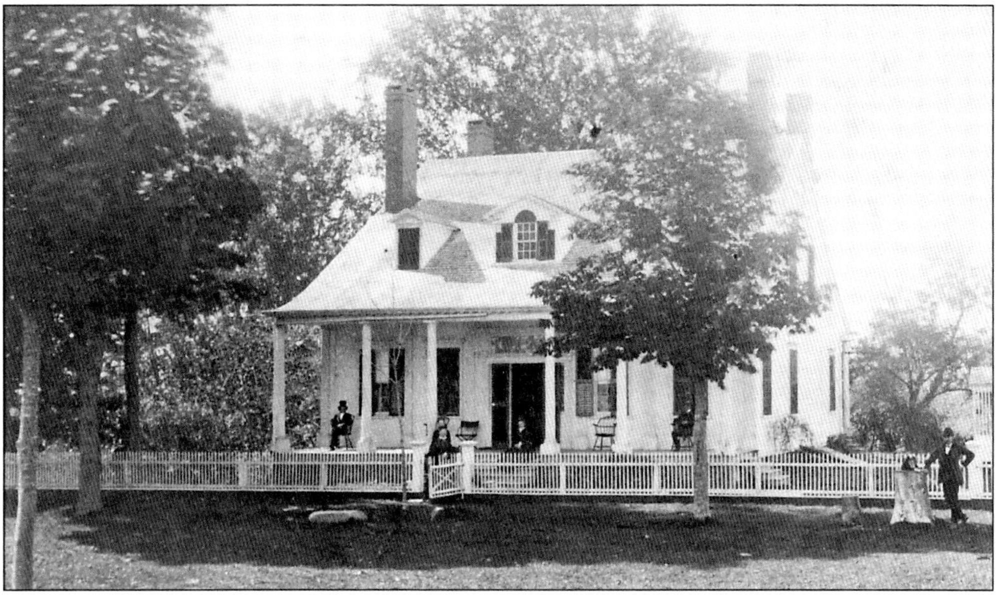

The Dey Parsonage, built in 1823 in the Federal style, is located at 55 Meeting House Lane. It takes its name from the Reverend Richard Varick Dey, minister of the Greenfield Hill Congregational Church from 1823 to 1828. This photograph is typical of those taken by itinerant photographers in the late 1800s.

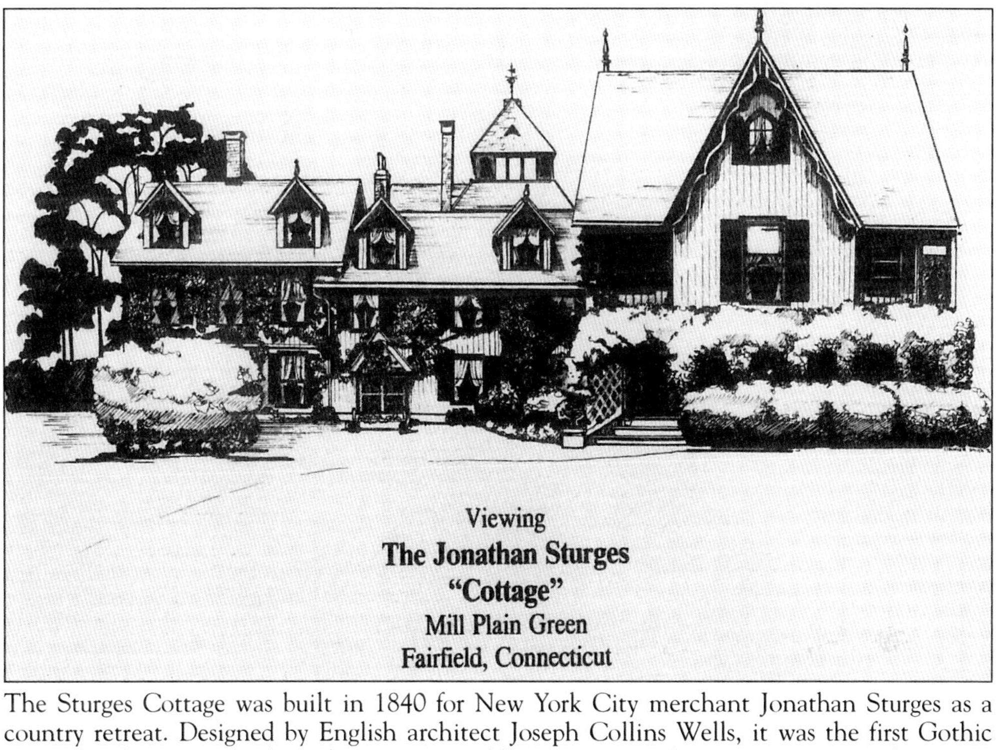

The Sturges Cottage was built in 1840 for New York City merchant Jonathan Sturges as a country retreat. Designed by English architect Joseph Collins Wells, it was the first Gothic Revival-style cottage built in this country. Additions were made in 1846, 1883, and 1890, so that it now boasts over thirty rooms, thirteen fireplaces, and eleven staircases. The original building is on the right.

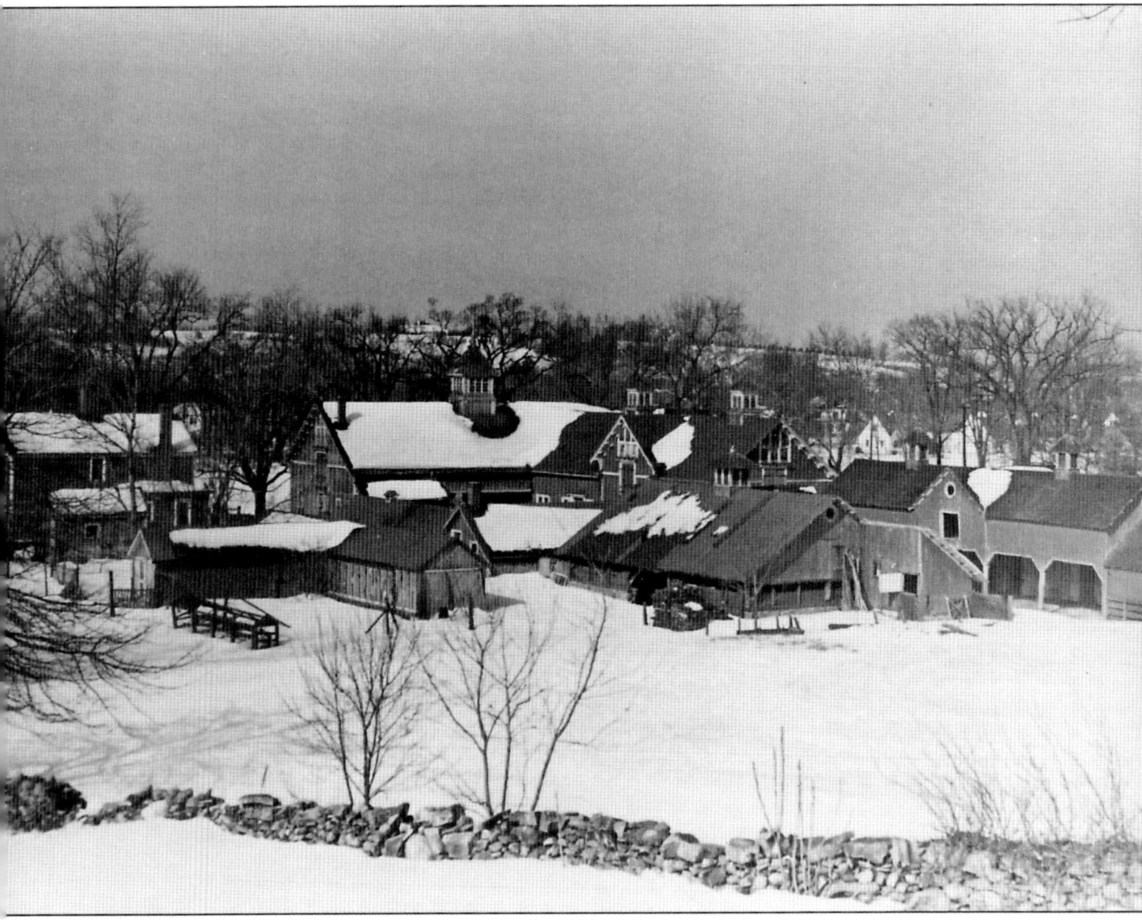

Frederick Sturges's Mount David Farm was located at 674 Mill Plain Road. Sturges, a son of Jonathan, was a New York City businessman who summered in Fairfield. The farm, established about 1878, raised vegetables, fruit, pigs, and cows and was managed by John Forsyth. Sturges's son, Frederick Jr., gave part of the farm to the Town for use as a public park.

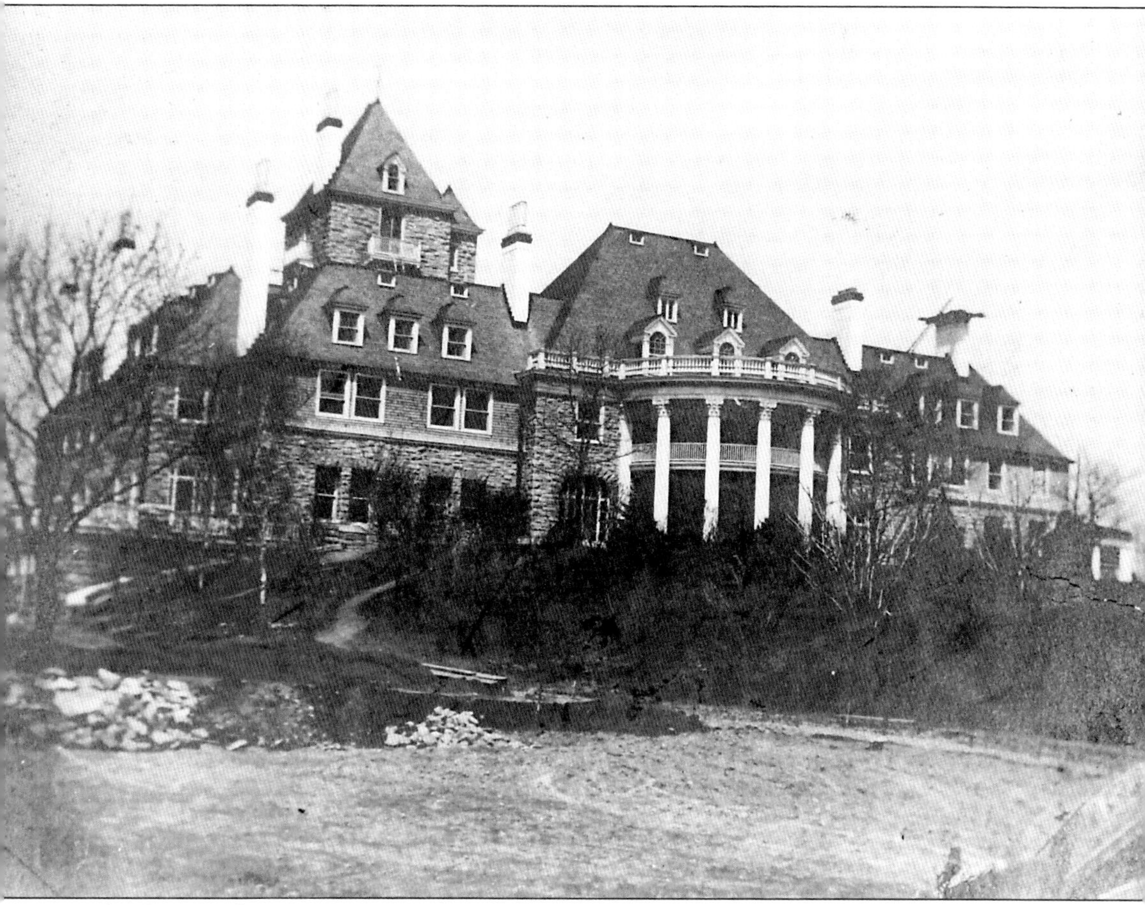

Mailands was a forty-room mansion built in 1907 by Oliver Gould Jennings, son of Oliver B. Jennings and brother of Annie B. The imposing building commanded a view of Long Island Sound. In 1941 the Society of Jesus purchased the estate and established Fairfield Preparatory School and Fairfield University. Today Mailands, now called McAuliffe Hall, houses University offices and its BEI School of Engineering.

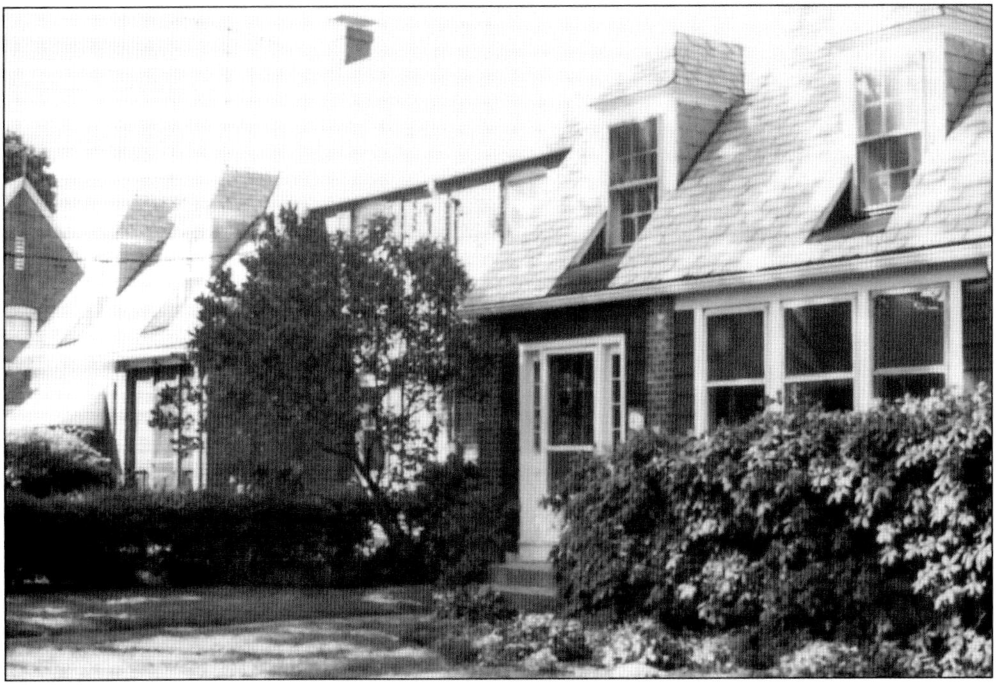

Houses in the Grasmere neighborhood are a significant reminder of our national mobilization for World War I. More than 100 single- and multi-family units were constructed by the United States Housing Corp. for employees of area manufacturers of war materiel. Designed by the architectural firm of Kilham & Hopkins, they were some of the earliest planned housing developments in the area. Similar clusters were built in Bridgeport. (Marcia Miner photograph, 1997.)

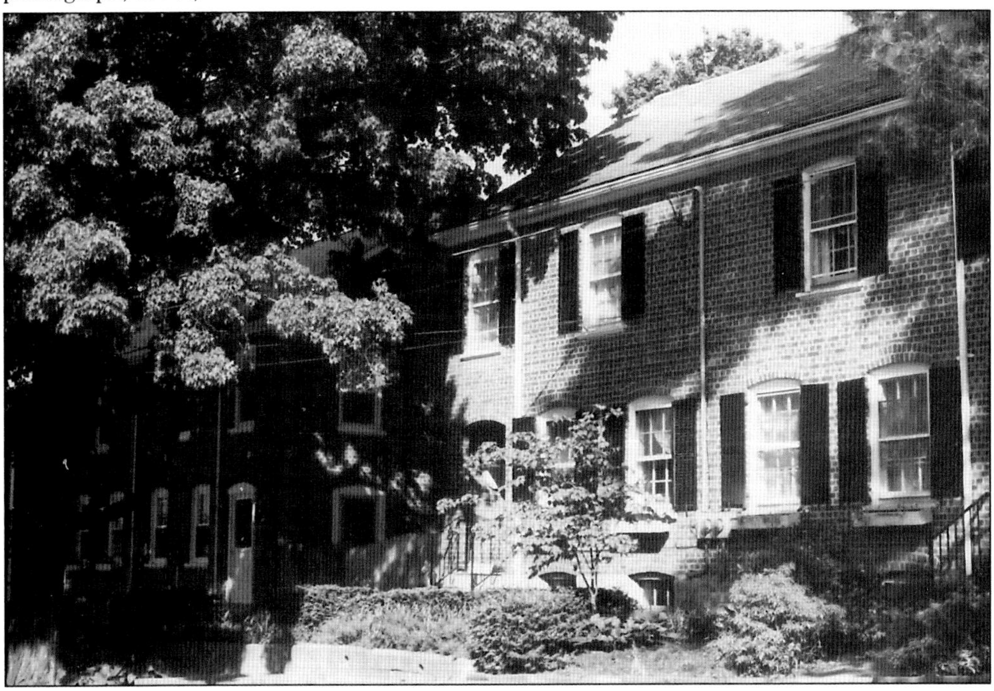

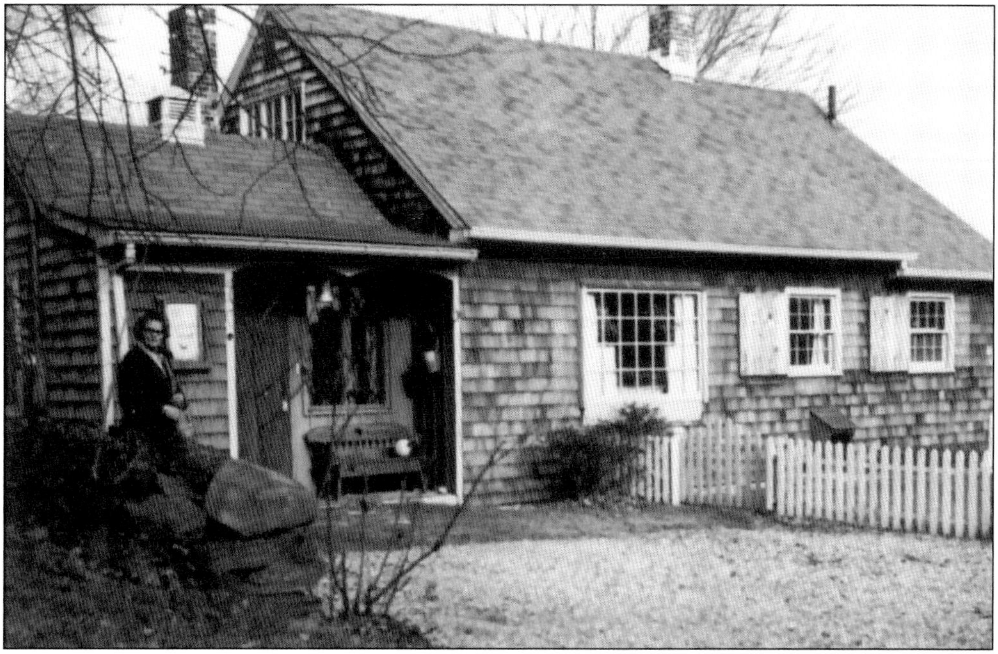

A style of home popular after World War II was the so-called Cape Cod, which could be built for a moderate price. Realtor Adelaide Barker sits in front of an attractive example on Gorham Road. (Charles Walsh photograph.)

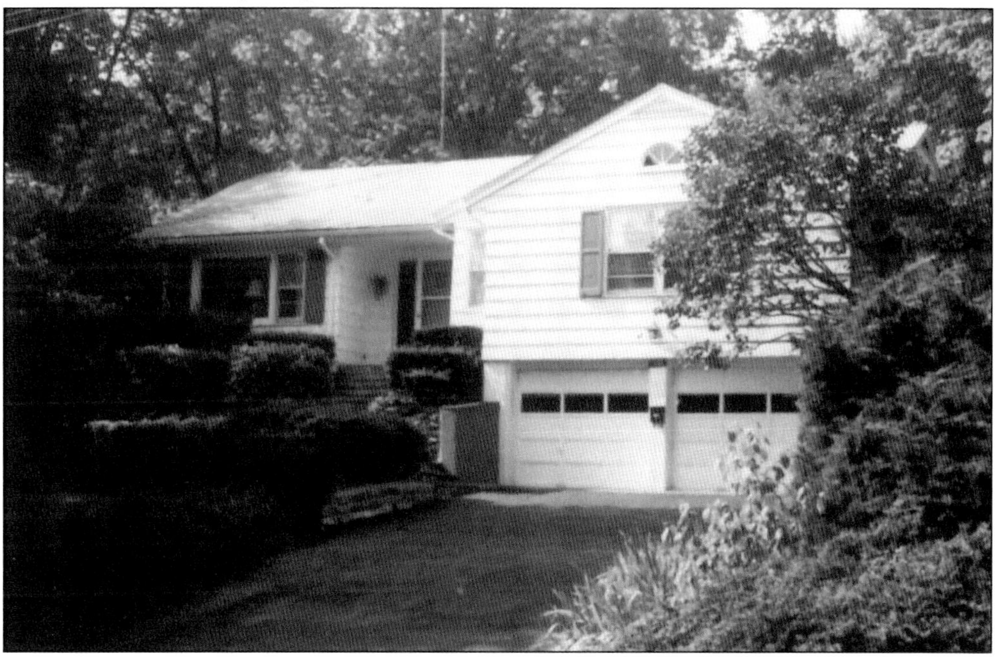

This house, located on Knollwood Drive, is an example of the split-level variety, popular in the post-World War II period. It provided a family recreation room at ground level, half a flight of steps below the living room level. Mr. and Mrs. Knute S. Lindfors, who operated the Green Comet Diner on Kings Highway from 1940 to 1970, called this home. (Charles Walsh photograph.)

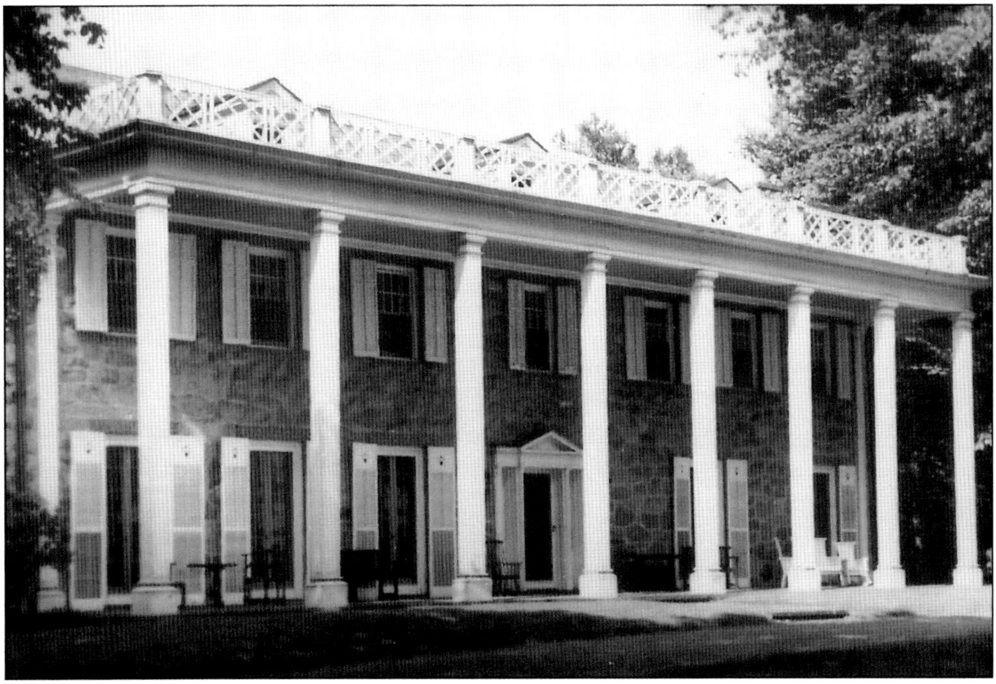

Edgar Webb Bassick built this home on Algonquin Road in the Stratfield area of Fairfield in 1908. The Bassick Company manufactured casters and cabinet and automobile hardware. Located near the Brooklawn Country Club and close to the Bridgeport line, this area attracted a number of Bridgeport industrialists.

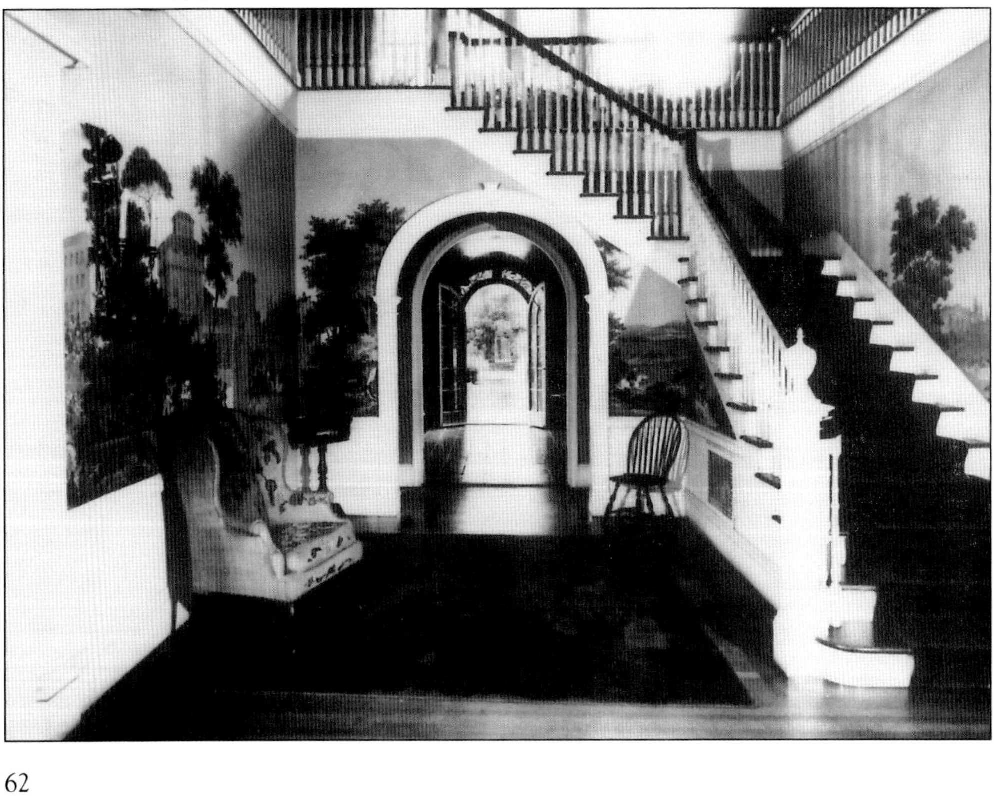

Four

Learning Never Ends

Opportunities for formal and informal education for all ages have long abounded in Fairfield. Formal schooling, both public and private, is supplemented by two excellent libraries and by programs offered by many organizations, including the Connecticut Audubon Society and the Fairfield Historical Society.

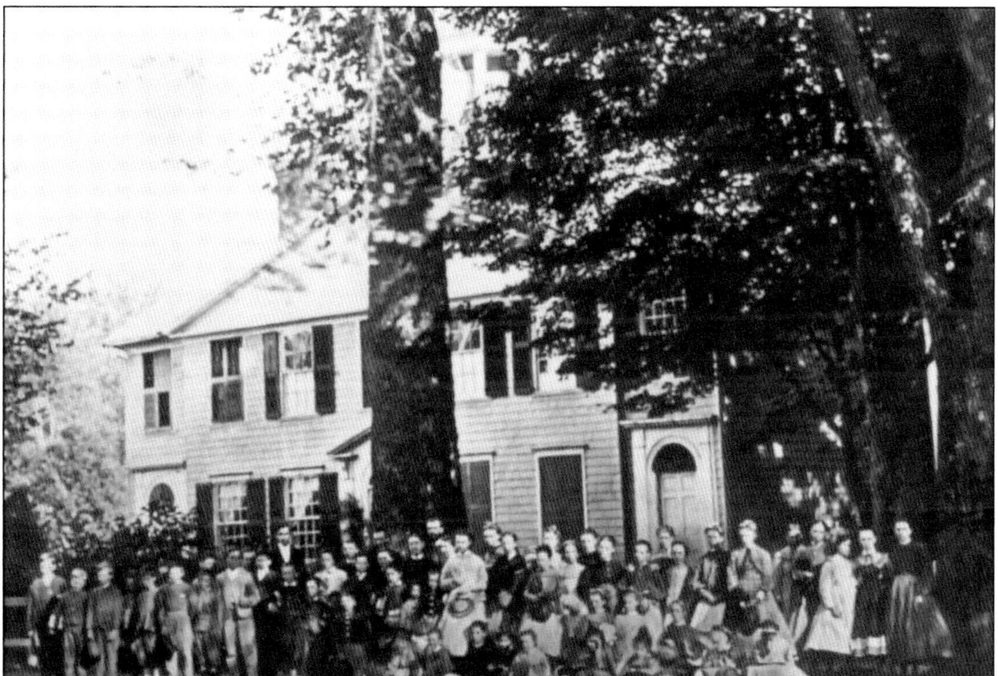

In 1817 Fairfield had sixteen primary schools and three academies: Fairfield Academy, Dwight Academy, and Black Rock Academy. Fairfield Academy (now commonly known as the Old Academy) was founded in 1804, and its first class included sixty scholars of both sexes. This 1865 image shows the building at its original site on the Old Post Road, nearly one hundred years before it was moved to its current location adjacent to the Town Hall. The Eunice Dennie Burr Chapter of the Daughters of the American Revolution meets here, and the Fairfield Historical Society uses it for educational programs.

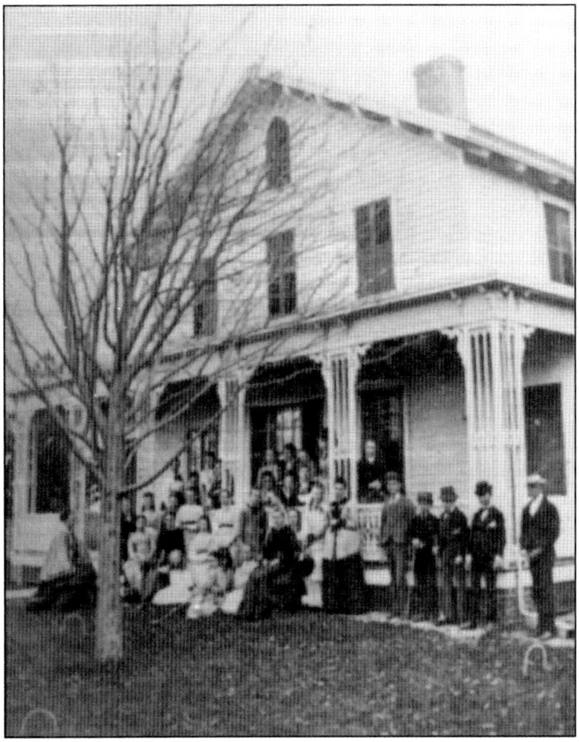

Miss Augusta Smith founded the Seaside Seminary at her home on Pequot Road in Southport. It was a boarding school for girls and a day school for both boys and girls. Students came from Southport, the countryside, and nearby villages, many commuting by train. (Cabinet card, c. 1874.)

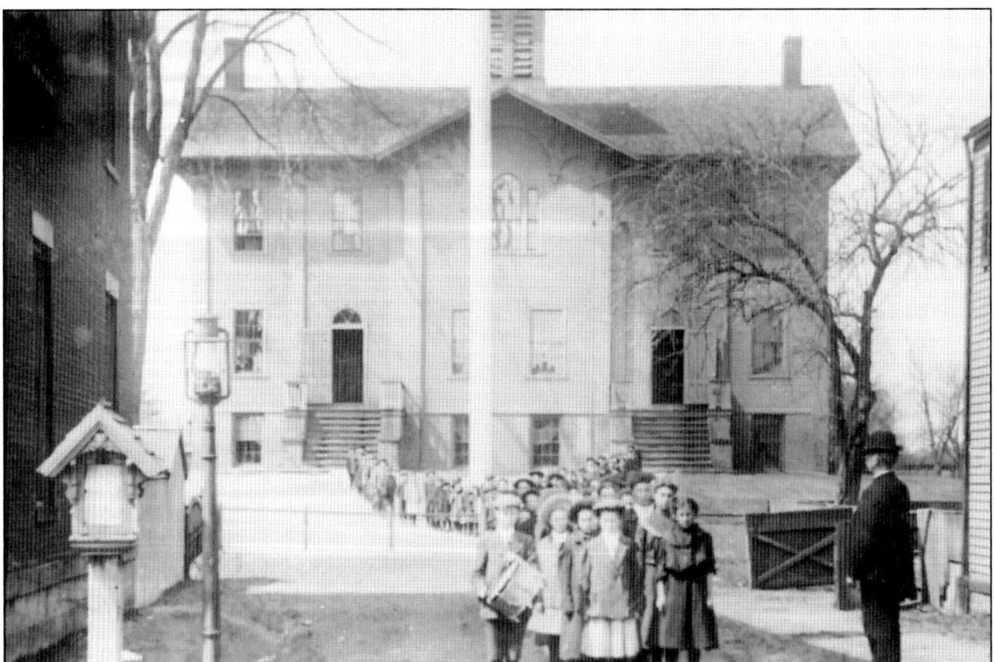

The Pequot School on Main Street in Southport was built in 1854. The building in this picture was replaced in 1918 by a one-story structure of buff-toned brick that was closed in the 1960s. Used for a period as school administrative offices, the building is now the site of the Eagle Hill School, a private institution for children with learning disabilities.

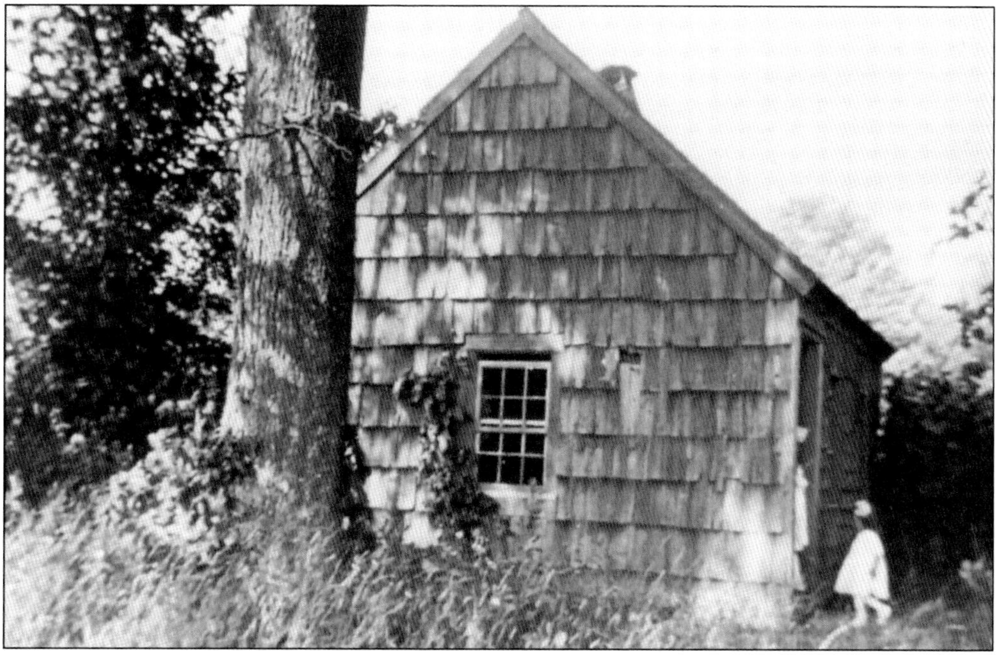

Pictured about 1920, the Deerfield District schoolhouse on Burr Street in the Greenfield Hill section of Fairfield was built in 1771 and used until about 1889. This is an early example of the neighborhood school, a concept that continues in a modified form for today's elementary schools.

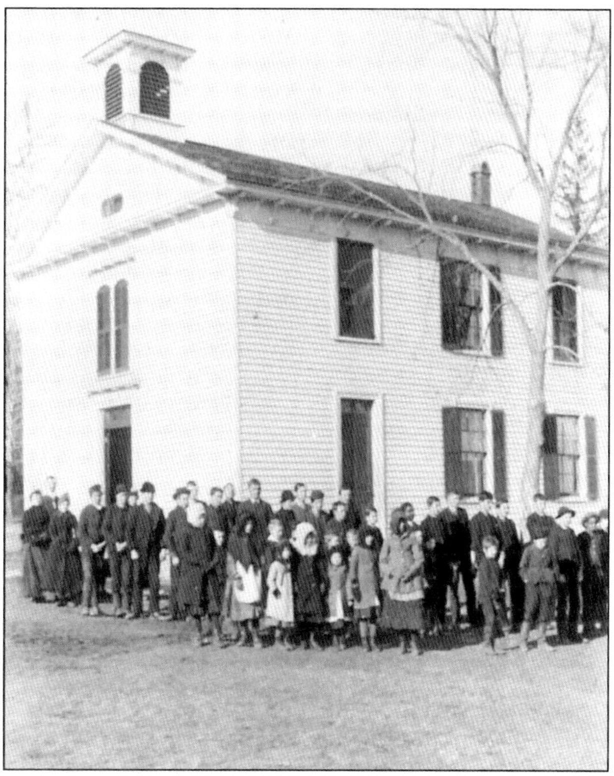

Timothy Dwight, pastor of the Greenfield Hill Congregational Church and later president of Yale College, founded the original Dwight Academy in 1786. The building seen in this photograph was constructed in 1854 after the Academy was taken over as a district school about 1835. The principal, W.E. Gardner, and assistant principal, Etta Perry, are at the left in this picture taken during the 1887/88 school year.

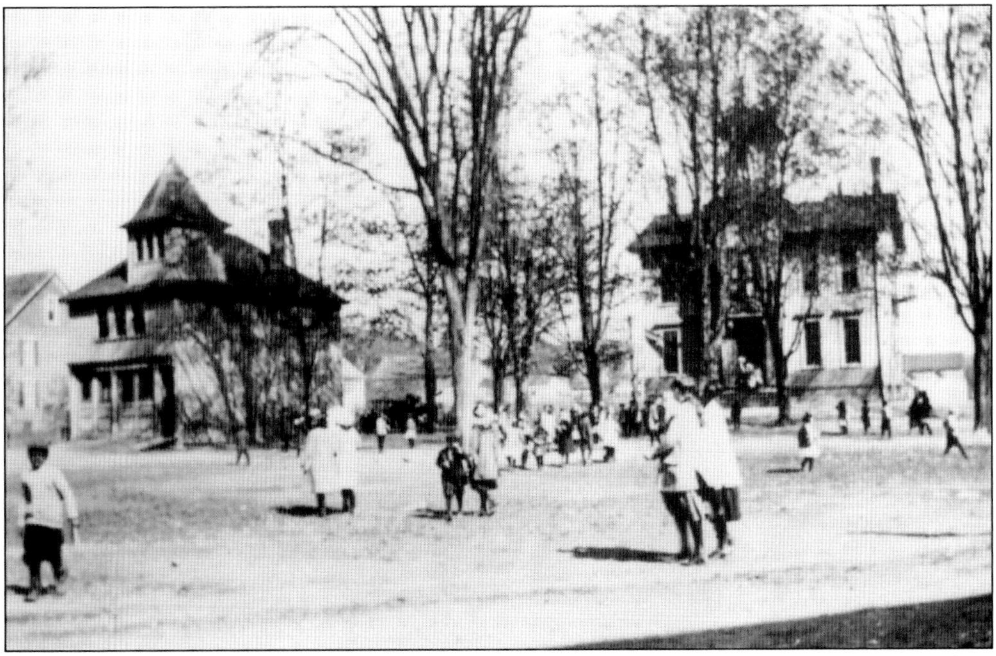

The Centre District School (to the right), renamed the Sherman School, stood on today's Sherman Green. The school and the green were named after Roger Minott Sherman, noted Fairfield attorney and judge. The first building, seen in this *c.* 1910 photograph, was replaced in 1913 by a brick structure that was razed in 1965.

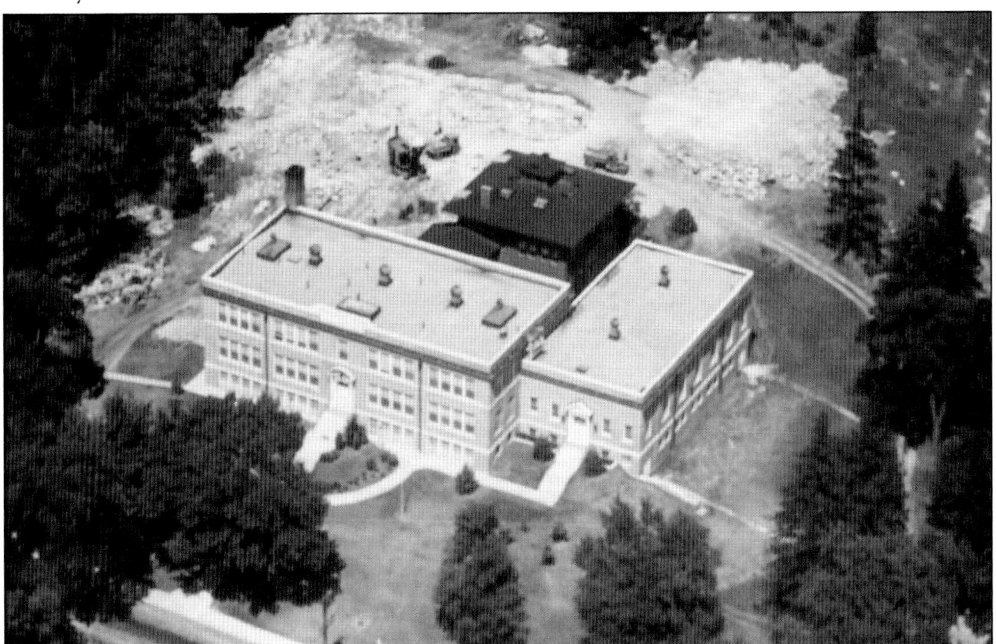

Fairfield's first high school was held in the basement of the Sherman School and moved in 1916 to the Brown residence on Unquowa Road. This house is seen in the upper center of this 1924 photograph of the newly constructed Roger Ludlowe High School. The Andrew Warde High School, opened in 1956, and Roger Ludlowe combined in 1987 to form Fairfield High School.

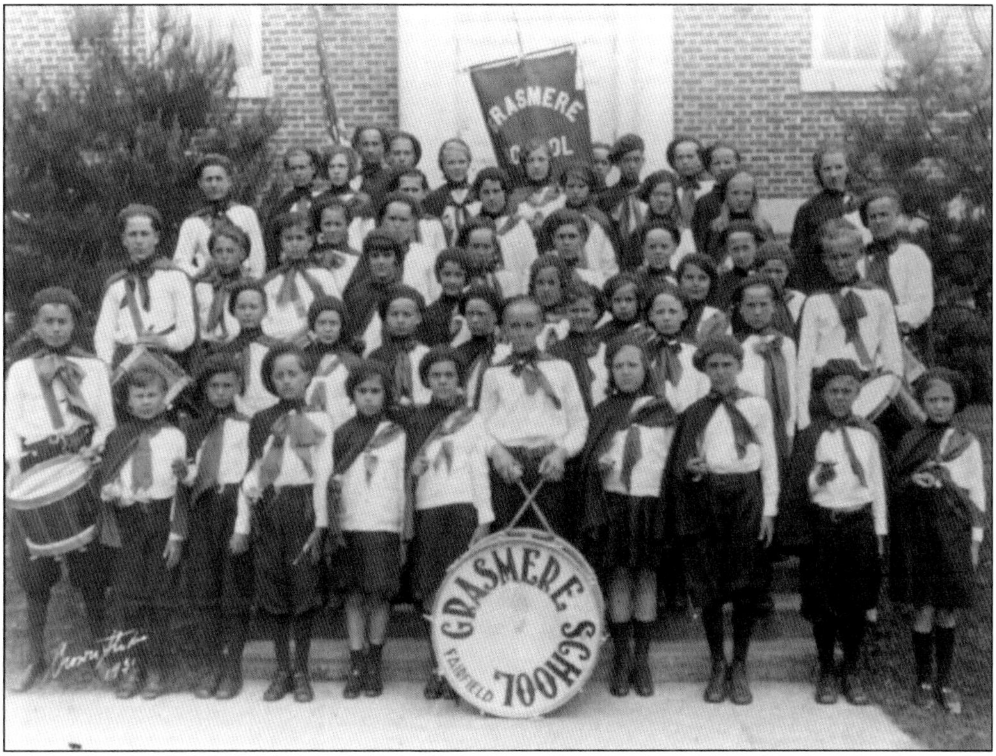

The Grasmere School band is shown in 1931. The building, closed as a school in 1981, was converted in 1989 to elderly housing. The federally funded Sullivan-McKinney Elder Housing complex was named for Fairfield First Selectman John J. Sullivan and U.S. Representative Stewart B. McKinney, both vocal advocates for the elderly.

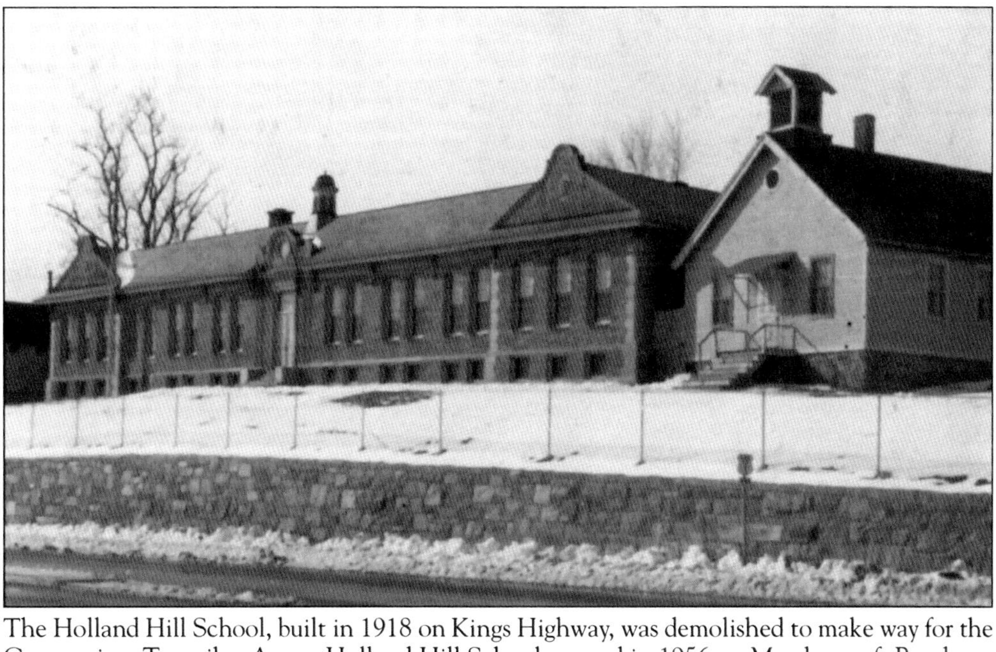
The Holland Hill School, built in 1918 on Kings Highway, was demolished to make way for the Connecticut Turnpike. A new Holland Hill School opened in 1956 on Meadowcroft Road.

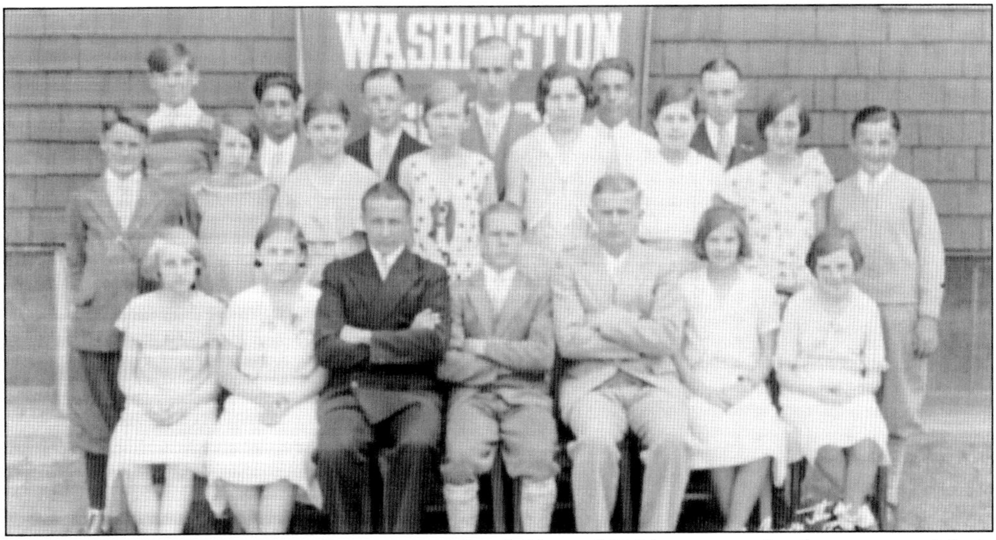

Members of the Washington Elementary School Class of 1931 pose on the front steps of their school located on Villa Avenue. The student signatures on the back of the photograph (shown below), addressed to their teacher, include "The most conceited boy of '31, Elmer Hansen" and "Your noisiest pupil, Laura Krosky '31."

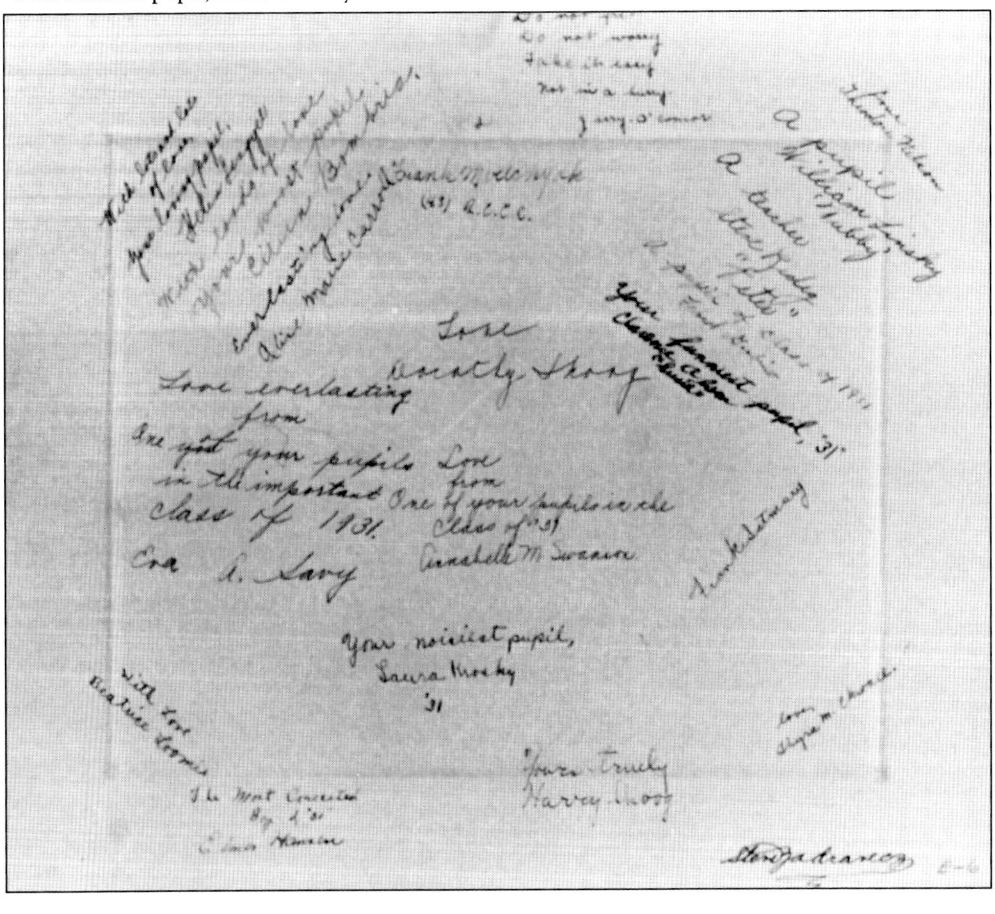

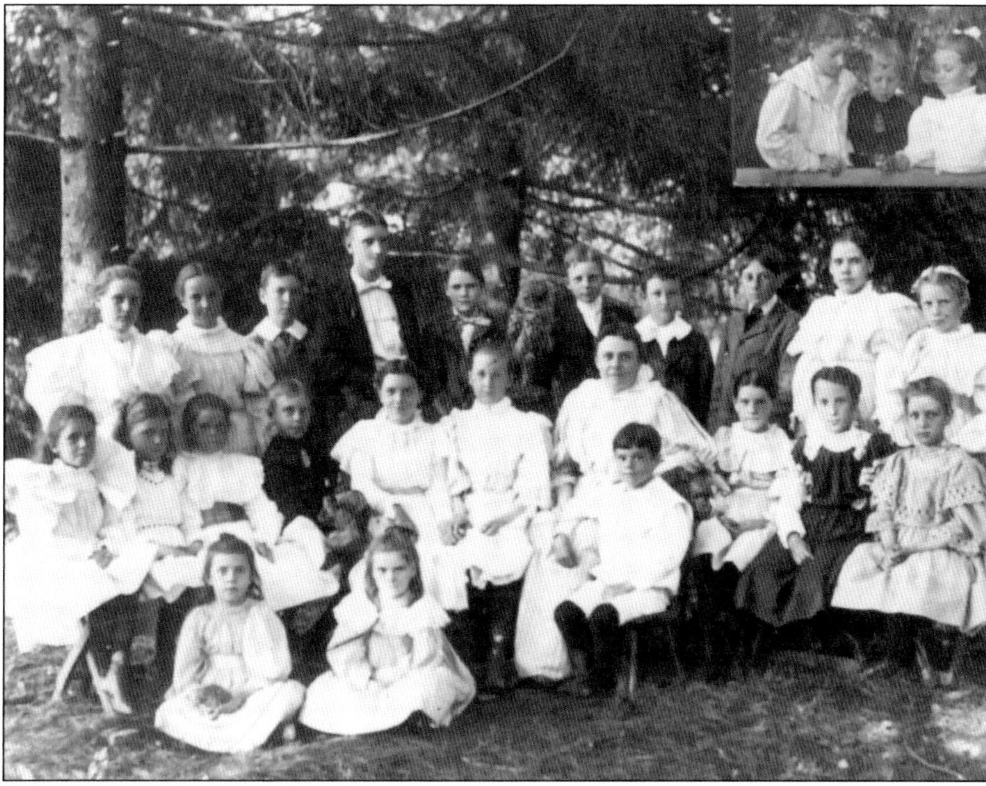

Mabel Osgood Wright founded the Birdcraft Sanctuary, part of the Connecticut Audubon Society, located on Unquowa Road. An activist in conservation, she promoted her cause through photography, writing, and teaching. Here she is shown with a bird study group in 1897.

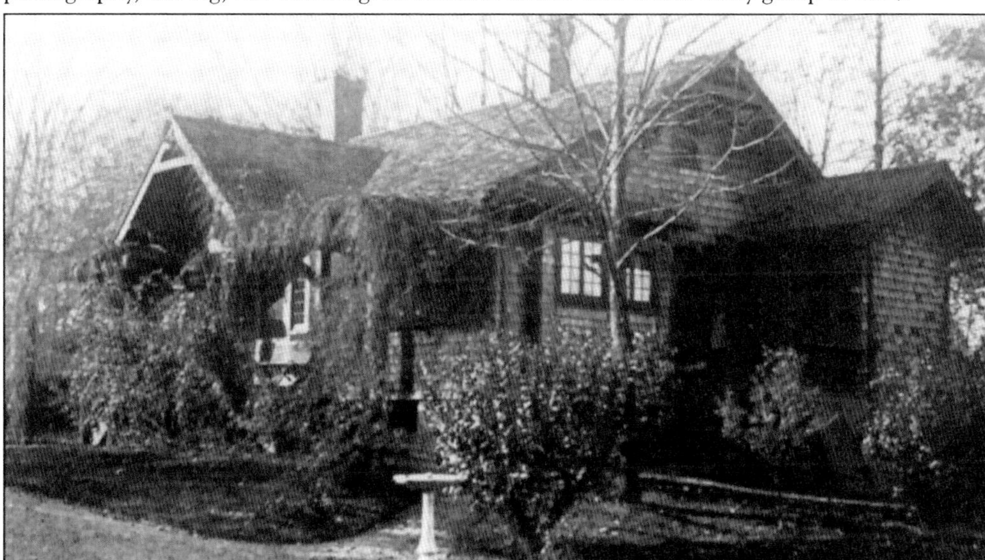

The sanctuary contains a caretaker's bungalow (seen above) and the Birdcraft Museum, an education center. Across the street stood founder Mabel Osgood Wright's family home, Mosswood, now the site of condominiums.

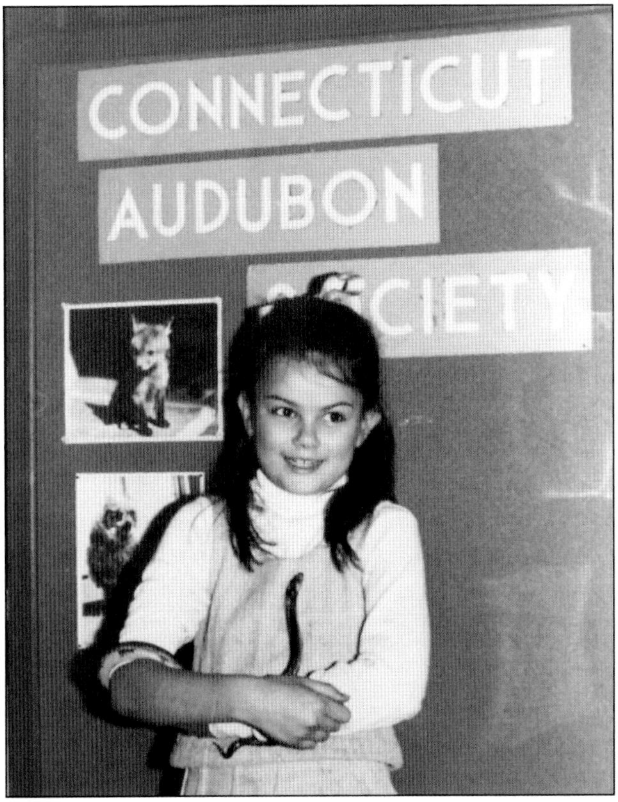

The Connecticut Audubon Society offers educational programs at its Burr Street headquarters. Here Kristen Bouton holds a California Striped King snake. (*Fairfield Citizen-News*, Hugh Smith photograph, 1978.)

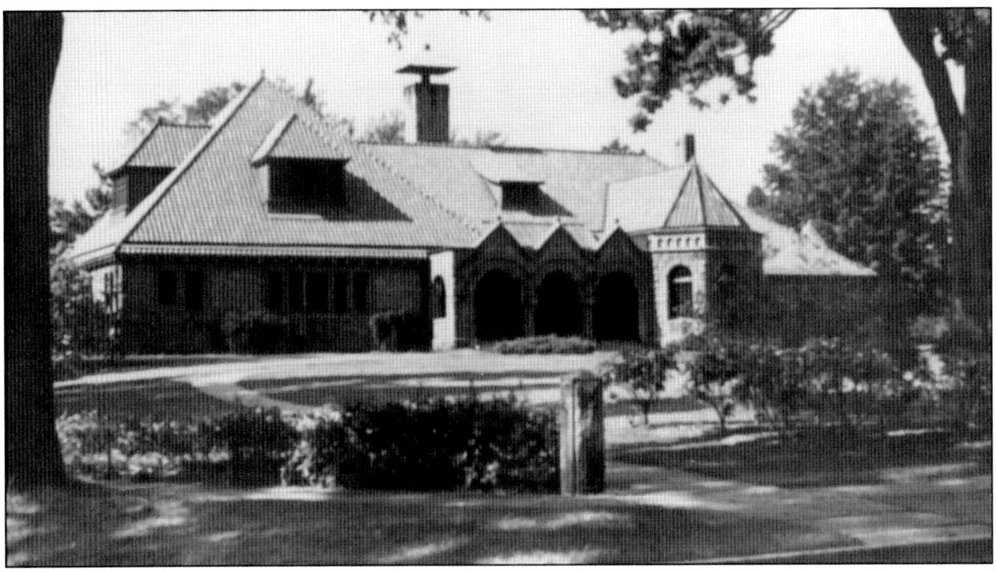

Mr. and Mrs. E.B. Monroe donated the funds for the Pequot Library in Southport. Constructed in 1887, the building was designed by the nationally renowned architect H.H. Richardson. It opened in 1894 for use as a library, reading room, lecture hall, and "something in the nature of a social headquarters" for Southport residents. The library is known for its rare book collection, its Audubon elephant folios, its stained-glass windows, and the almost perfect acoustics in the auditorium.

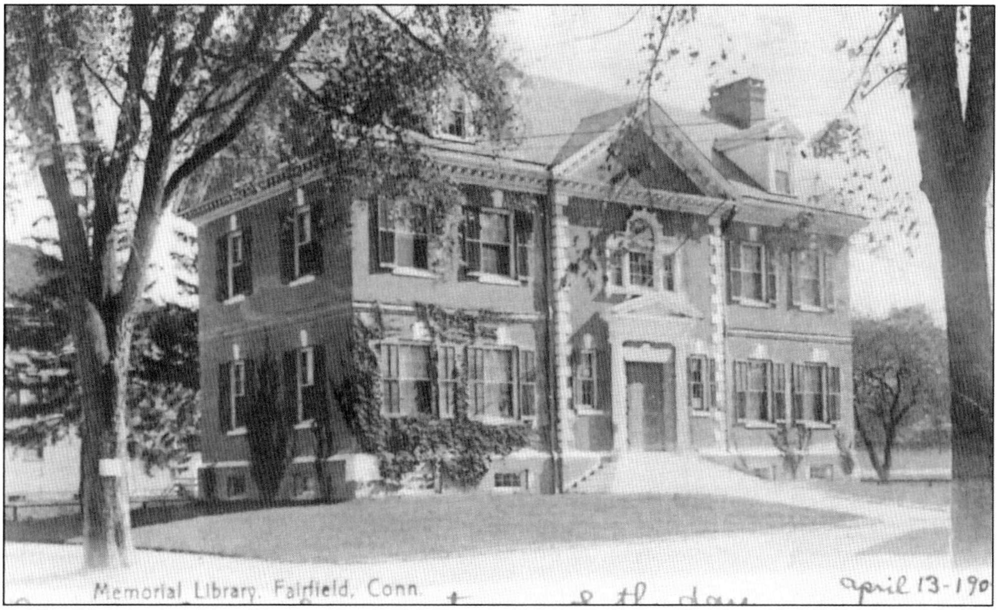

Fairfield's Memorial Library was founded in 1876 and moved to this building on the Old Post Road in 1903. In 1950 the library was turned over to the Town and became the Fairfield Public Library. The single building, shown in this c. 1904 postcard, has undergone a number of additions to accommodate the growing population and the concomitant increase in collections and services.

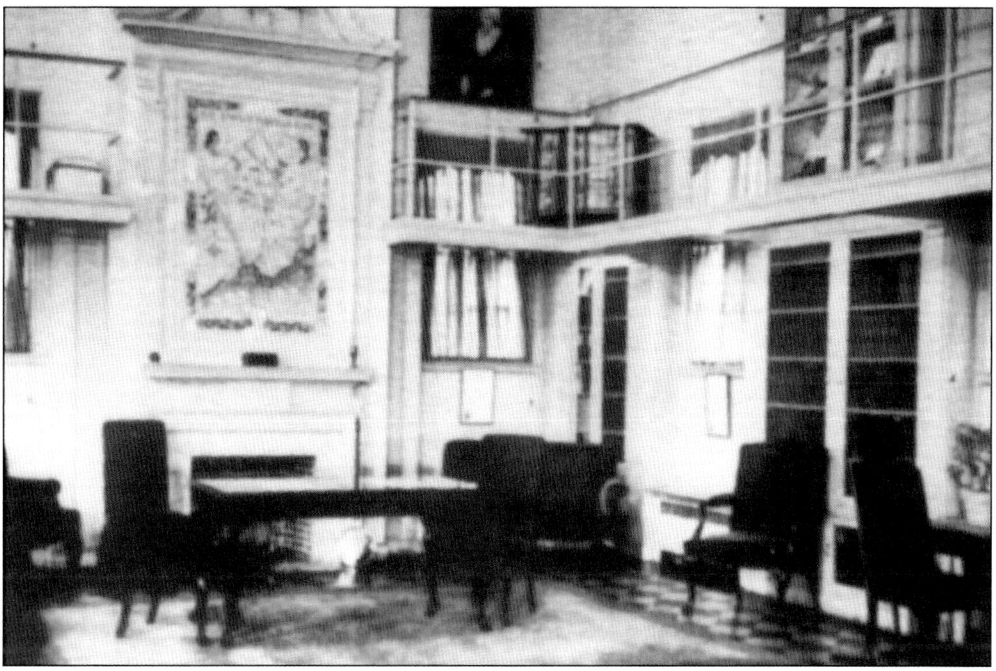

The Fairfield Historical Society, founded in 1903, first operated from the second floor of the Fairfield Memorial Library. In 1930 it moved downstairs to a new wing provided by Oliver G. Jennings. Today, the historical society has its headquarters in the heart of the Old Post Road Historic District, across from the old Town Hall.

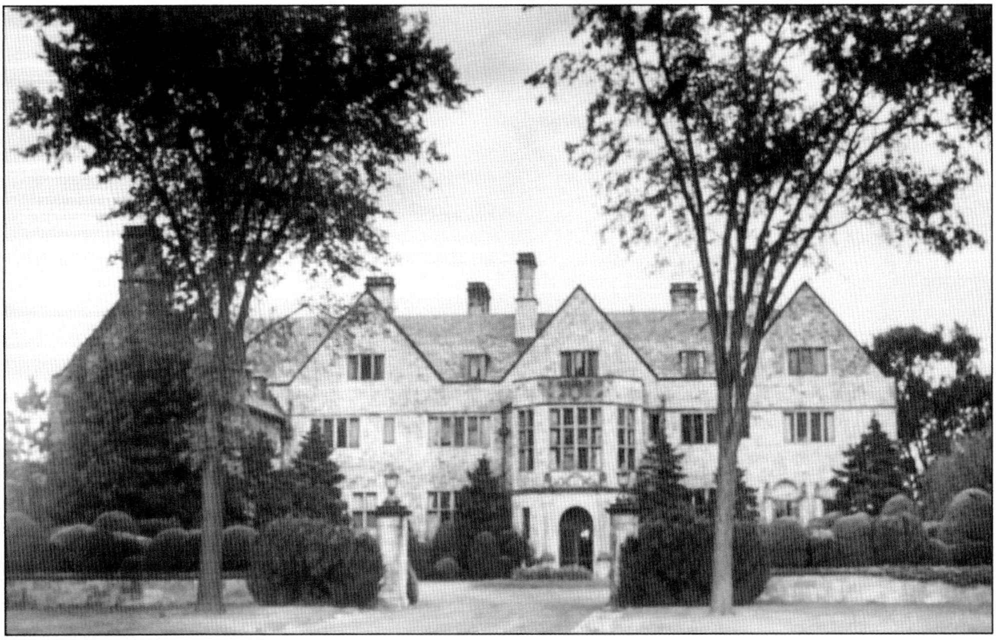

Built by Walter B. Lashar in 1920, the former Hearthstone Hall (named for its thirteen fireplaces) is now Bellarmine Hall, the chief administrative building for Fairfield University. The Society of Jesus purchased the estate together with the adjacent O.G. Jennings property as a site for a boys' high school and a university. Before its conversion to offices, the house served as the on-campus residence of the university's Jesuit priests. (Courtesy of Fairfield University.)

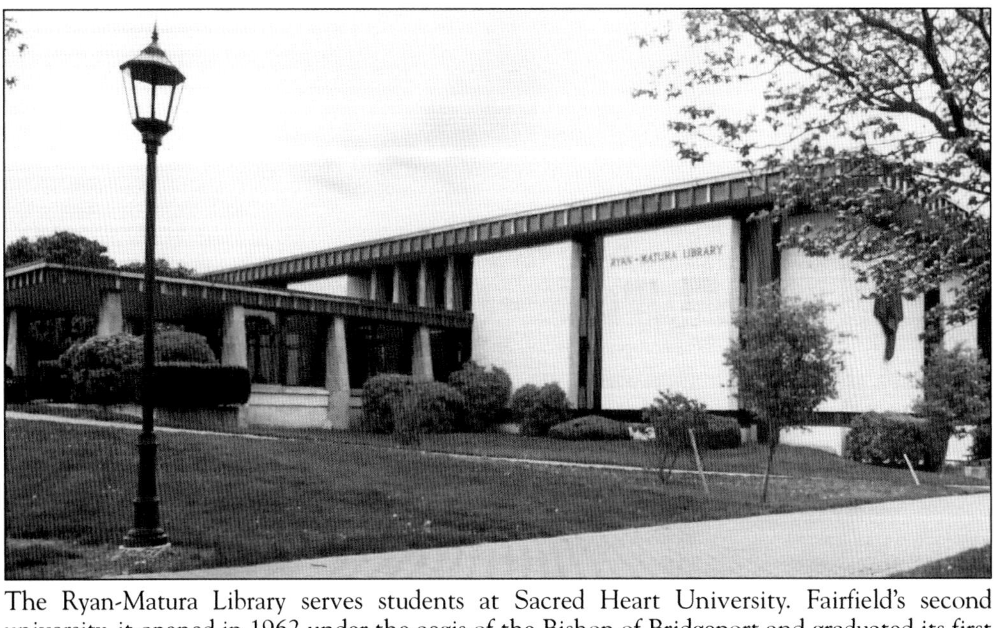

The Ryan-Matura Library serves students at Sacred Heart University. Fairfield's second university, it opened in 1962 under the aegis of the Bishop of Bridgeport and graduated its first class of 112 in 1967. First a commuter school, Sacred Heart has expanded to provide graduate programs and accommodate residential students. (Courtesy of Sacred Heart University, Michael Bisceglie photograph.)

Five

Enterprising Fairfield

Fairfield's location along the Connecticut coast and in the Boston-New York corridor has been a major factor in its economic development. The early farmers and craftsmen traded among themselves, then agricultural products such as the Southport Globe Onion were exported to New York City and beyond. Industry, which grew in the years around the two World Wars, has been largely replaced today with retail trade.

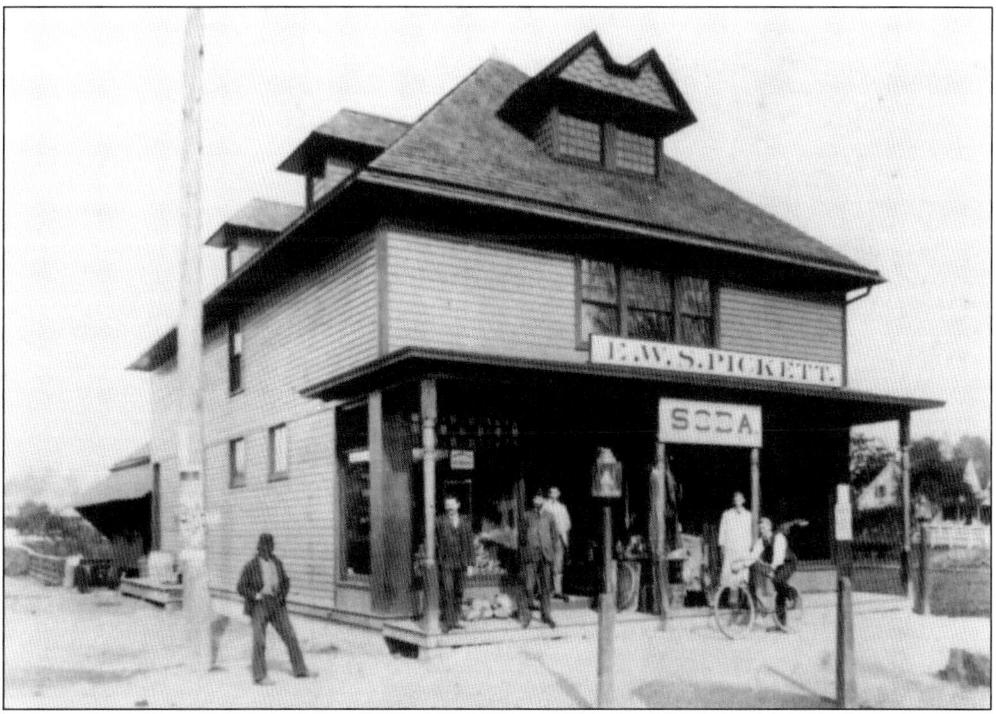

Edwin W.S. Pickett operated a grocery store at this spot at the corner of Post Road and Sanford Street from 1887 to 1904. Pickett also served as postmaster, fire chief, and a real estate and insurance agent. The building was destroyed by fire in 1911. (Instantaneous Photo-View Co., New York City, c. 1895.)

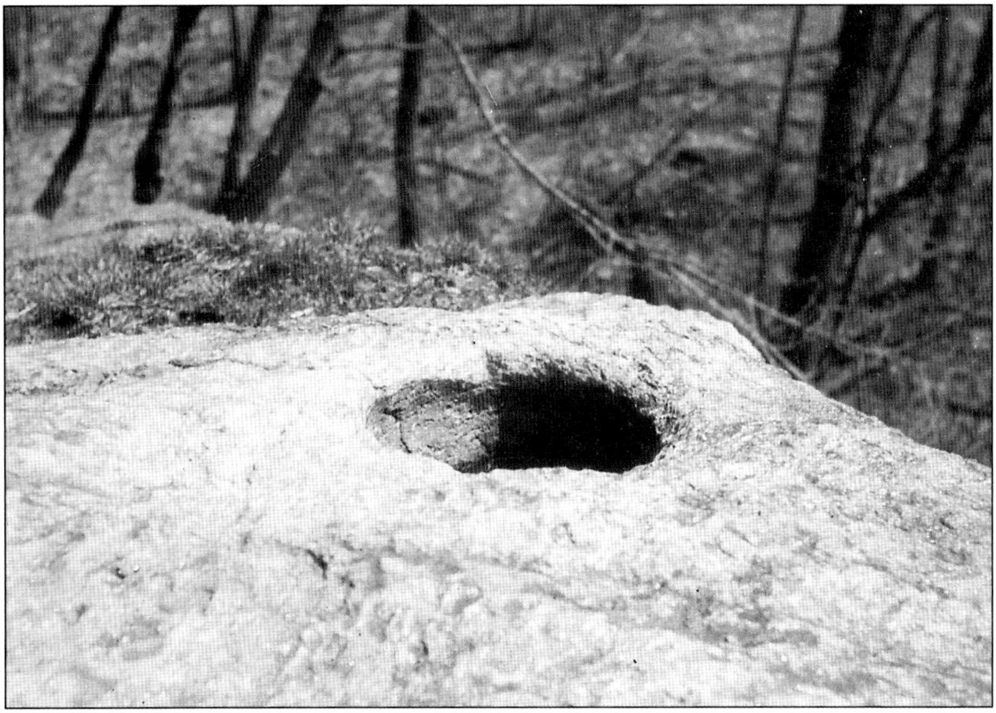

Native Americans lived in the area called Fairfield before Europeans settled here in 1639. The Mohegan-Pequots lived in small villages where the women planted corn and beans and the men hunted and fished. According to legend, women used this natural hole known as Samp Mortar Rock for grinding their corn into samp or meal.

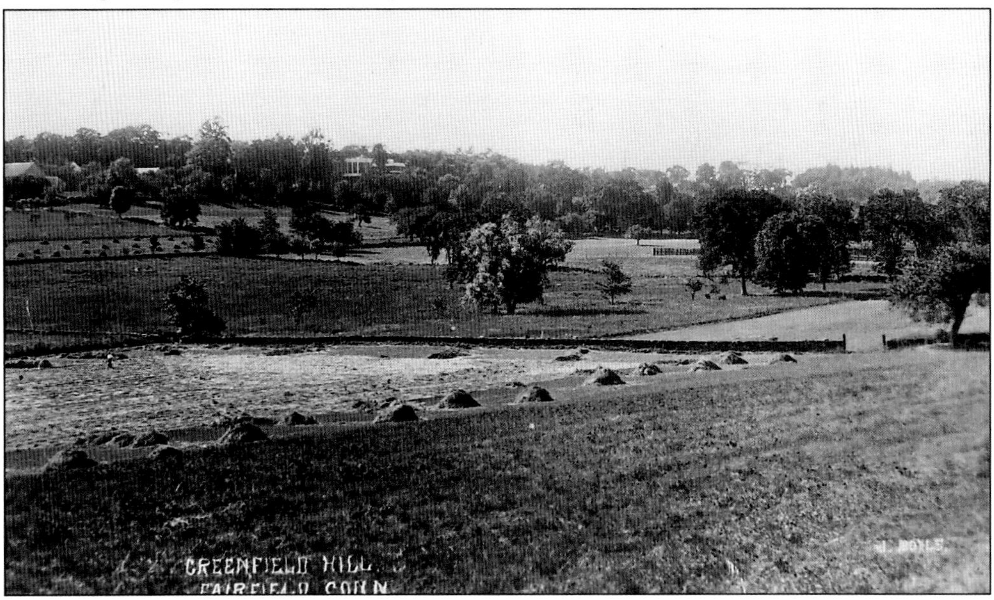

Timothy Dwight built his home, Verna, on Greenfield Hill. In 1796 Isaac Bronson bought the property, and over the generations his descendants expanded the holdings into a farm of more than 200 acres. The rounded porch seen in the background of this *c.* 1900 photograph was the house at Verna when occupied by Frederic Bronson Jr.

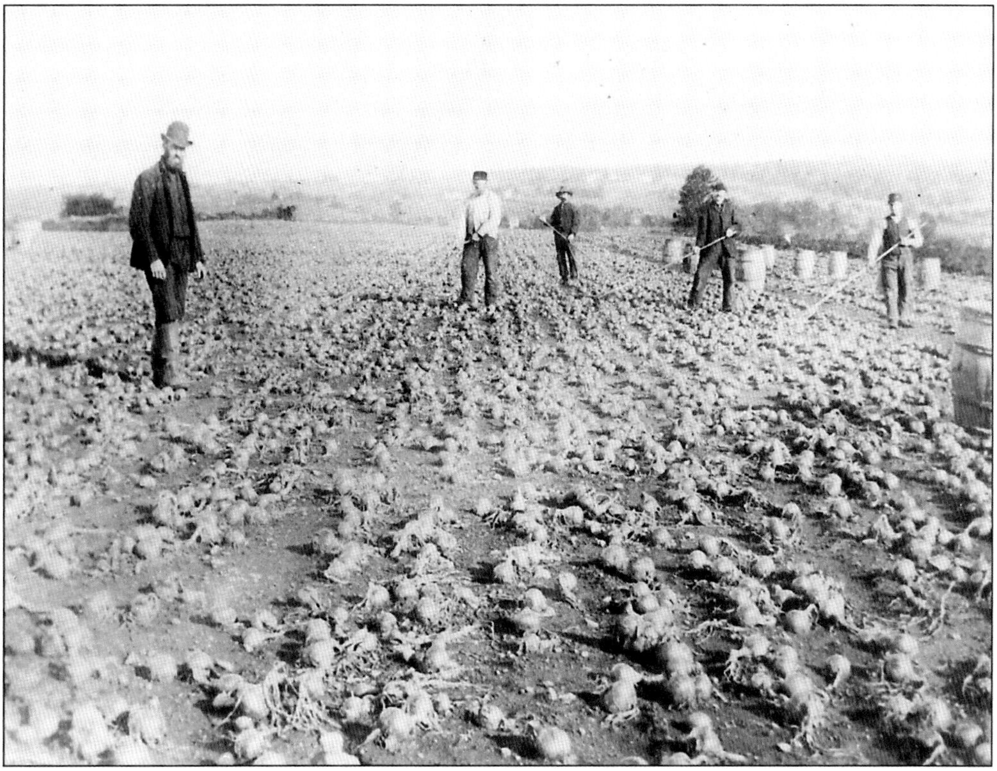

Hired hands cultivate onions on the Buckingham farm on the north side of Mill Hill about 1890. Onions were a major crop for Fairfield's farmers in the nineteenth century. During the Civil War, about 100,000 bushels of onions were raised in Southport. The Southport Globe Onion earned a worldwide reputation for its shape and its keeping qualities. You can still order the Southport Onion through a catalog today.

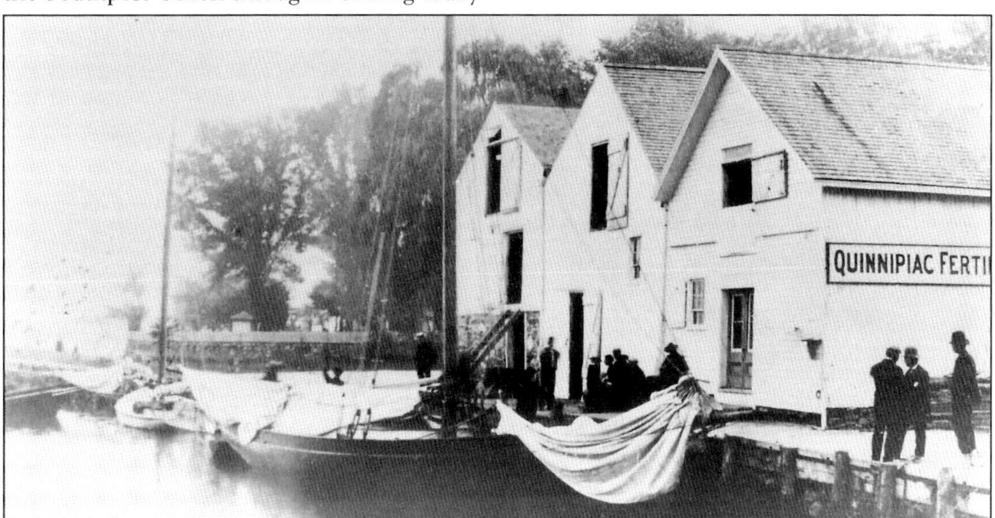

Merchants shipped onions from sheds along Southport harbor similar to the ones pictured in this c. 1890 photograph. Warehouses dominated the shoreline in the 1800s. Vessels such as the sloop *James K. Polk* and the schooner *Estelle* carried the cargo to New York City.

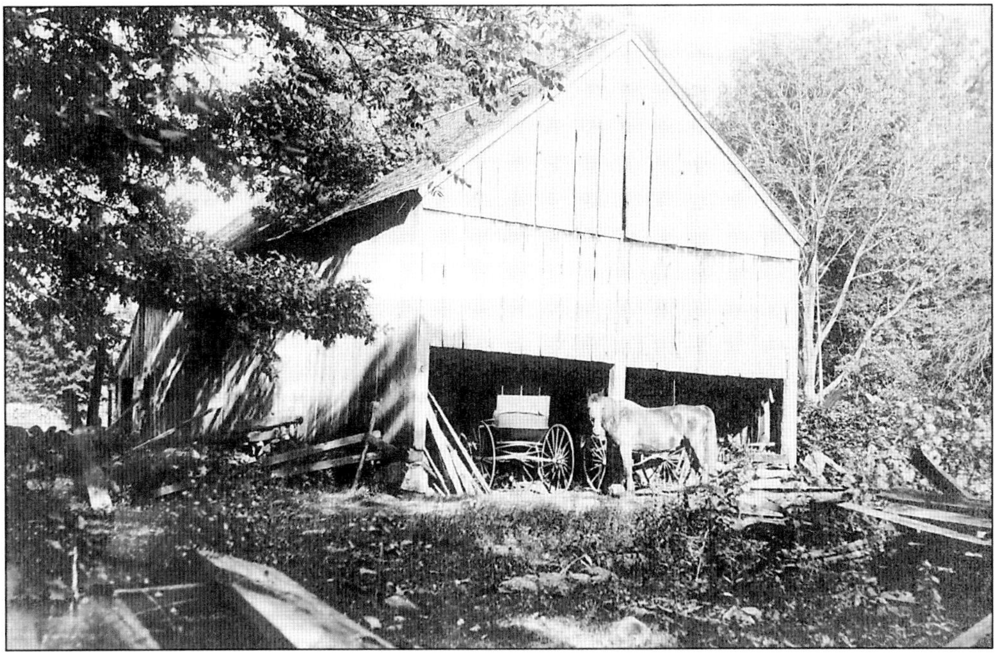

Abbie Wakeman operated a farm until it was purchased by the Bridgeport Hydraulic Company to make way for the Hemlock Reservoir. Photographed in September 1910, the farm was located east of Black Rock Turnpike.

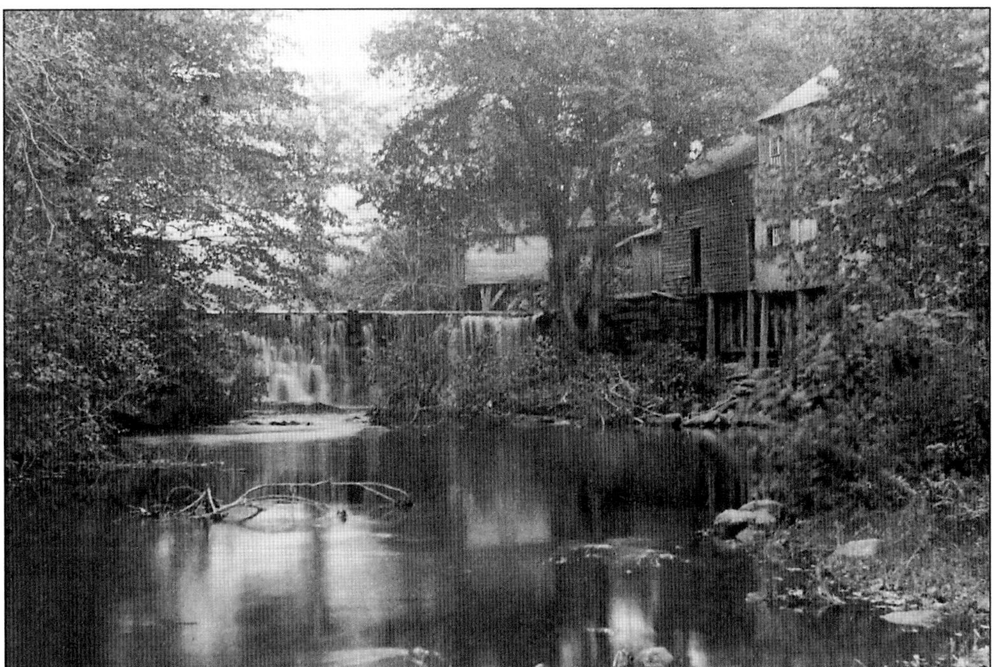

Farmers took their corn and grain to neighborhood mills for grinding. The town regulated the establishment and operation of all mills along the rivers within its boundaries from 1639. Wilson's Mill, at the corner of Congress Street and Black Rock Turnpike, now lies under the Merritt Parkway. (Mabel Osgood Wright photograph, c. 1905.)

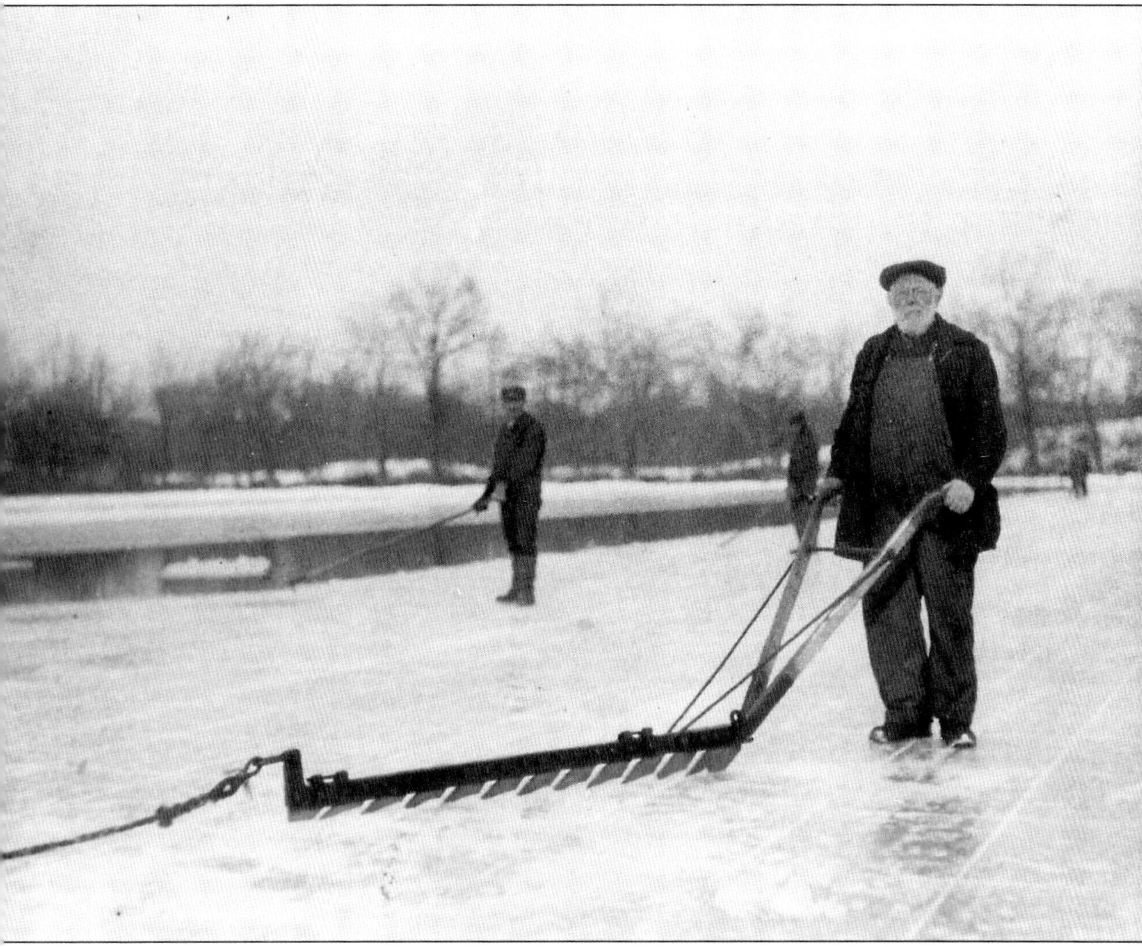

Benjamin F. Bulkley Sr. scores the surface prior to cutting blocks of ice from Sasco Lake about 1910.

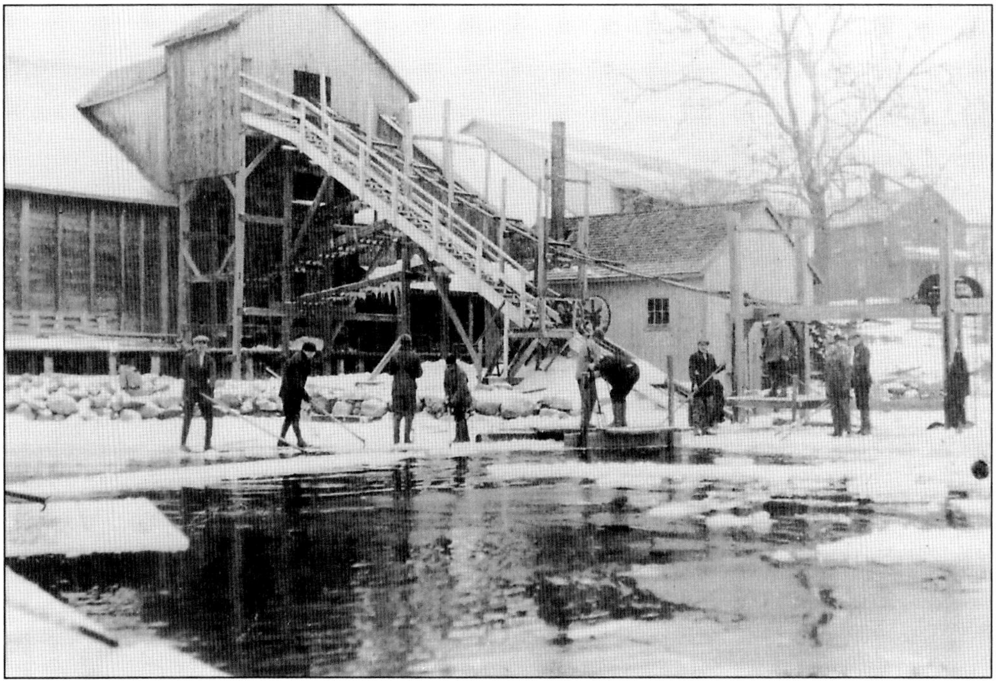

Ice blocks were floated to the Bulkley Ice House, where a conveyor moved them into position for storage. Ice was insulated with sawdust so it would last through the summer to supply the household icebox.

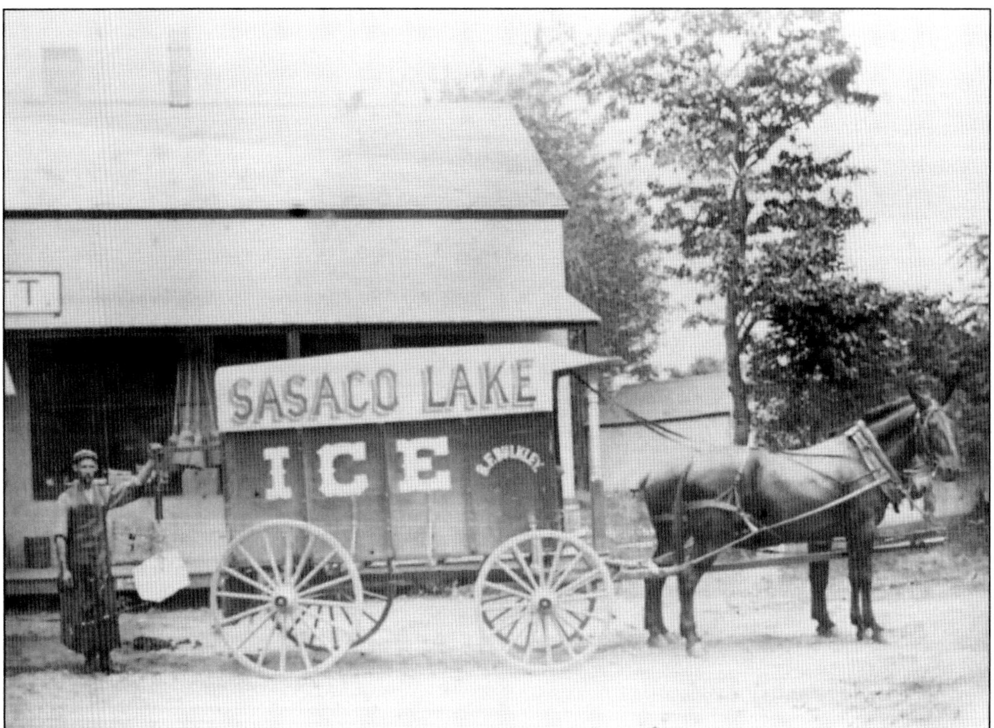

Bulkley's Sasaco Lake Ice company delivered ice to local hardware and general stores *c.* 1890.

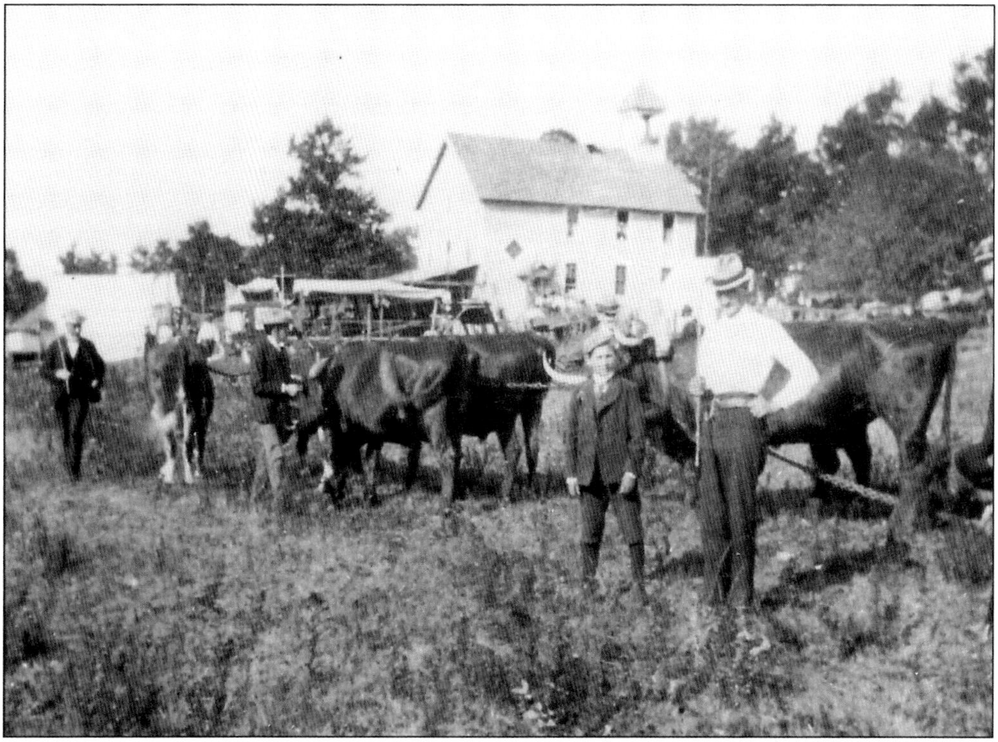

Patrons of Husbandry, commonly called the Grange, hosted annual fairs where farmers displayed their goods and entered into friendly competitions, such as the oxen pull seen here, about 1900. The Greenfield Hill Grange still holds an annual fair, although on a much smaller scale, indicative of the decline of and waning interest in agriculture in Fairfield.

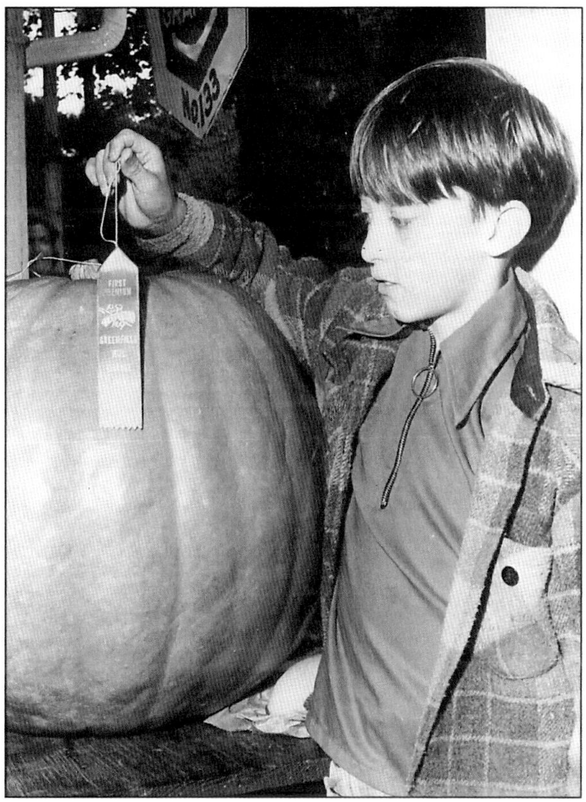

In 1981 John Maxneo, age ten, won a blue ribbon at the Greenfield Hill Grange Fair for growing the largest pumpkin. The behemoth took four months to grow and weighed 90 pounds. (*Fairfield Citizen-News* photograph.)

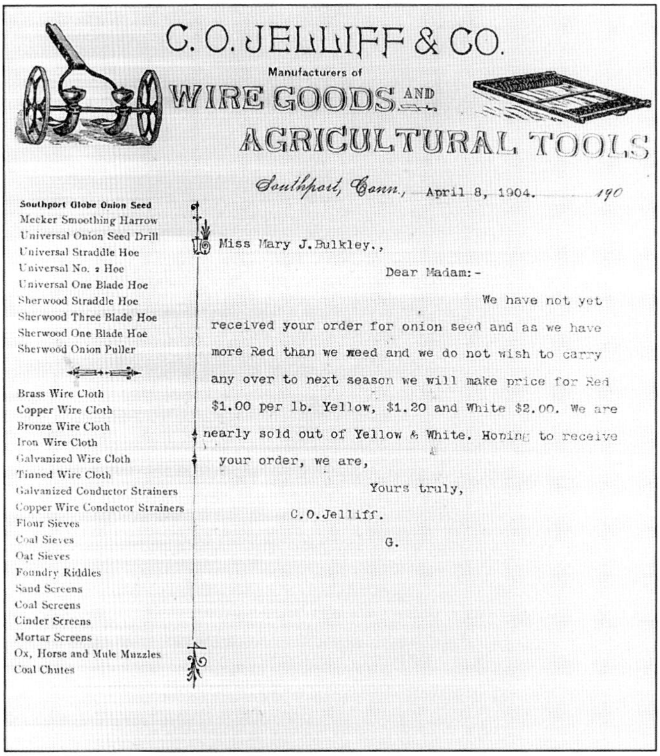

C. O. JELLIFF & CO.

Manufacturers of

WIRE GOODS AND AGRICULTURAL TOOLS

Southport, Conn., April 8, 1904. 190

Southport Globe Onion Seed
Mecker Smoothing Harrow
Universal Onion Seed Drill
Universal Straddle Hoe
Universal No. 2 Hoe
Universal One Blade Hoe
Sherwood Straddle Hoe
Sherwood Three Blade Hoe
Sherwood One Blade Hoe
Sherwood Onion Puller

Brass Wire Cloth
Copper Wire Cloth
Bronze Wire Cloth
Iron Wire Cloth
Galvanized Wire Cloth
Tinned Wire Cloth
Galvanized Conductor Strainers
Copper Wire Conductor Strainers
Flour Sieves
Coal Sieves
Oat Sieves
Foundry Riddles
Sand Screens
Coal Screens
Cinder Screens
Mortar Screens
Ox, Horse and Mule Muzzles
Coal Chutes

Miss Mary J. Bulkley.,

Dear Madam:-

We have not yet received your order for onion seed and as we have more Red than we need and we do not wish to carry any over to next season we will make price for Red $1.00 per lb. Yellow, $1.20 and White $2.00. We are nearly sold out of Yellow & White. Hoping to receive your order, we are,

Yours truly,

C.O.Jelliff.

G.

Farmers purchased both their onion seed and the necessary agricultural equipment from C.O. Jelliff & Co., one of the oldest continuously operating manufacturing firms in Fairfield. (Letterhead, 1900.)

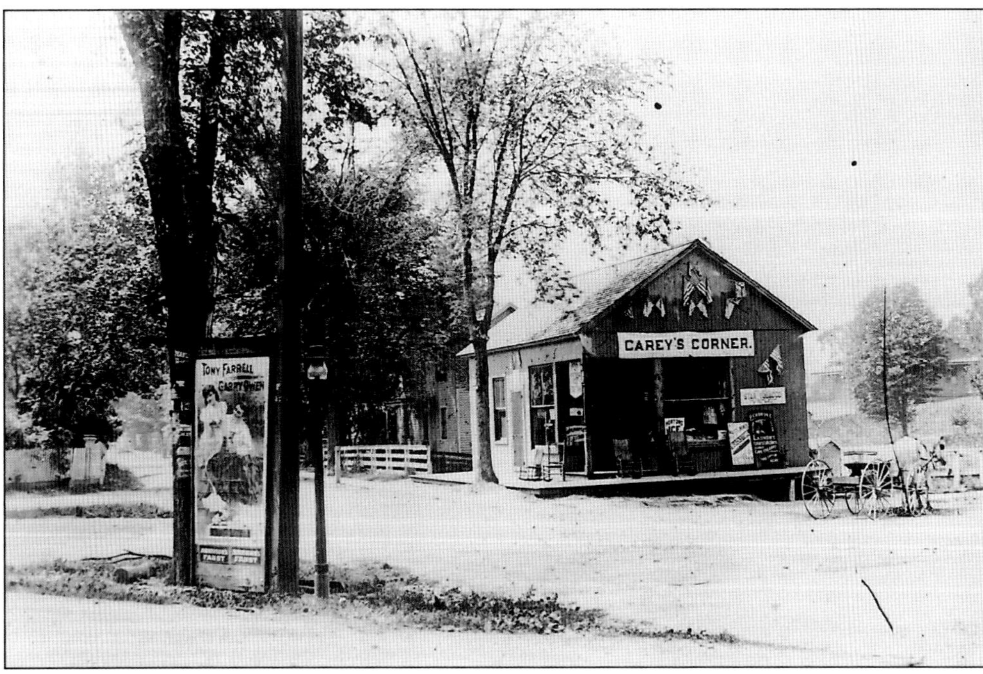

Tom Carey managed a confectionery store in Disbrow's Block on Main Street in Southport before building his own store nearby in 1894. He gave his name to the intersection of Main Street and Pequot Avenue, Carey's Corner, where Switzer's Pharmacy is located today. This photograph is of Carey's second store, built after 1898.

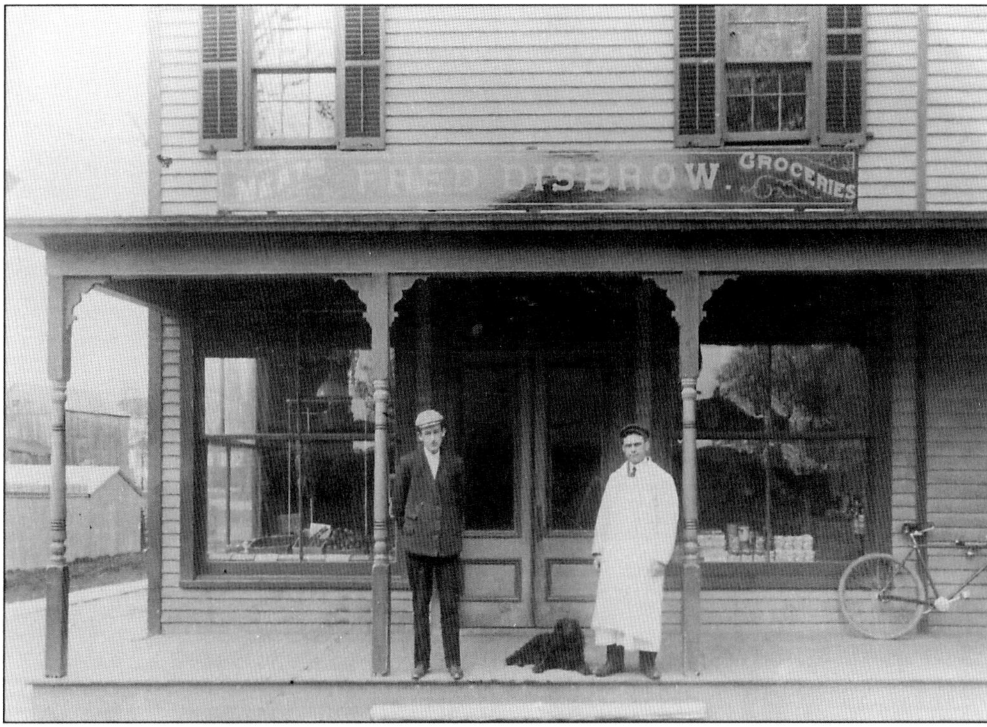

Theodore Becker, a clerk at Disbrow's meat market, poses on the front porch with his dog Prince about 1904. Fred A. Disbrow's store was on Main Street in Southport. Charles E. Bulkley ran a confectionery and ice cream parlor in the portion of the building seen beyond the chainless bicycle.

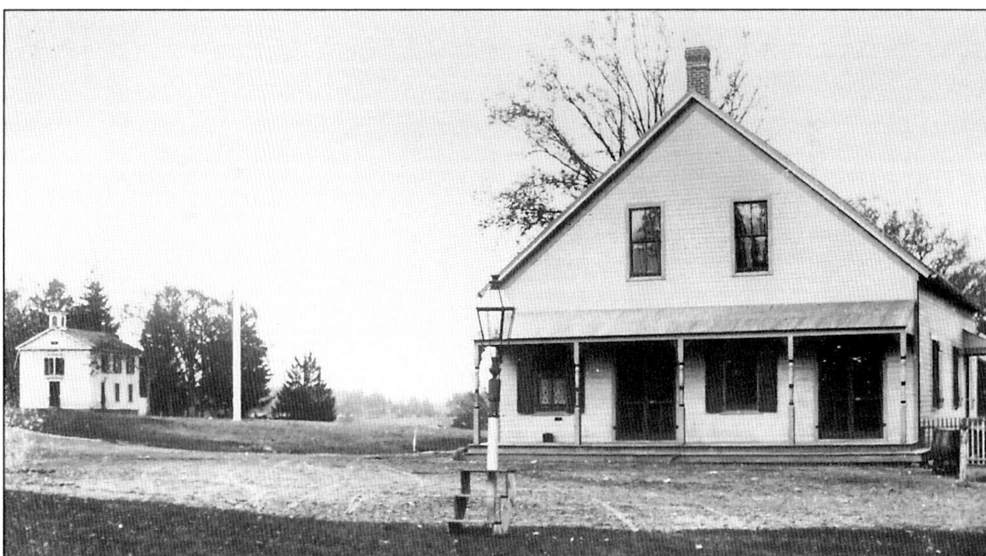

Barzilla Banks opened a store on Bronson Road at the intersection of Old Academy Road in 1869. His son, William, and his daughters, Georgianna and Mary Elizabeth, continued to run the combination general store and post office until 1929. The building, pictured in 1880, was later moved to Hillside Road and converted into a home.

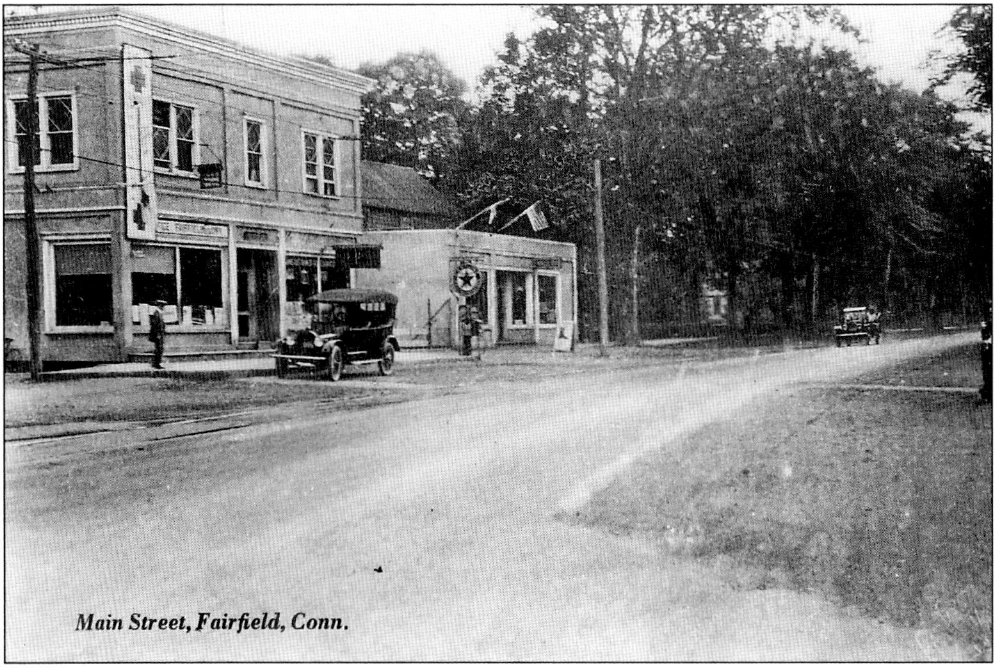

The post office and Henderson's Texaco station stood at the corner of Reef Road and the Post Road (then called Marine Avenue and Spring Street) about 1915. Henderson's was one of the first gas stations in town. (Postcard.)

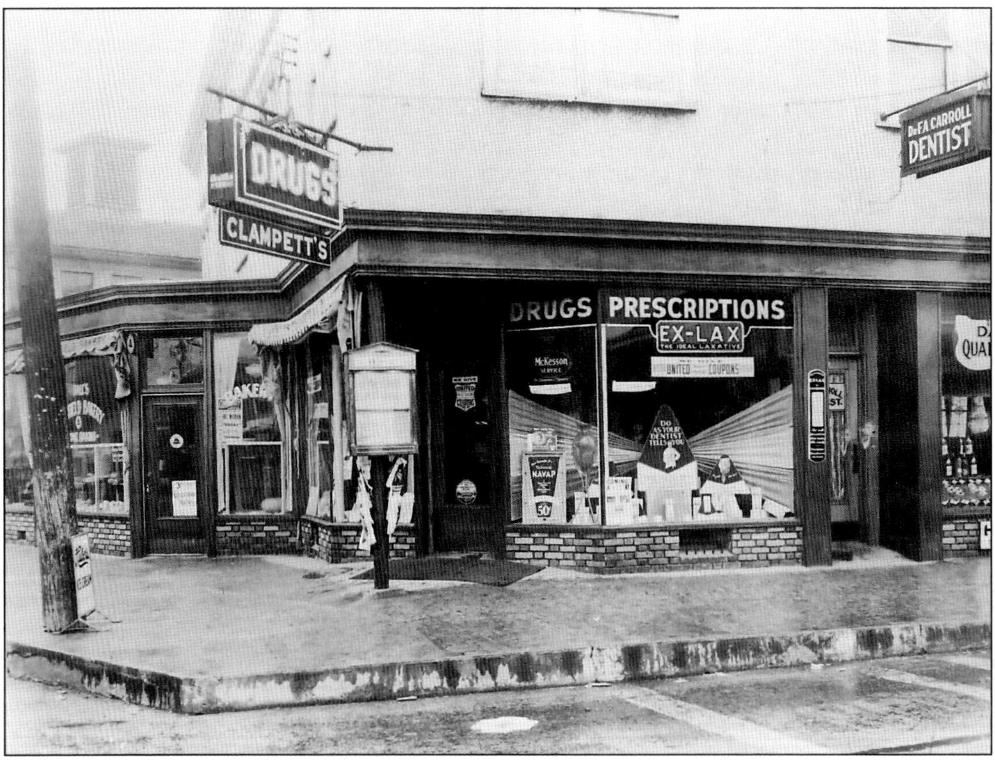

The same corner in 1932 was home to Clampett's Drug Store.

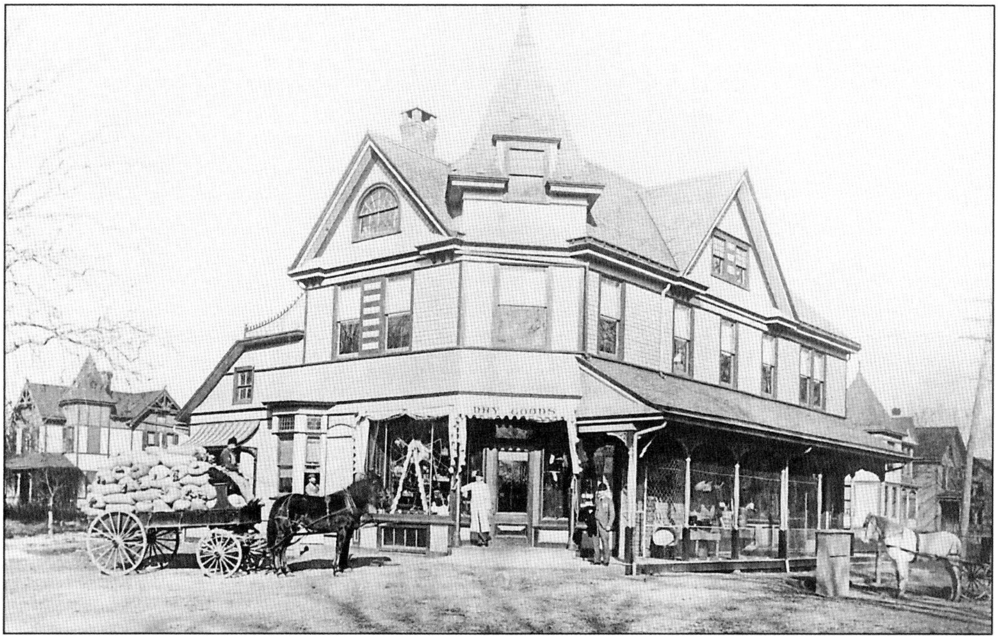

Benjamin Betts sold dry goods, groceries, and general merchandise from his store at the corner of Unquowa Place and the Post Road, seen in 1894. The business was founded about 1844 by Benjamin's father, Moses G. Betts. Benjamin offered delivery service to the beach during the summer.

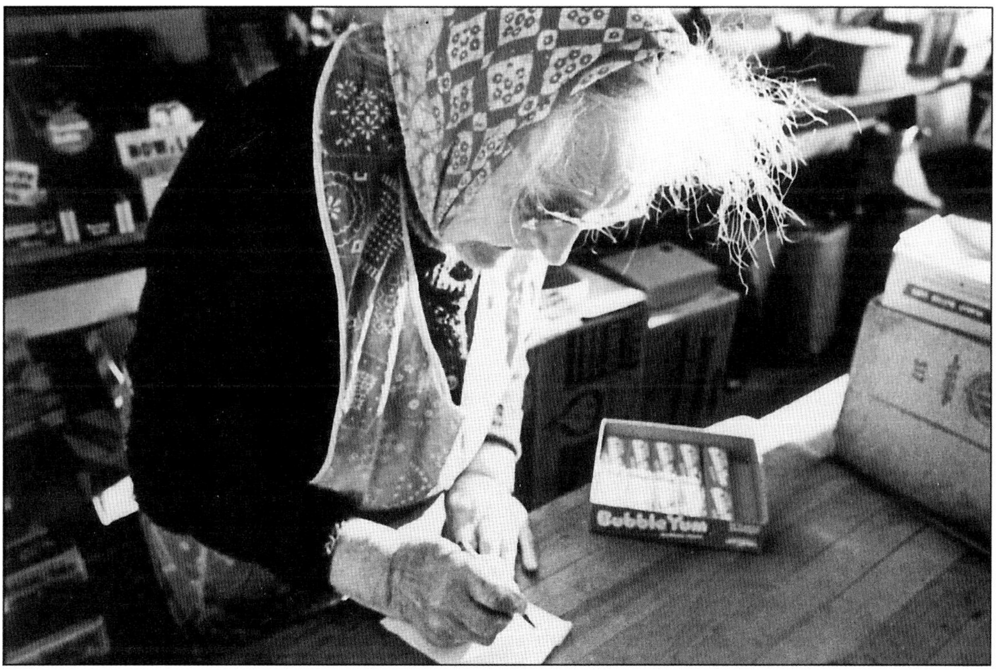

Grasmere storekeeper Mary Salamon opened her small market on Churchill Street in 1920. Born in Hungary, Mrs. Salamon came to Bridgeport when she married in 1909. Competition from major chain stores and inflation threatened her enterprise in 1977, but she stayed open to sell candy to youngsters who came in daily. (*Fairfield Citizen-News* photograph.)

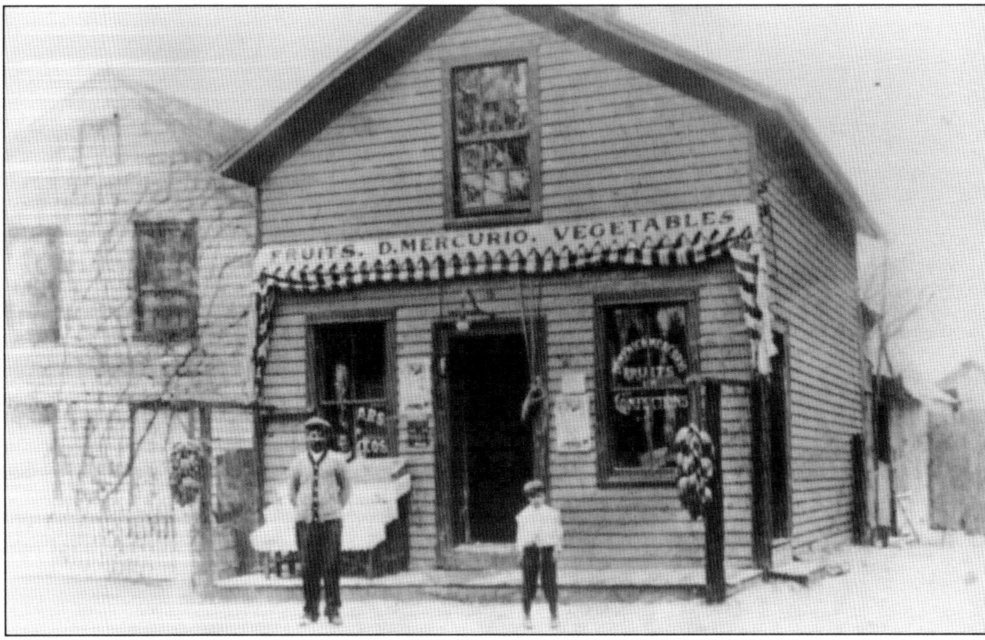

Mercurio's is the oldest continuously operating family-owned business in Fairfield. Domenic Mercurio sold fruits and vegetables from his first store on the Old Post Road. He moved the store to its Post Road location in 1913 and turned operations over to his children in 1928. Sons Jimmy and Domenic Jr. expanded the store to its present size and continued the personalized service and home delivery that characterized the business from its start. (Below: George P. Weising photograph, 1945.)

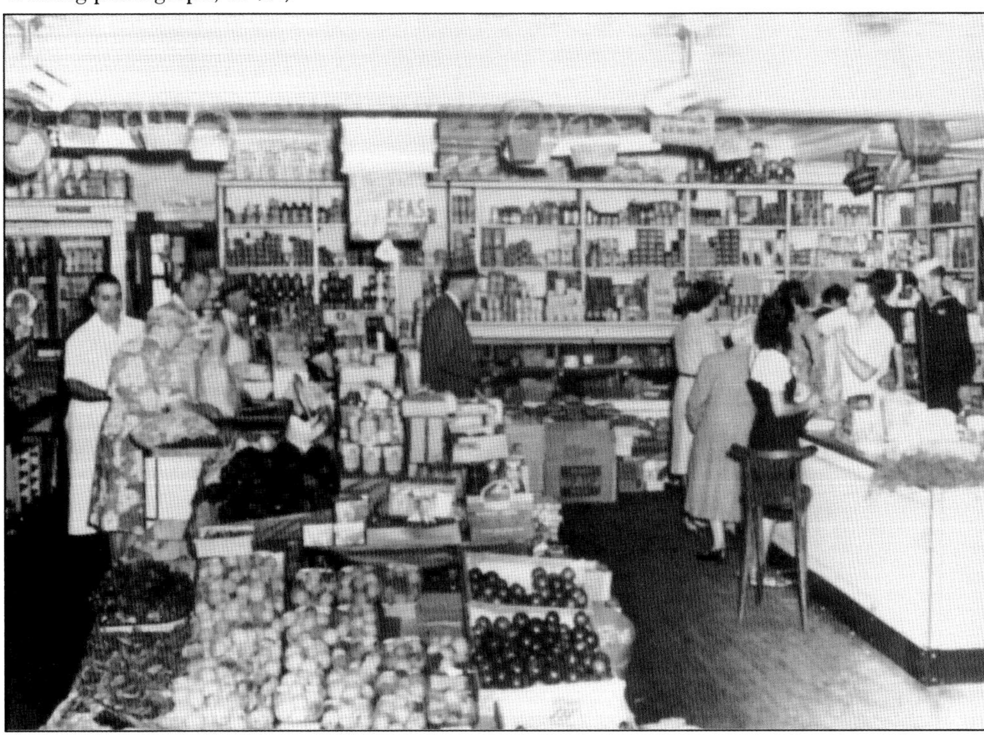

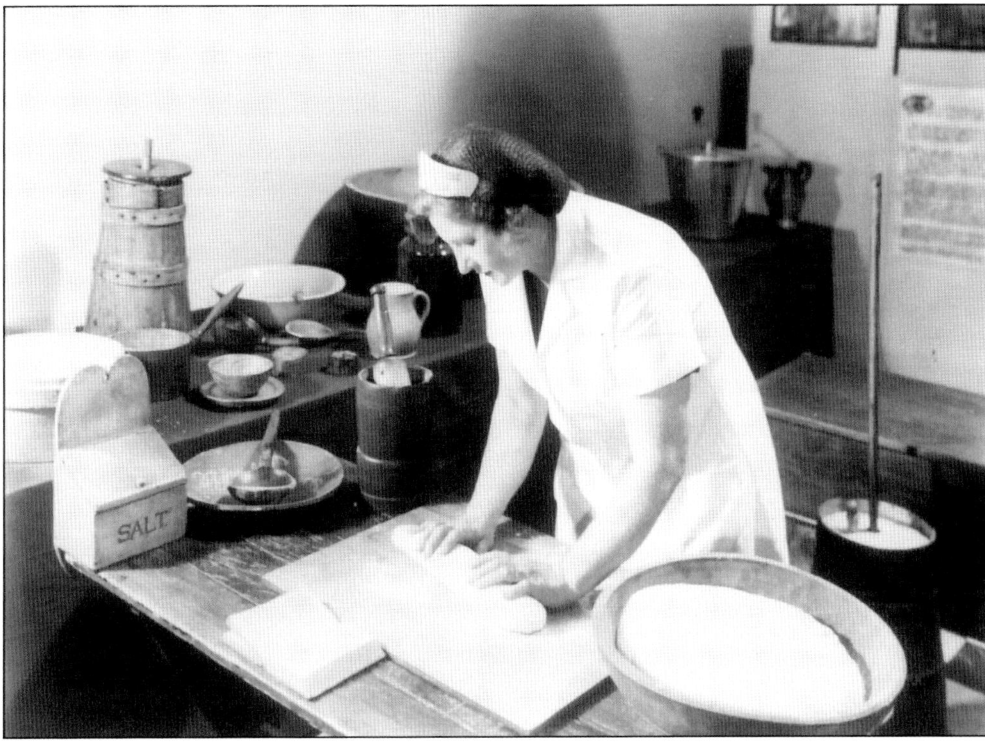

In 1937 Margaret Rudkin of Fairfield baked her first loaf of bread, using natural ingredients. That summer she took a basket of loaves to Mercurio's Market. The bread sold out before Mrs. Rudkin reached her home, Pepperidge Farm, on Sturges Highway. Demand for the fresh bread exceeded Mrs. Rudkin's ability to make it in her kitchen, and she founded Pepperidge Farm Bakery, which now has its headquarters in Norwalk.

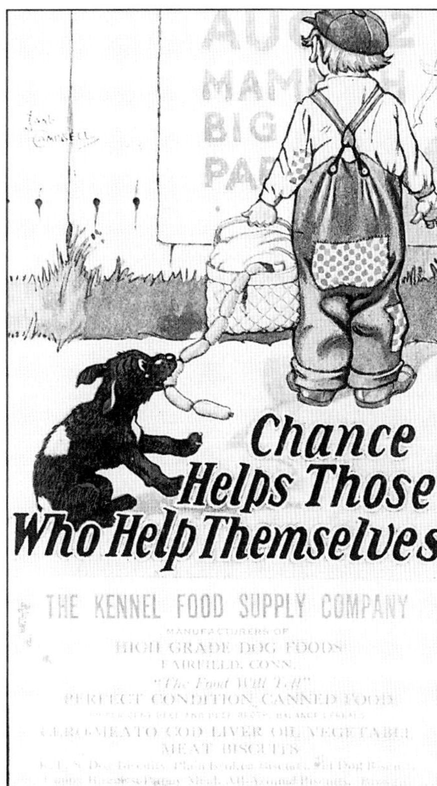

Simon C. Bradley fed his prime hunting dogs biscuits he baked in his own kitchen. Other dog owners requested more biscuits than Bradley could supply, so he built a plant on Mill River, just below the Sturges Road bridge. The company (Kennel Food Supply) continued after Bradley's death in 1936, expanding its product line to include canned dog food, rabbit pellets, wild bird food, and "Chim" crackers for monkeys. Hygrade Food Products of Detroit bought the business and moved it to Ohio in 1959. (Advertising blotter, *c.* 1920.)

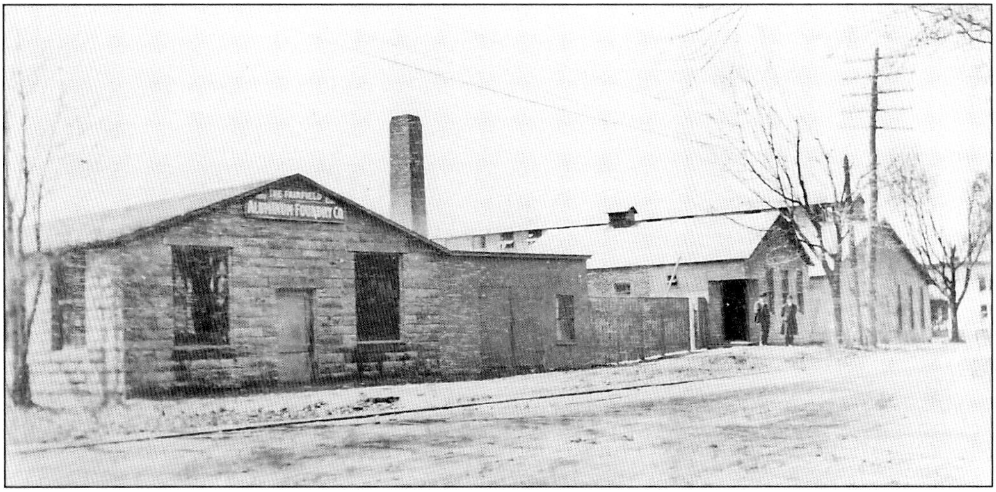

Fairfield Aluminum Foundry Company started in Southport in 1907 and moved to the Post Road the following year. Taken over by the Aluminum Company of America in 1922, the company produced aircraft parts and parts for ships and railway cars. Eastern European immigrants made up a significant portion of the work force after 1924. The company moved to Bridgeport in 1957. (Postcard, *c.* 1910.)

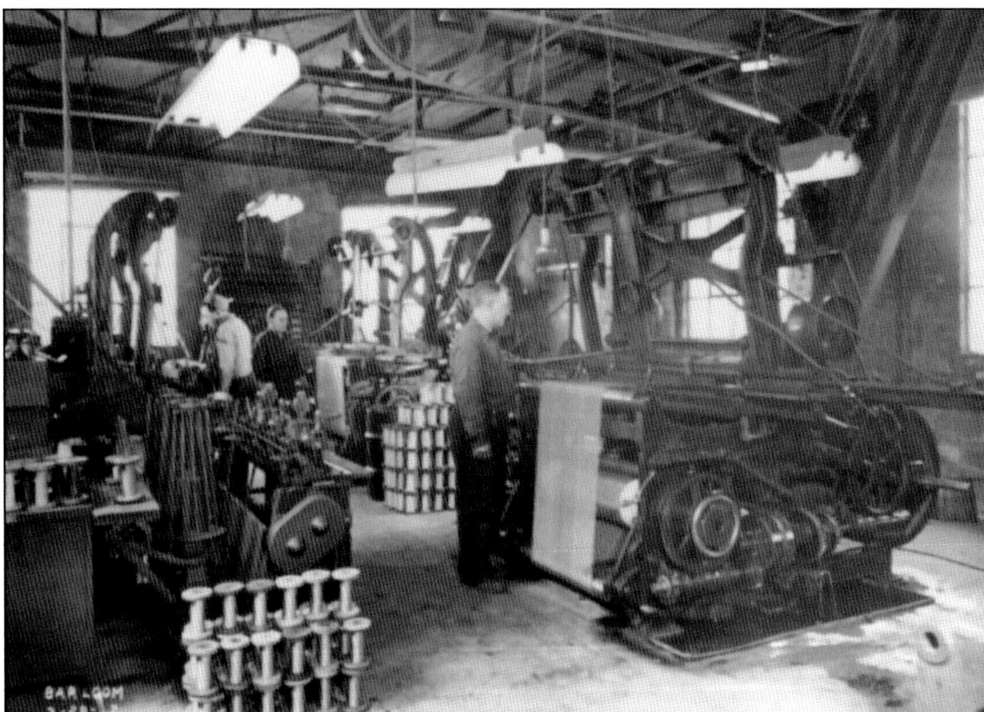

Rolock Inc. was founded in Southport in 1924 as DeMattia Wire Works. Rolock was DeMattia's trademark, becoming the company name in 1929. The company manufactures woven wire mesh baskets and trays for industrial heat treating processes. The plant moved to its current location on Kings Highway in Fairfield in the mid-1940s. This picture of the corner of the weaving department, taken in 1947, shows bar looms which wove medium grades of wire cloth.

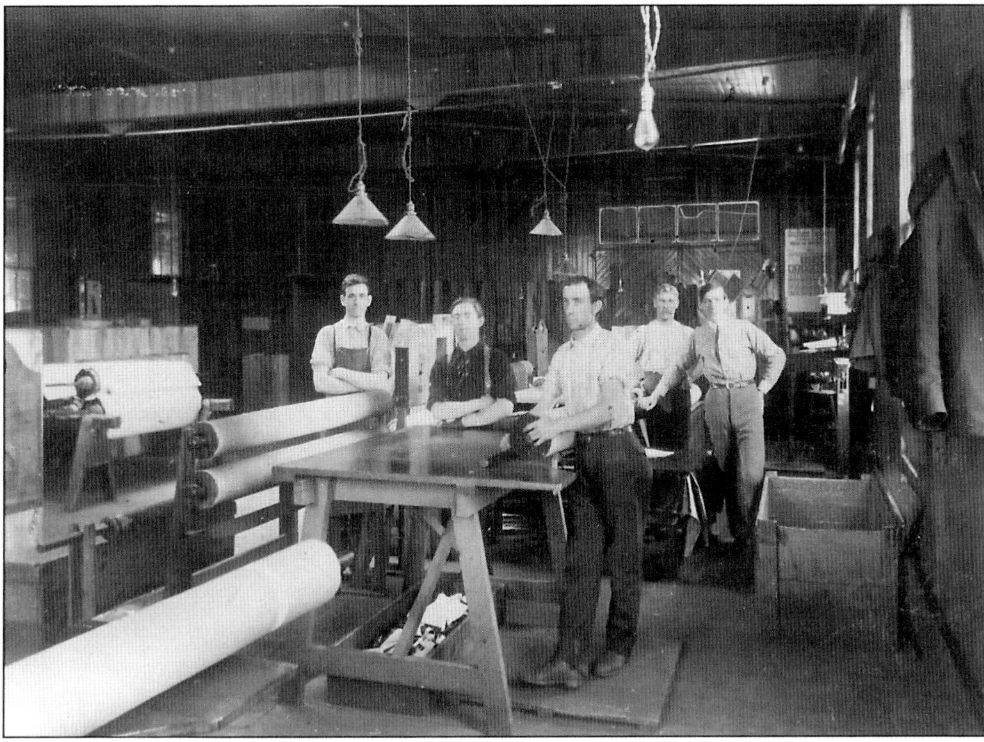

Fairfield Rubber Company, founded in 1879, made rubber-coated fabrics for raincoats, upholstery, work aprons, and carriage tops. Three men identified in this 1908 photograph of the inspection room are Antone Mickut, John Mullins, and Oscar Mullins.

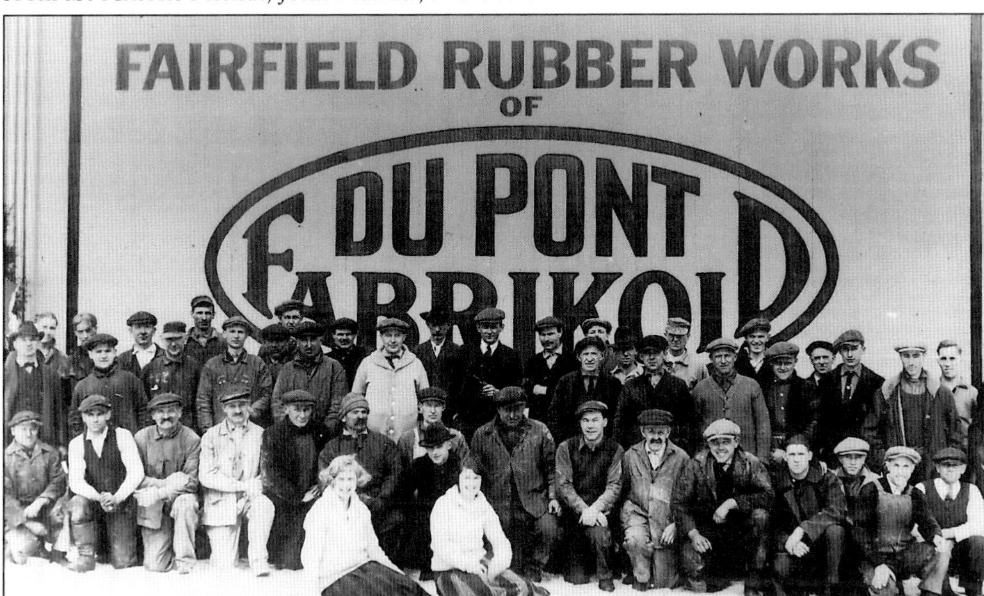

E.I. duPont de Nemours purchased Fairfield Rubber Works in 1916 and changed its name to DuPont Fabrikoid. The company continues today as Fairprene Industrial Products Co. Inc. at its original location on Mill Plain Road.

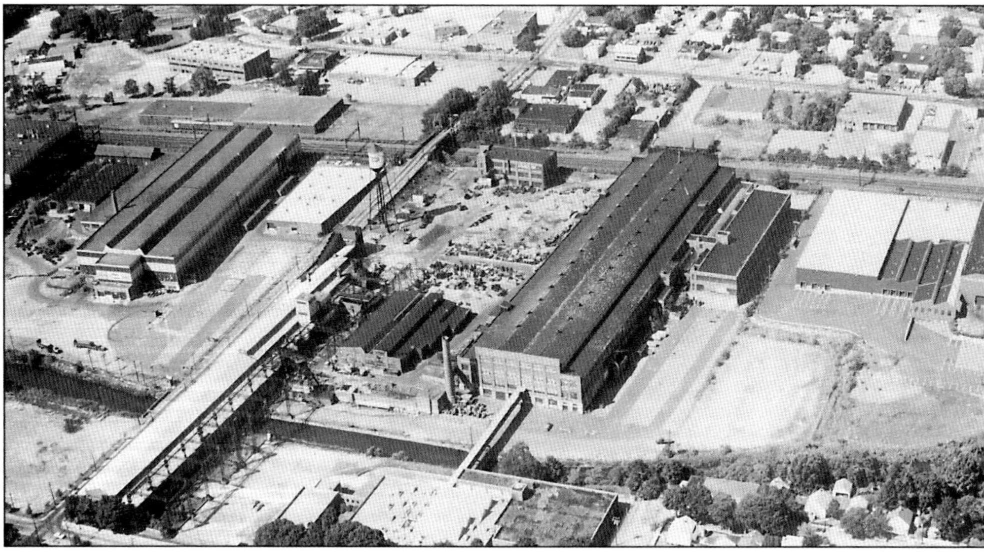

The extent of the Bullard Company plant can be seen in this 1982 aerial view, looking north toward the Black Rock Turnpike interchange of the Connecticut Turnpike (I-95). Note the proximity of the railroad, one of the features that attracted the company to this site.

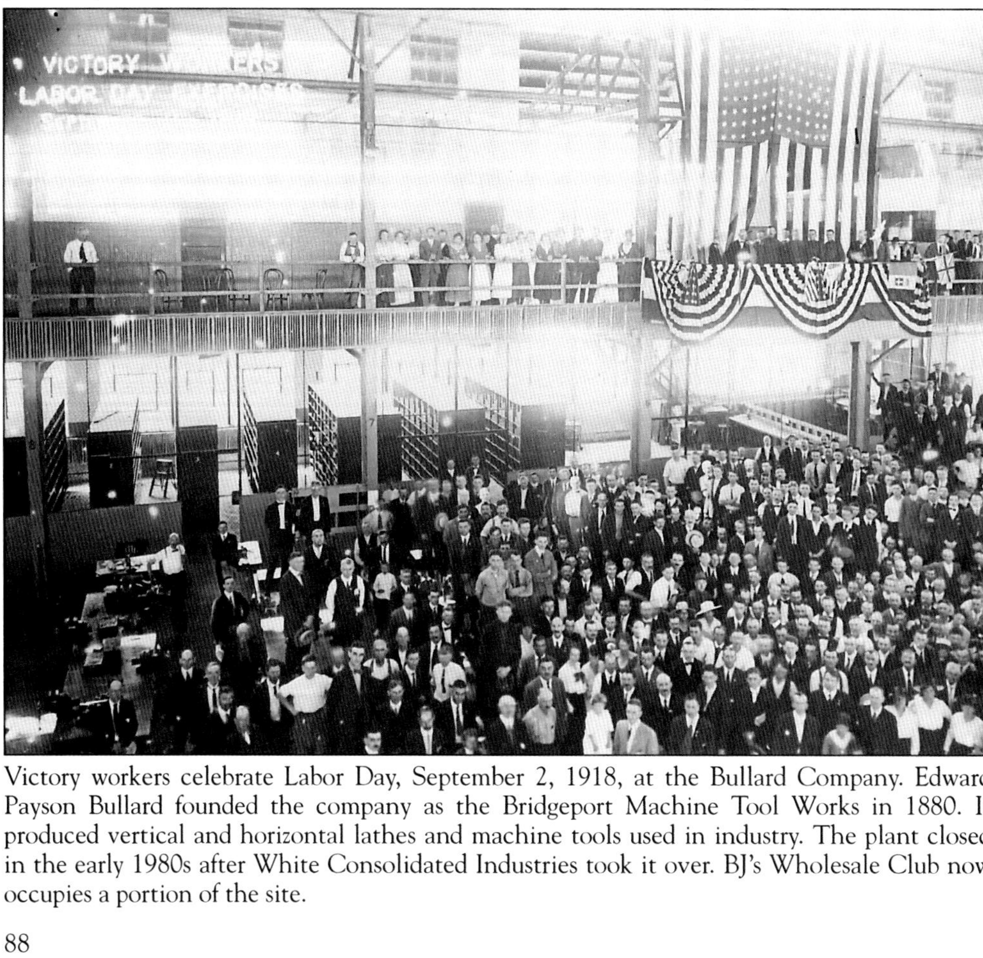

Victory workers celebrate Labor Day, September 2, 1918, at the Bullard Company. Edward Payson Bullard founded the company as the Bridgeport Machine Tool Works in 1880. It produced vertical and horizontal lathes and machine tools used in industry. The plant closed in the early 1980s after White Consolidated Industries took it over. BJ's Wholesale Club now occupies a portion of the site.

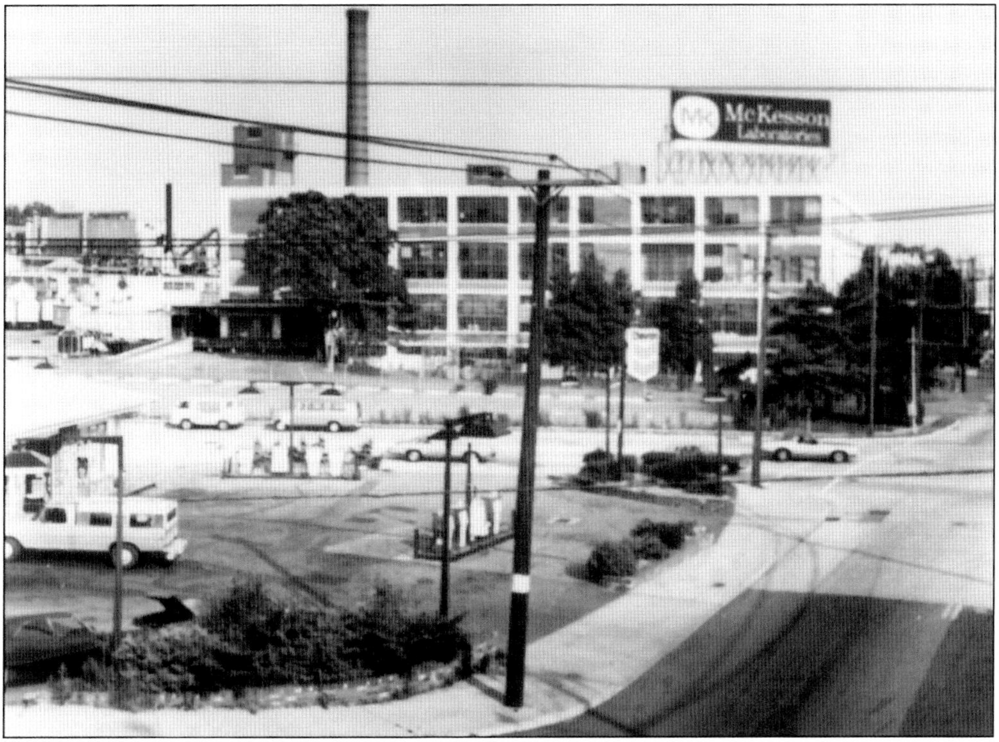

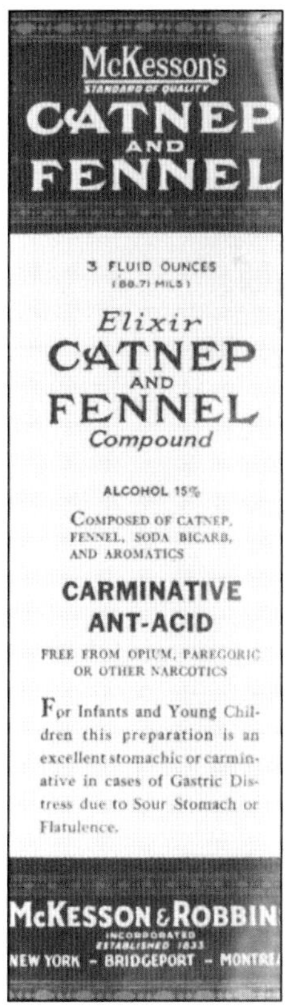

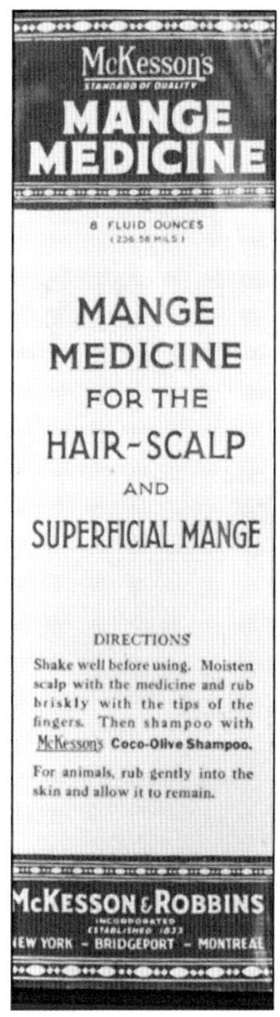

Drugs and cosmetics for world distribution were made at McKesson & Robbins's Fairfield plant. The company employed hundreds of men and women from Fairfield and the surrounding towns before closing in 1988. Home Depot is now located where the plant stood. These package labels indicate the variety of products produced at McKesson & Robbins.

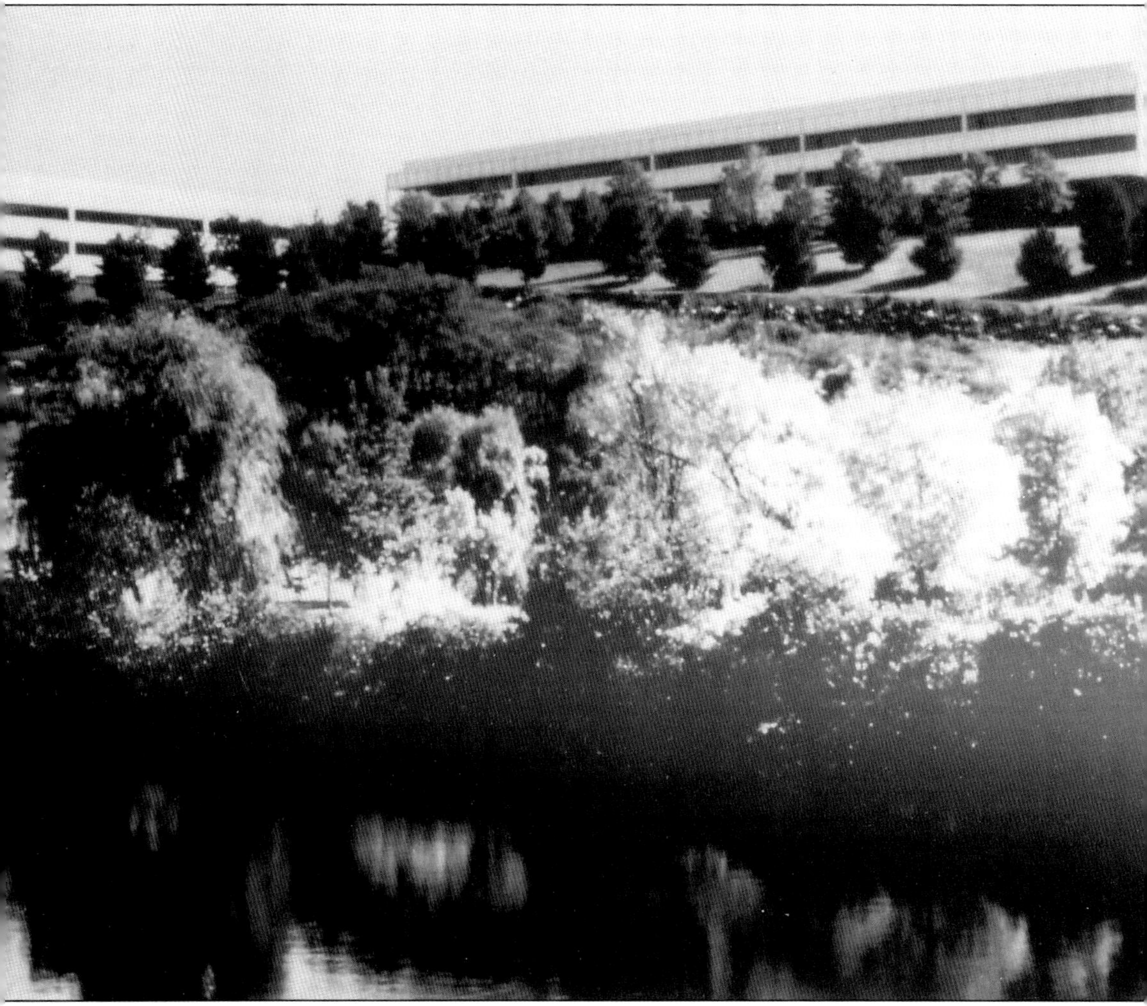

In 1974 General Electric moved its corporate headquarters to a location on a rise south of exit 46 on the Merritt Parkway in Fairfield. The company donated 30 acres of the 100-acre site to the Town for its open space program. The beautifully landscaped grounds had been a source of gravel during the construction of I-95.

Six

Going Places

Location has made Fairfield a convenient place to live for those pursuing careers in many places. Railroad tracks, an interstate highway, and a parkway across the town—these byways have made major intrusions on neighborhoods, but they are lifelines for the residents.

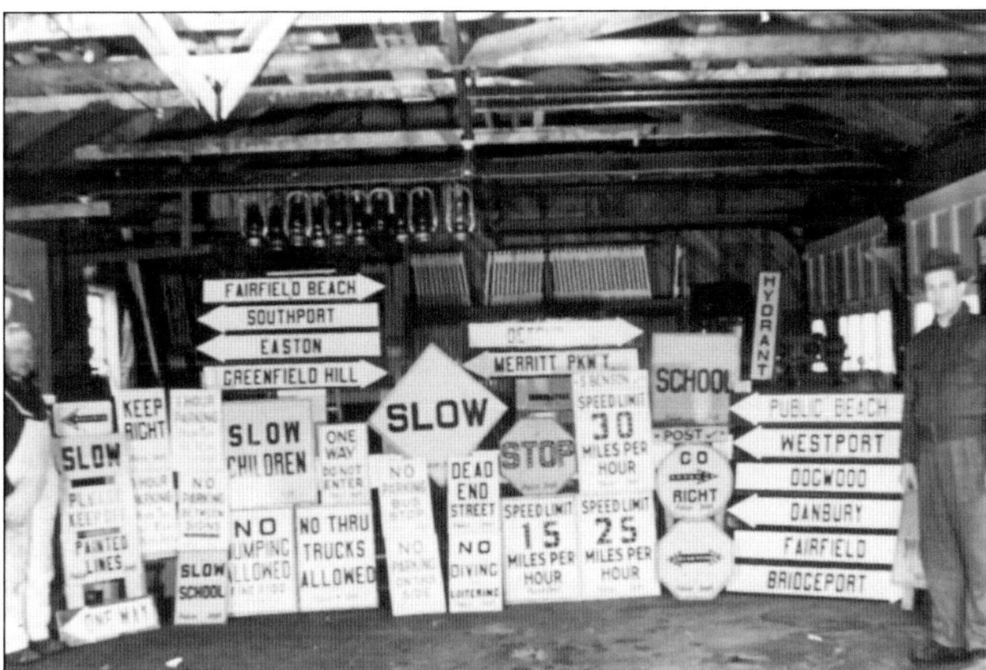

The proliferation of automobiles after World War II and the increase in the volume of traffic required more control, leading to more signs. Bill Burr and friend survey the signs at the town garage about 1950.

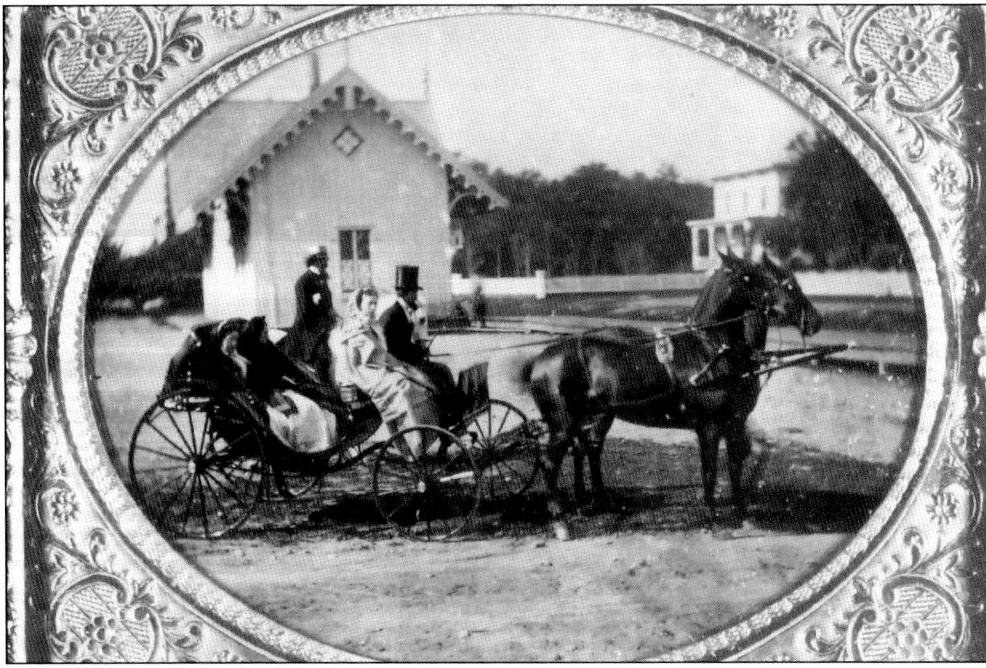

Passengers wait for the train at the Southport station. The single-track railroad from New Haven to New York opened in 1848, and the passenger station, seen in this quarter-plate daguerreotype, was built that same year. This station, moved 80 feet east when double tracks were installed in 1852, burned in 1884.

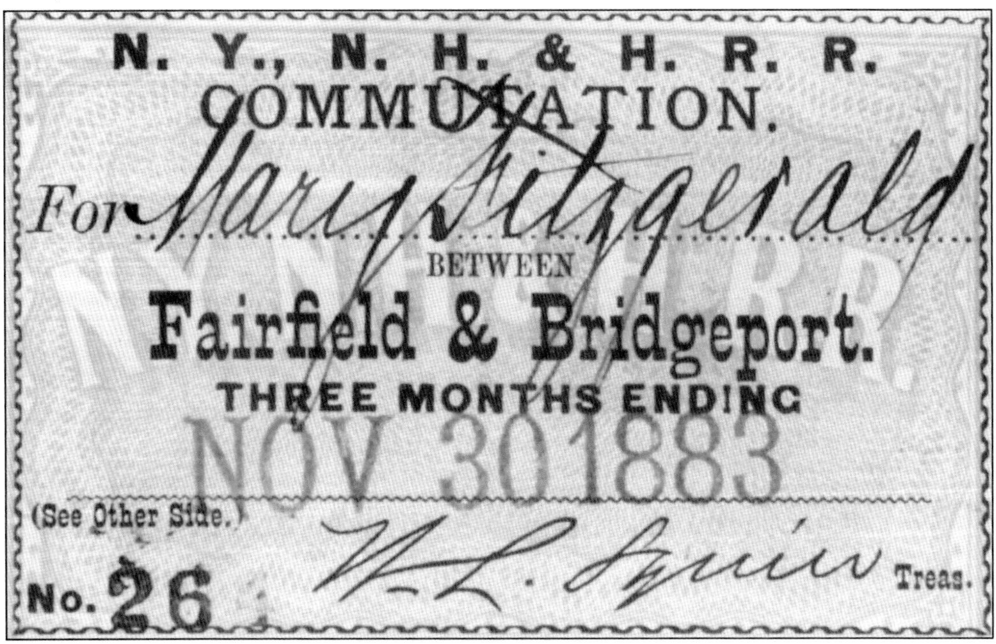

The holder of this 1883 commutation ticket could only get on or off at the stations listed on the face of the ticket, and could only use regular weekday passenger trains. Fairfield residents took the train to Bridgeport to work in the factories or retail shops or to go shopping. Today the majority of commuters who take the train have destinations west of Fairfield.

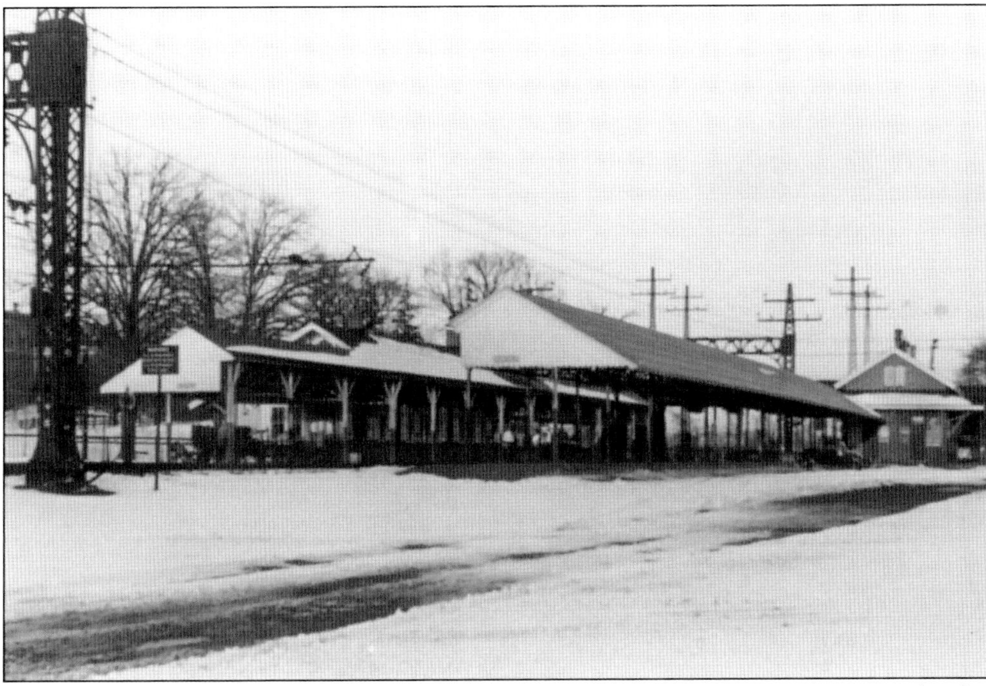

The passenger stations in Fairfield, seen in this 1941 photograph, are the same ones used today, although the platforms have been raised to accommodate newer train designs.

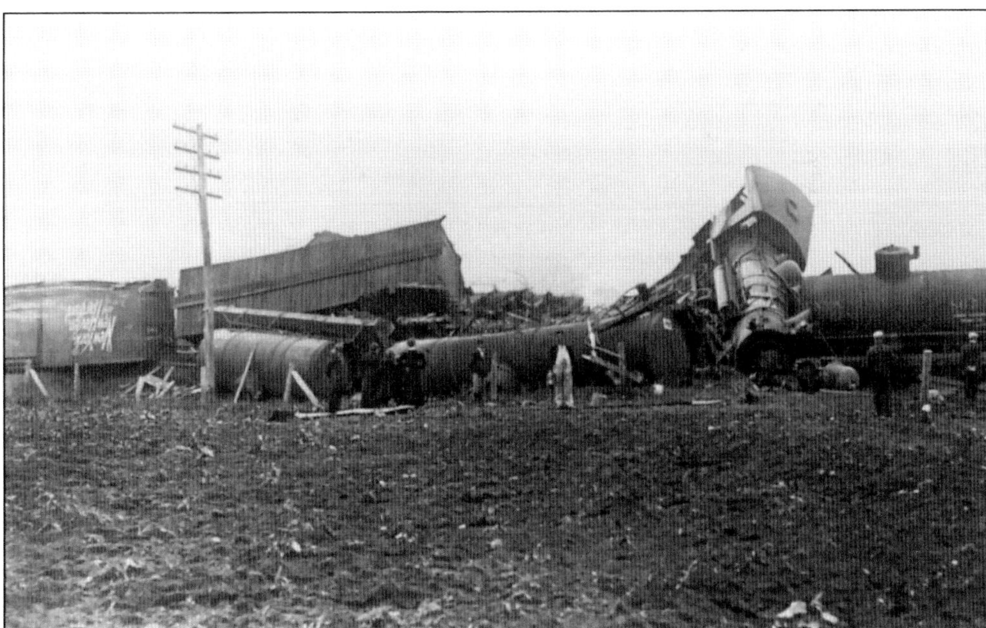

On June 7, 1911, four freight trains collided in Fairfield. Five men were killed and seven injured in the disaster that resulted in a pile of rail cars 35 feet high. This accident was one of a series that plagued the New York, New Haven & Hartford Railroad in the space of one year.

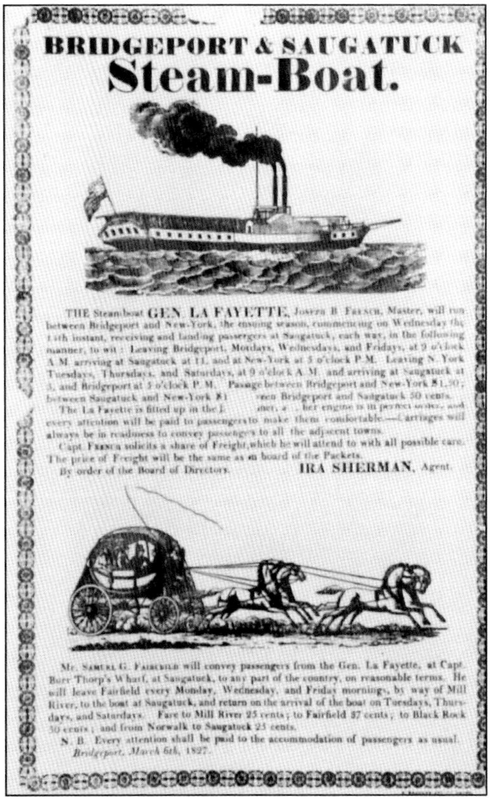

BRIDGEPORT & SAUGATUCK

Steam-Boat.

THE Steamboat **GEN. LA FAYETTE,** Joseph B. French, Master, will run between Bridgeport and New-York, the ensuing season, commencing on Wednesday the 14th instant, receiving and landing passengers at Saugatuck, each way, in the following manner, to wit: Leaving Bridgeport, Mondays, Wednesdays, and Fridays, at 9 o'clock A.M. arriving at Saugatuck at 11, and at New-York at 5 o'clock P.M. Leaving N. York Tuesdays, Thursdays, and Saturdays, at 9 o'clock A.M. and arriving at Saugatuck at 3, and Bridgeport at 5 o'clock P.M. Passage between Bridgeport and New-York $1,50; between Saugatuck and New-York $1 [illegible] een Bridgeport and Saugatuck 50 cents.

The La Fayette is fitted up in the [illegible] ner, a [illegible] her engine is in perfect order, and every attention will be paid to passengers to make them comfortable.—Carriages will always be in readiness to convey passengers to all the adjacent towns.

Capt. French solicits a share of Freight, which he will attend to with all possible care. The price of Freight will be the same as on board of the Packets.

By order of the Board of Directors. **IRA SHERMAN,** Agent.

Mr. Samuel G. Fairchild will convey passengers from the Gen. La Fayette, at Capt. Burr Thorp's Wharf, at Saugatuck, to any part of the country, on reasonable terms. He will leave Fairfield every Monday, Wednesday, and Friday mornings, by way of Mill River, to the boat at Saugatuck, and return on the arrival of the boat on Tuesdays, Thursdays, and Saturdays. Fare to Mill River 25 cents; to Fairfield 37 cents; to Black Rock 30 cents; and from Norwalk to Saugatuck 25 cents.

N. B. Every attention shall be paid to the accommodation of passengers as usual.

Bridgeport, March 6th, 1827.

Before the opening of the railroad, Fairfield residents could travel to New York City in the comfort of a steamboat for $1.50. The boat left Bridgeport on Monday, Wednesday, and Friday for the eight-hour trip and returned the next day. (Broadside.)

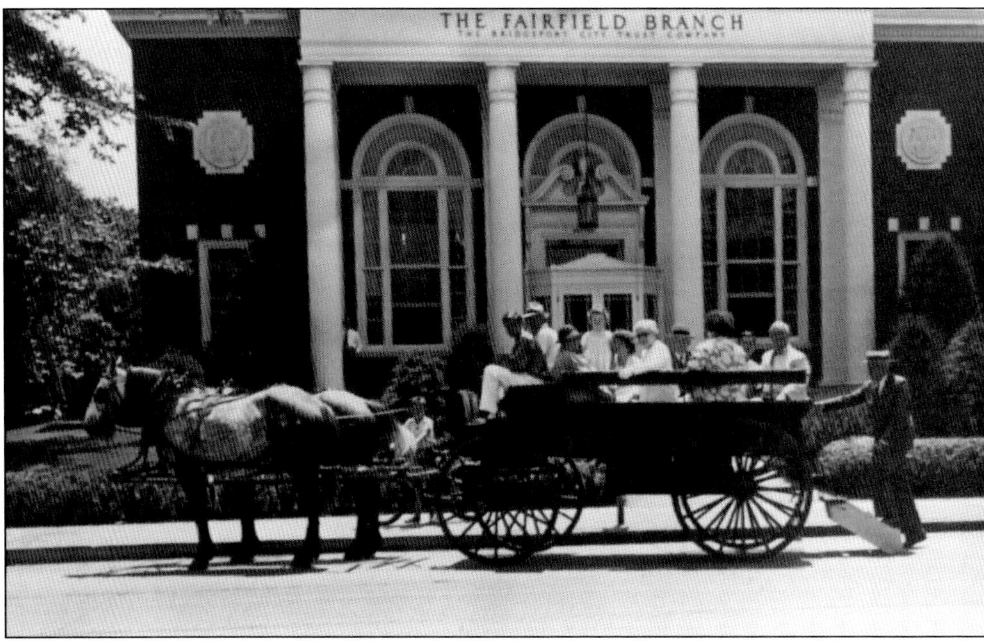

During the gas shortages of World War II, the Fairfield Beach Club provided an alternative mode of transportation for its members. In this July 1943 image, Albert S. Banks drives the wagon that took members from the town center to the beach.

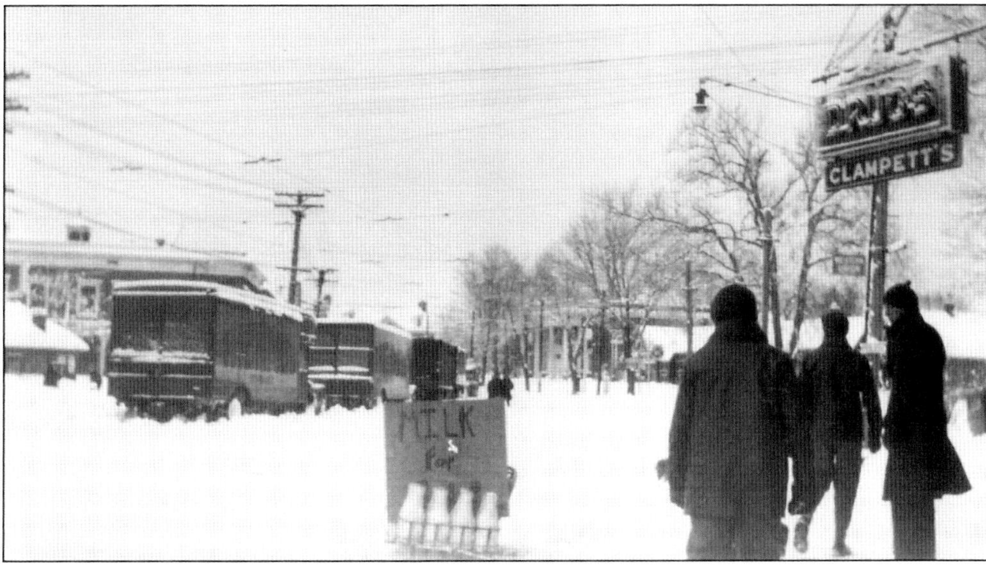

In 1934 a blizzard virtually halted vehicular traffic along the Post Road, although it did not stop enterprising storekeepers or pedestrians. Note McGarry's blacksmith shop on the far left, nearly hidden by snow.

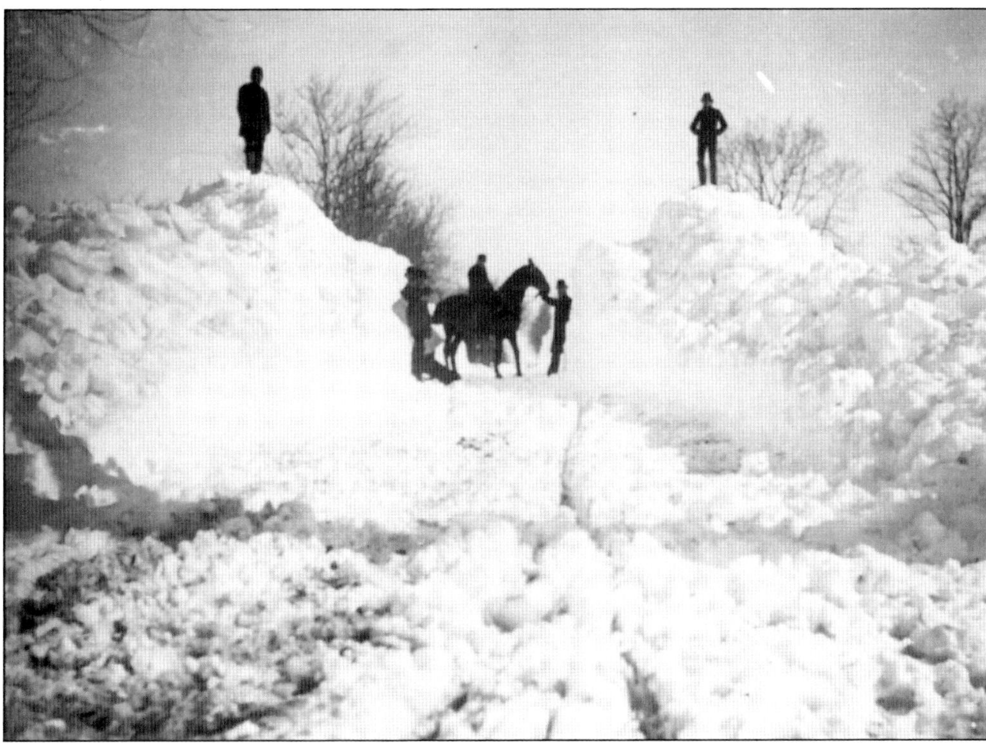
The Blizzard of 1888 (March 11–15) suspended travel for days. Boats delivered newspapers to Southport because trains could not get through. Five feet of snow reportedly fell, but winds created drifts of 15 to 20 feet. John Henry Beach noted in his diary on Wednesday, March 14th, "commence digging out. Turned out with 18 men to open the road got down as far as Sam. Beach ['s house] and gave up."

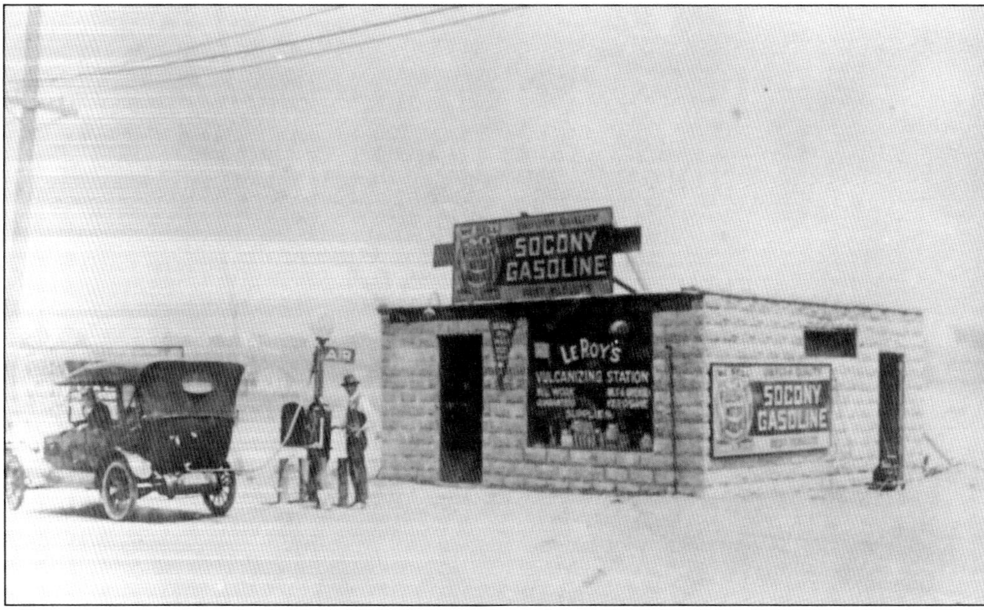

Drivers crossing Ash Creek from Bridgeport to Fairfield could fill up their cars at LeRoy Miner's Vulcanizing Station located on the Post Road. (Postcard, *c.* 1918.)

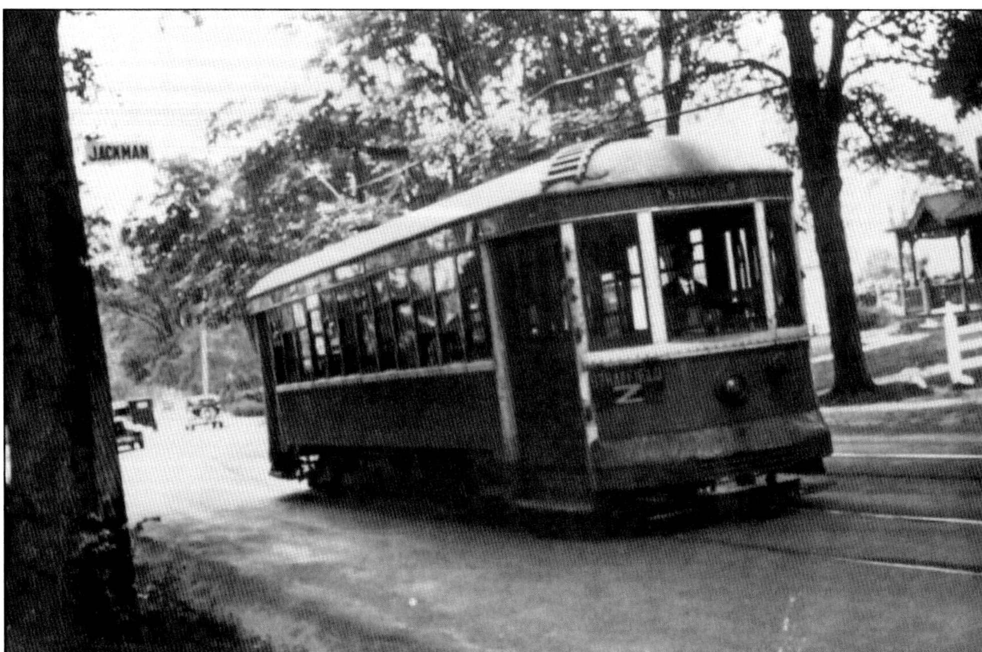

Trolleys provided inexpensive and clean transportation between Bridgeport, Stratford, Fairfield, and Norwalk. Many Fairfield residents recall taking the trolley to Bridgeport to attend high school, take music lessons, or go shopping. This trolley travels along Stratfield Road near Jackman Avenue about 1930.

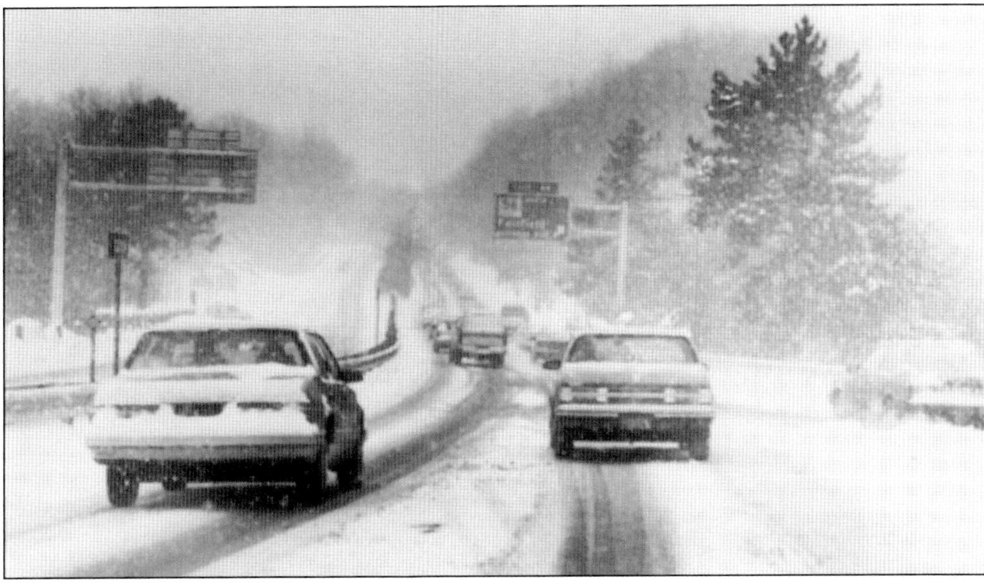

Morning rush hour traffic clogs the westbound lanes of the Merritt Parkway on January 8, 1988. Even the construction of the new Connecticut Turnpike failed to ease congestion on this scenic highway. (*Fairfield Citizen-News* photograph.)

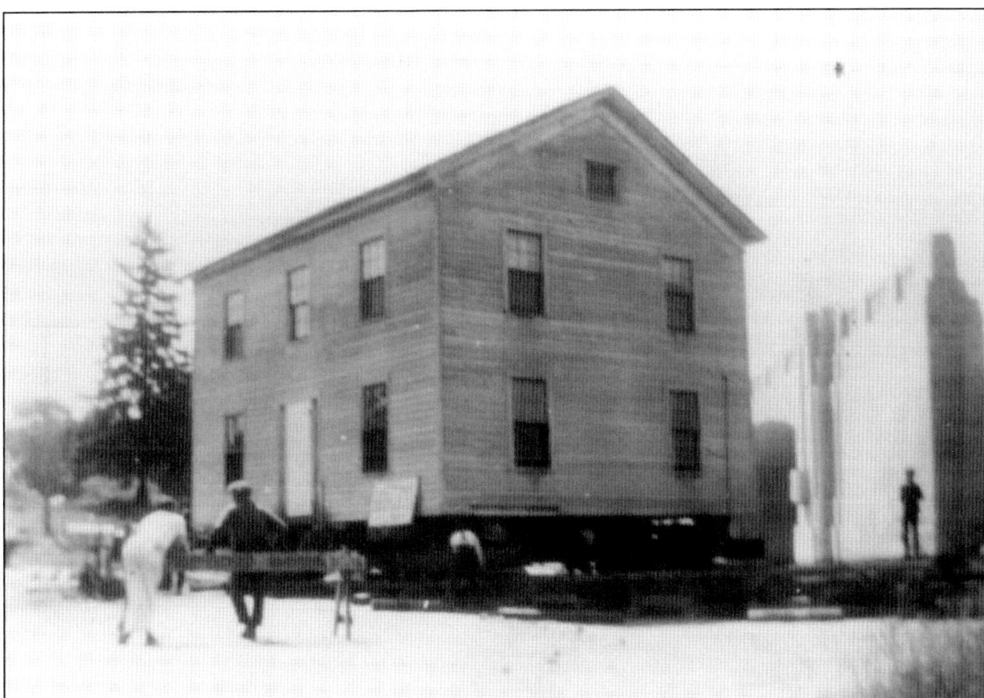

The construction of the Merritt Parkway, the first major limited-access highway built in Connecticut, displaced a number of houses. This house, ready for moving, stood at the site of the Lacey Fulling Mill on the Mill River. The parkway, opened in 1938 and limited to automobiles, was designed to relieve congestion on Route 1 (the Post Road). Noted for its unique bridge designs, the parkway is on the National Register of Historic Places.

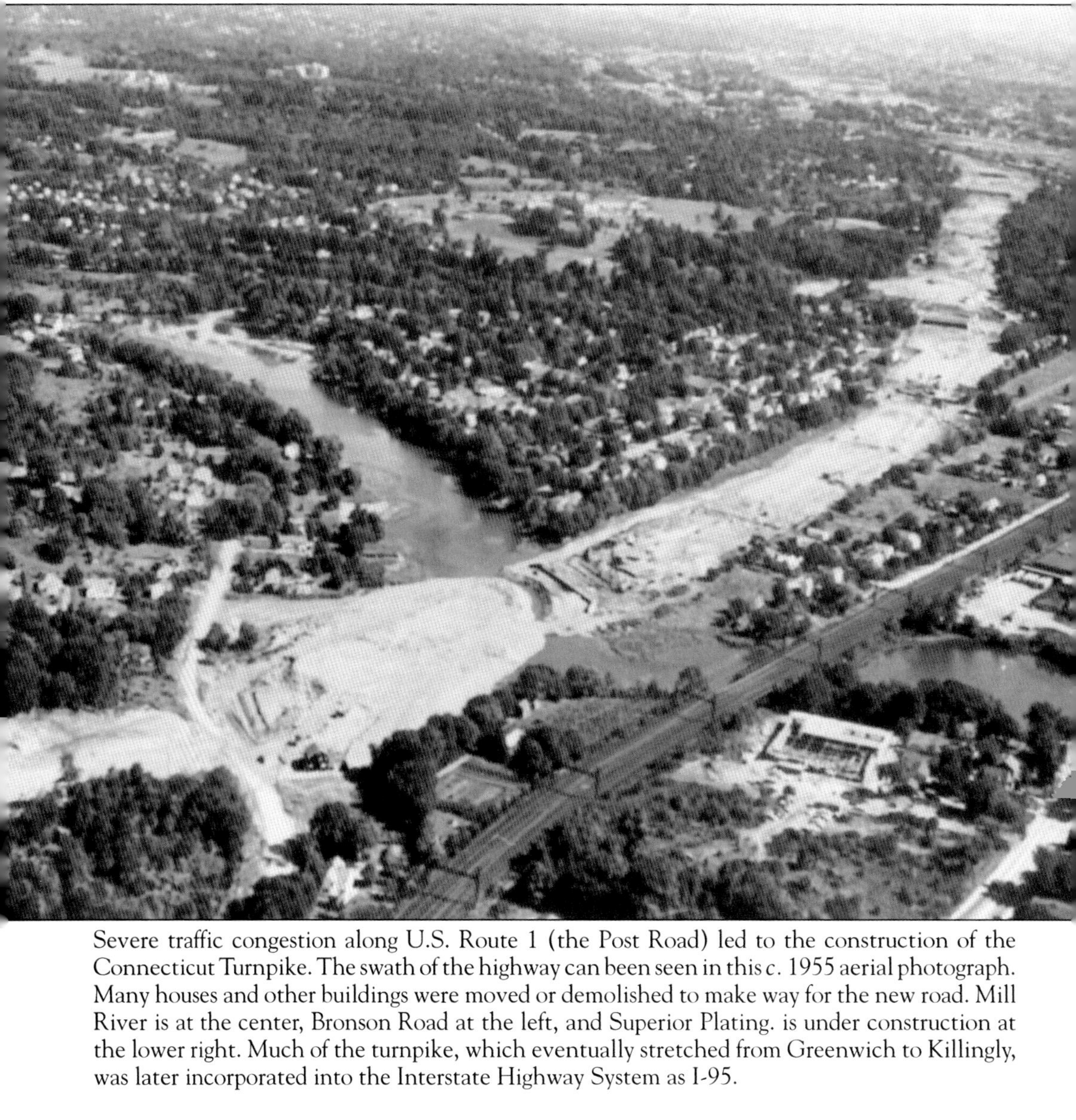

Severe traffic congestion along U.S. Route 1 (the Post Road) led to the construction of the Connecticut Turnpike. The swath of the highway can been seen in this *c.* 1955 aerial photograph. Many houses and other buildings were moved or demolished to make way for the new road. Mill River is at the center, Bronson Road at the left, and Superior Plating. is under construction at the lower right. Much of the turnpike, which eventually stretched from Greenwich to Killingly, was later incorporated into the Interstate Highway System as I-95.

Seven

Pleasures and Pastimes

The topography of Fairfield, from the shore to the hills, has drawn people to town for relaxation and recreation for generations. Long Island Sound offers beaches, boating, and fishing. Anglers also revel in the area's rivers and streams. Parks and dedicated open space are sites for games, picnicking, and walking.

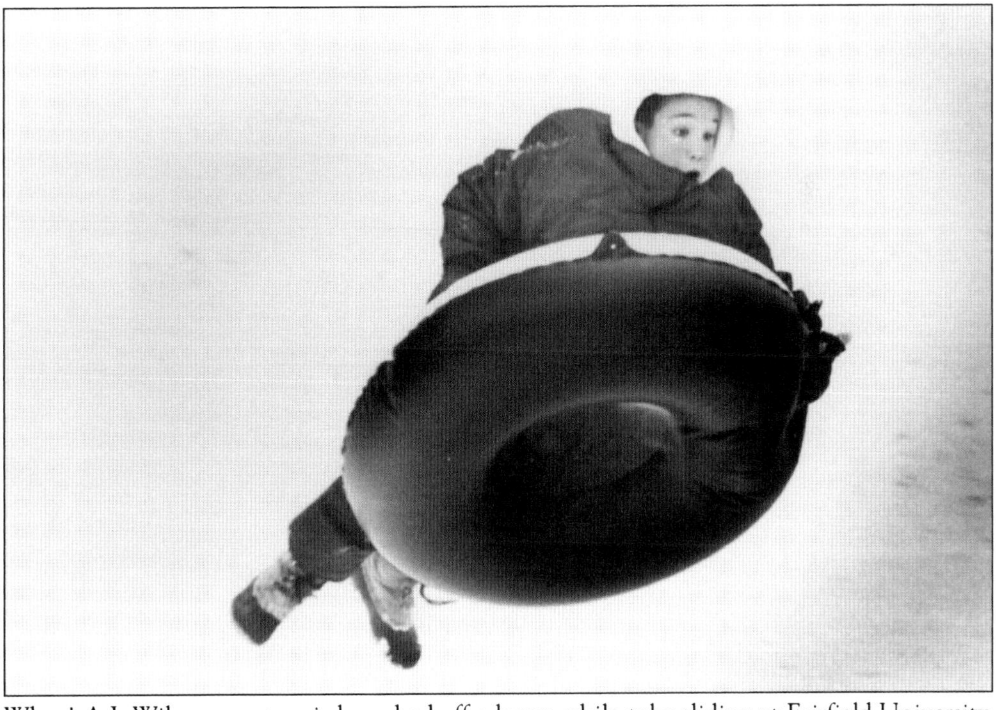

Whee! A.J. Wilson, age ten, is launched off a bump while tube sliding at Fairfield University. (*Fairfield Citizen-News*, D'Elia photograph, 1990.)

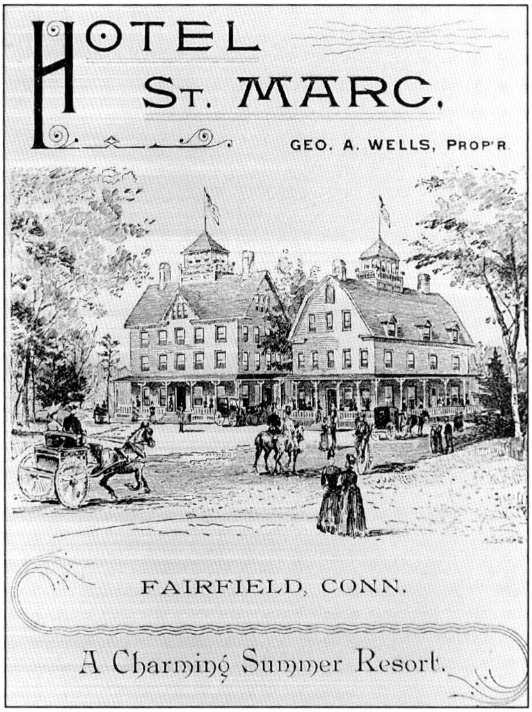

The Hotel St. Marc, "located in the center of beautiful Fairfield, is the best appointed and liberally managed Hotel in the State, and is now one of the finest in New England, situated in the most charming town on the New York and New Haven R.R. It is a favorite summer resort of New York families who seek its pure air, wholesome fare, varied scenery and delicious quiet it so freely affords." (Advertising brochure, *c.* 1890.)

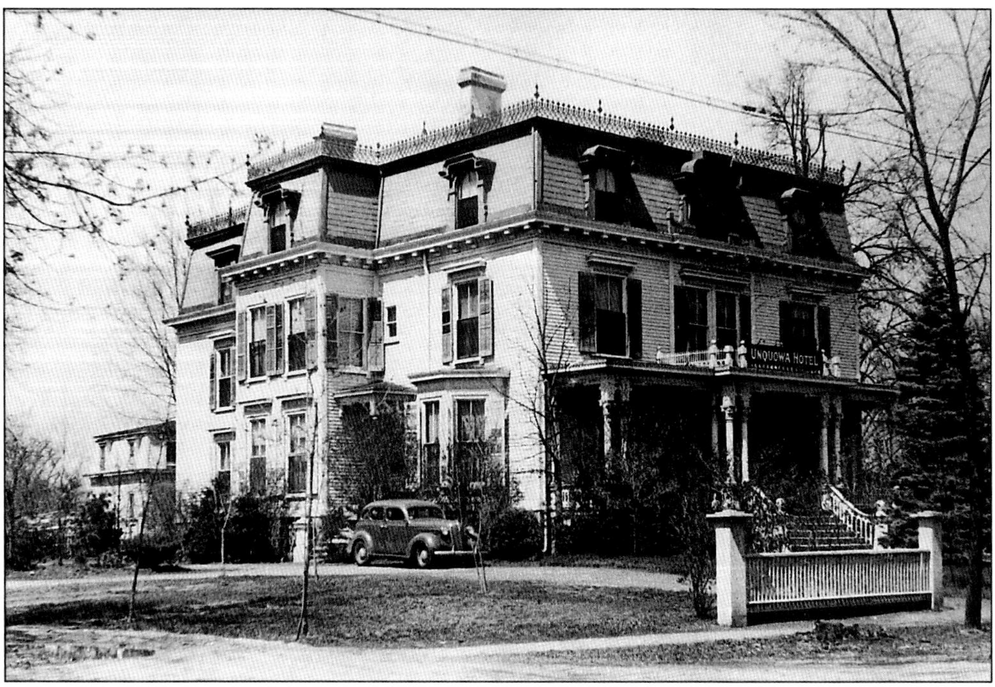

James Mott, founder of the Mott Manufacturing Co., built this twenty-three-room private home in 1868. By 1910 it housed the Hargrove School for Boys, a college preparatory school. In 1913 Mrs. Harriet S. Donovan purchased the building and turned it into the Unquowa Hotel; it became a boardinghouse in 1966. The town condemned the building in 1991 and demolished it three years later.

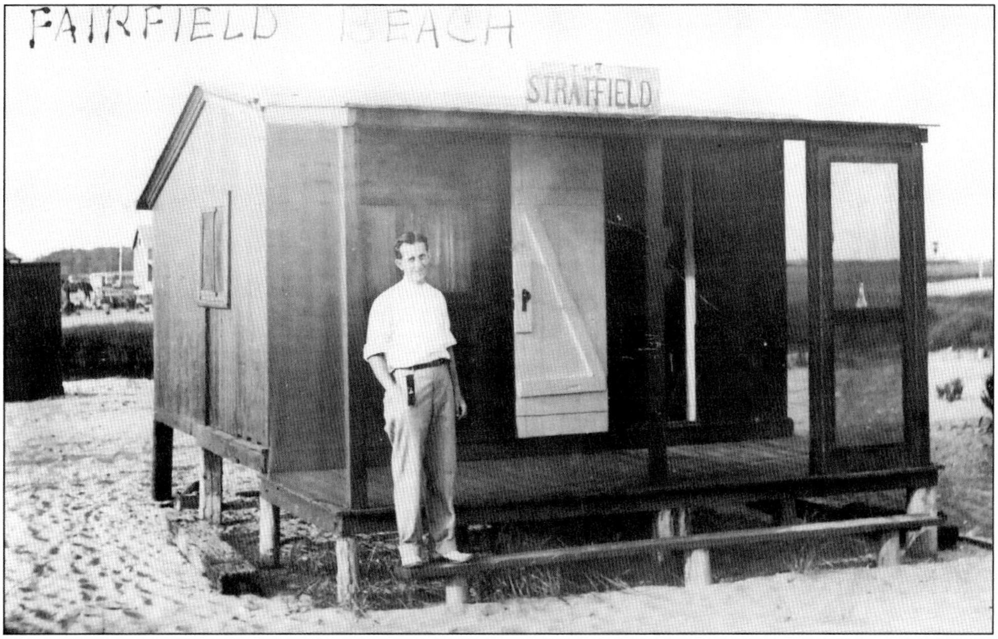

The "Stratfield" cottage at Fairfield beach probably took its name from the Stratfield Hotel in Bridgeport rather than the section of Fairfield called Stratfield. This cottage is typical of the more temporary structures found at the beach before World War II. (Courtesy of the Connecticut Historical Society.)

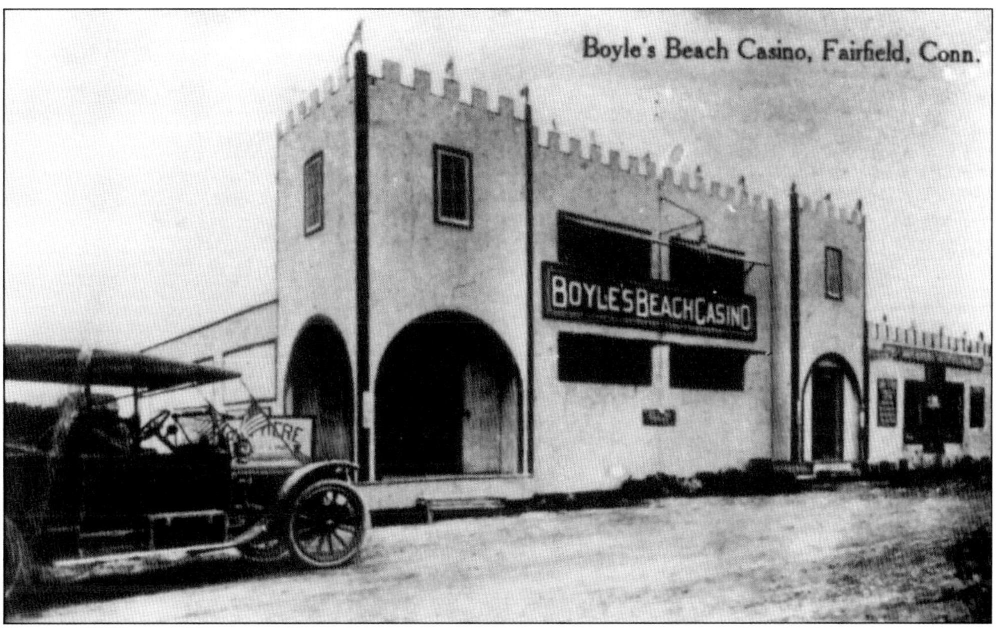

John Boyle ran a large and lively dance hall across the street from Little Danbury, a group of cottages along the beach at Fairfield. Boyle's Beach Casino was located at the corner of Reef Road and Fairfield Beach Road. (Postcard, 1913.)

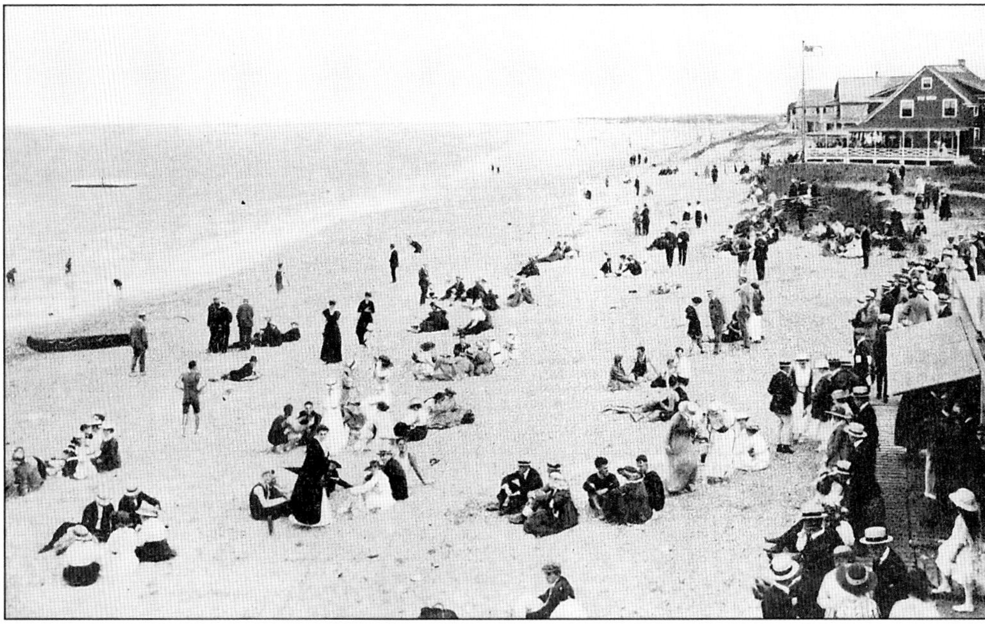

Fairfield's beach became a mecca for summer vacationers in the late nineteenth century. Bathers depicted on this postcard enjoy the sun and sand about 1900.

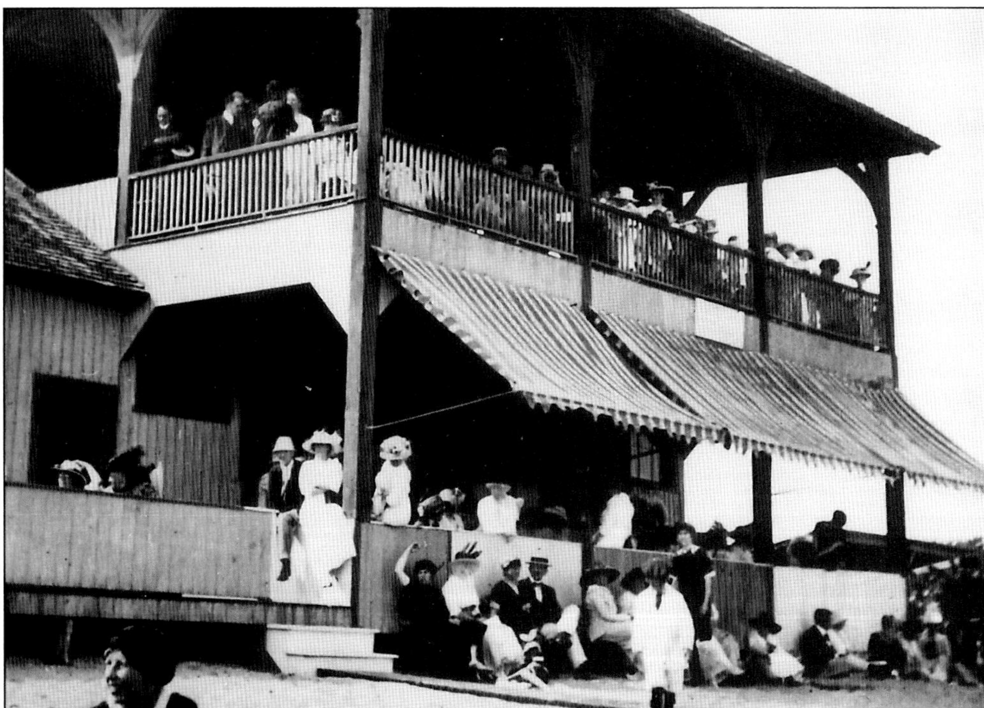

The Fairfield Beach Company was incorporated in 1886 as a private membership club. The pavilion, seen in this *c.* 1895 photograph, suffered through fire and storm and was rebuilt several times. The present Fairfield Beach Club includes an Olympic-sized swimming pool and tennis courts.

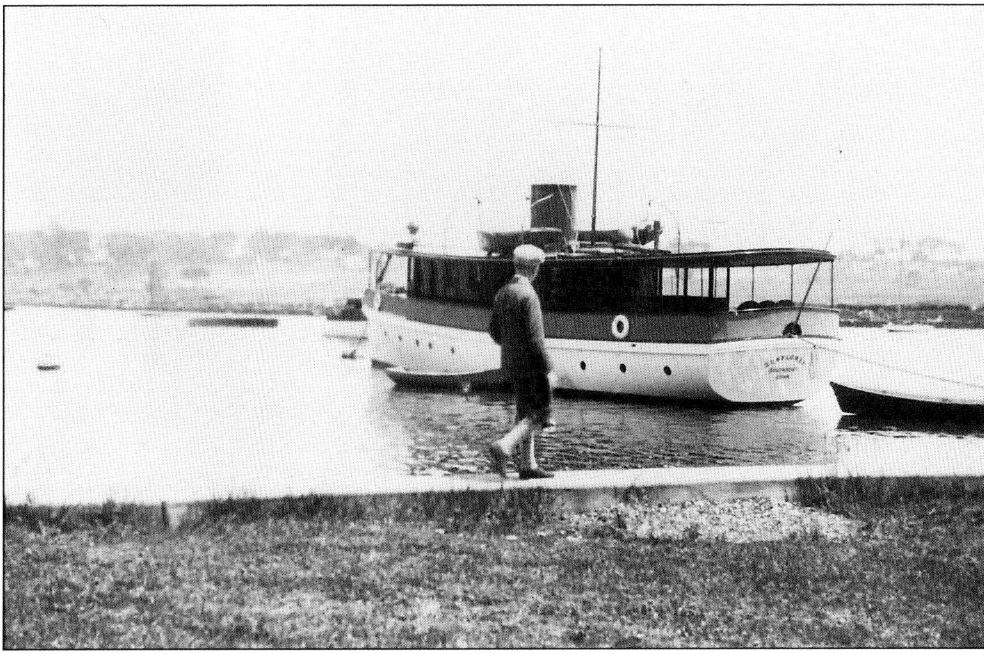

The steam launch *Sunflower*, moored in Southport in 1929, illustrates the harbor's transformation from commercial shipping to pleasure boating during the early part of the twentieth century.

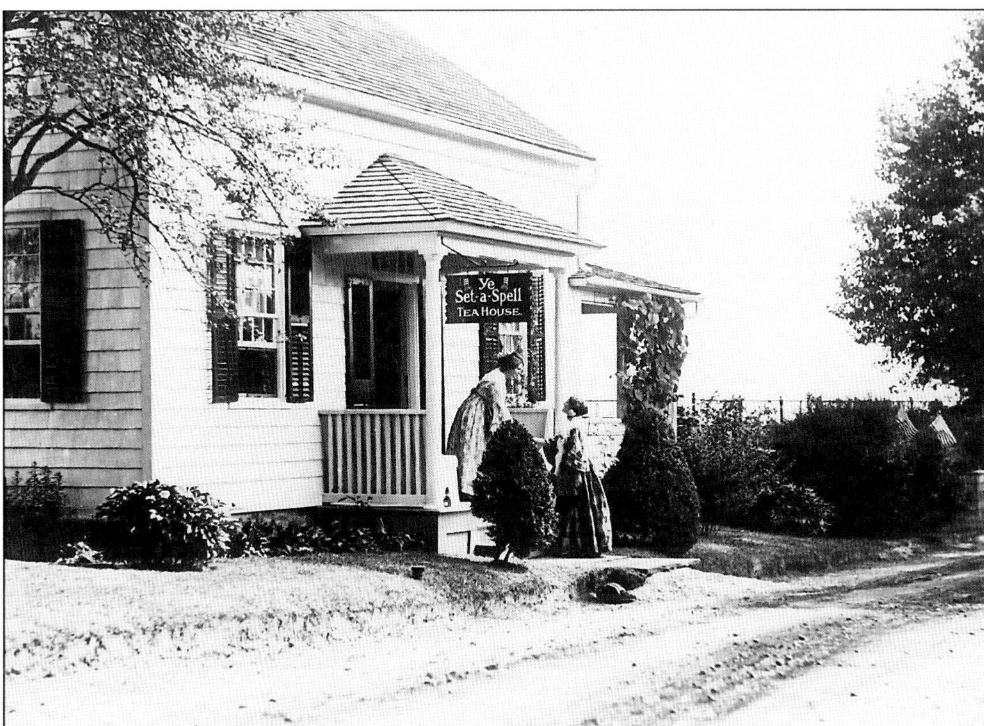

A pleasant spot to spend a summer afternoon was the Ye Set-a-Spell Tea House on Southport Harbor. (Postcard, *c.* 1920.)

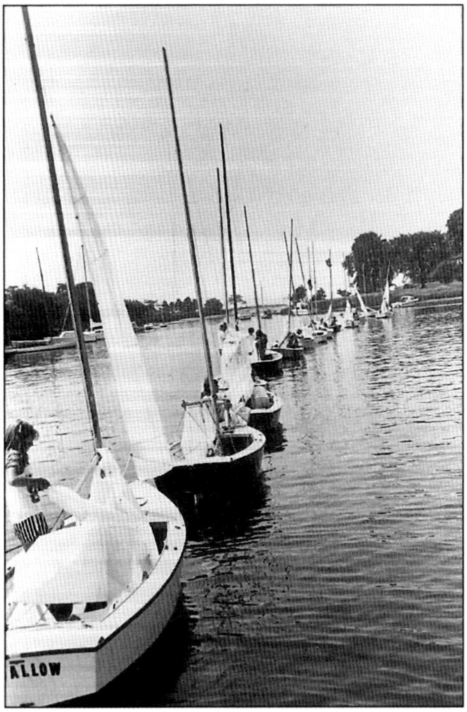

The Pequot Yacht Club offers sailing lessons and holds regattas during the summer. It was organized in 1921 as a successor to the Bachelors' Comfort and Married Men's Rest. The club's property along the shore of Southport Harbor was once the site of warehouses. (*Fairfield Citizen-News*, Coolen photograph, *c.* 1984)

The Cascades is one of several town-owned open spaces available for recreation. This popular fishing spot is located north of Lake Mohegan. (*Fairfield Citizen-News* photograph, 1974.)

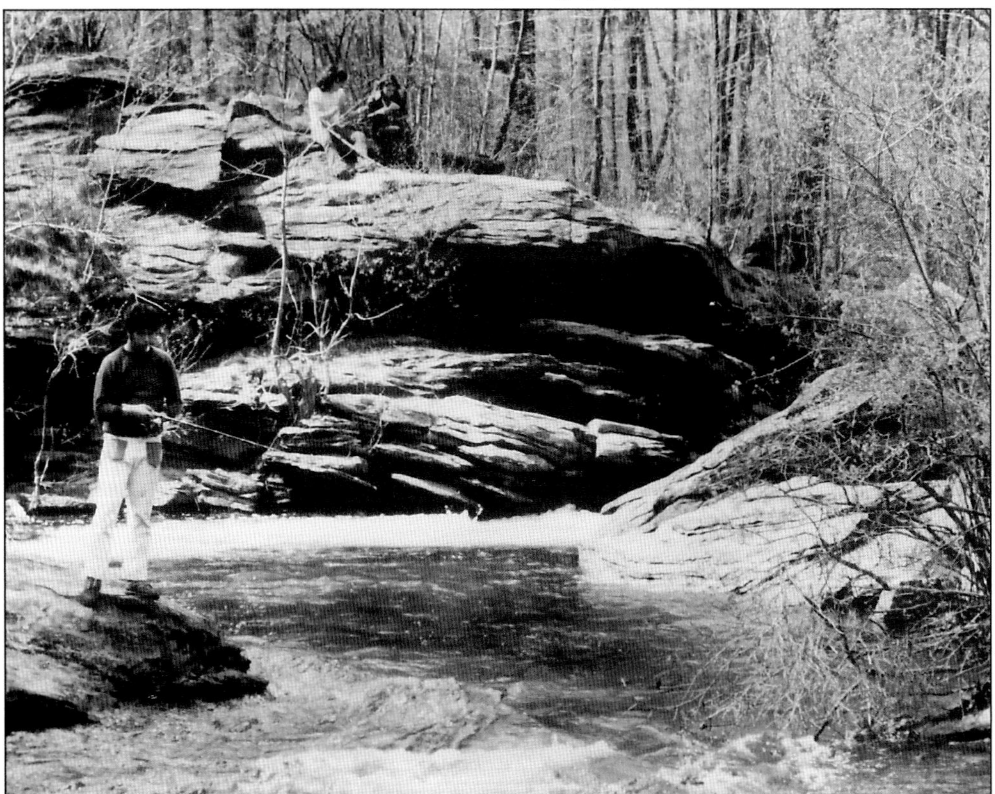

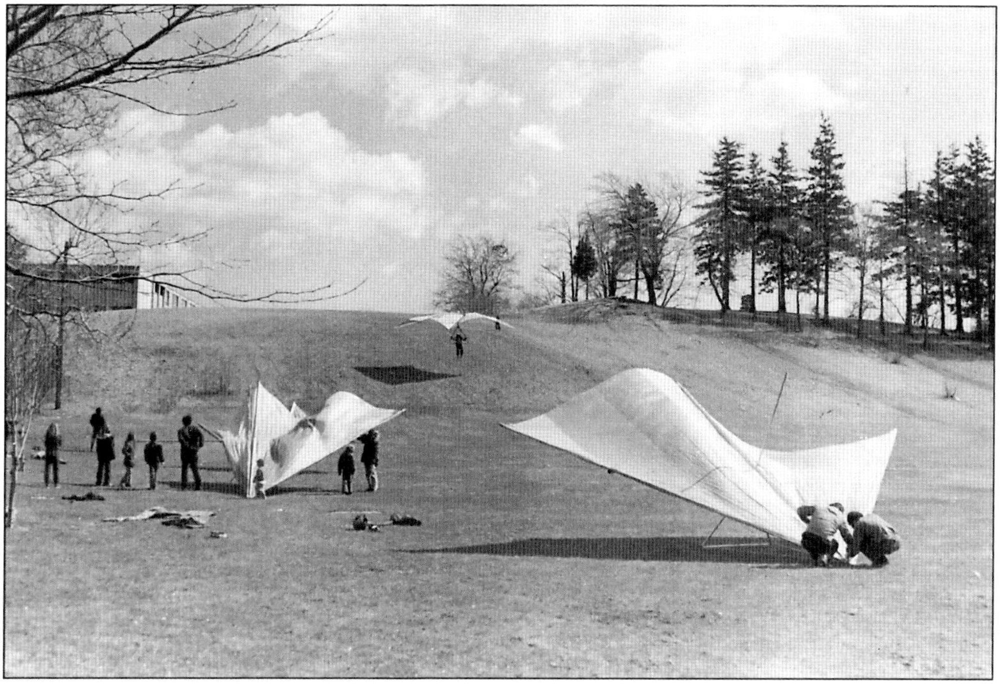

Hang-gliders use the facilities at Sturges Park in 1976. Visible at the upper left is the former Roger Ludlowe High School. When the town's two high schools were consolidated in 1987, this building became a community center. It will house board of education offices and a middle school by 1998.

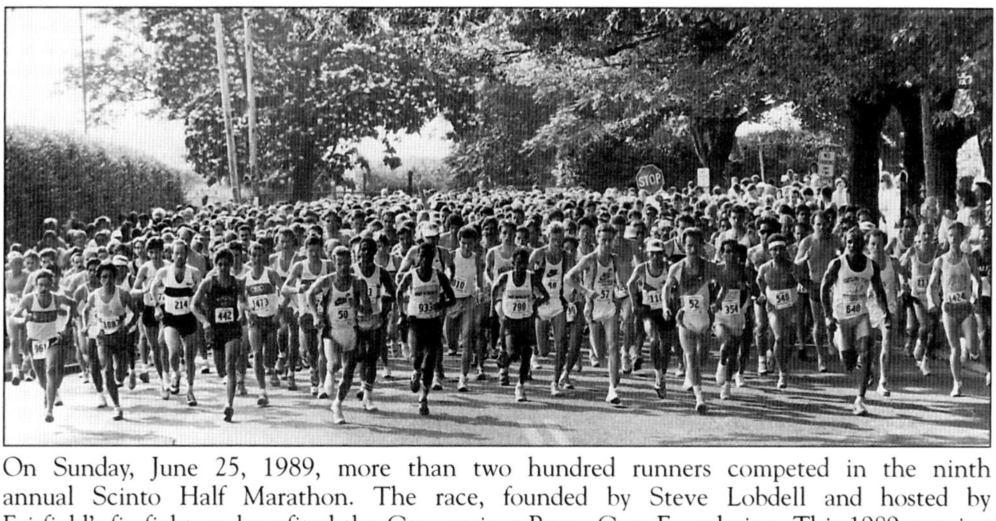

On Sunday, June 25, 1989, more than two hundred runners competed in the ninth annual Scinto Half Marathon. The race, founded by Steve Lobdell and hosted by Fairfield's firefighters, benefited the Connecticut Burns Care Foundation. This 1989 running of the race included the first United States Women's Half Marathon Championship. (*Fairfield Citizen-News* photograph.)

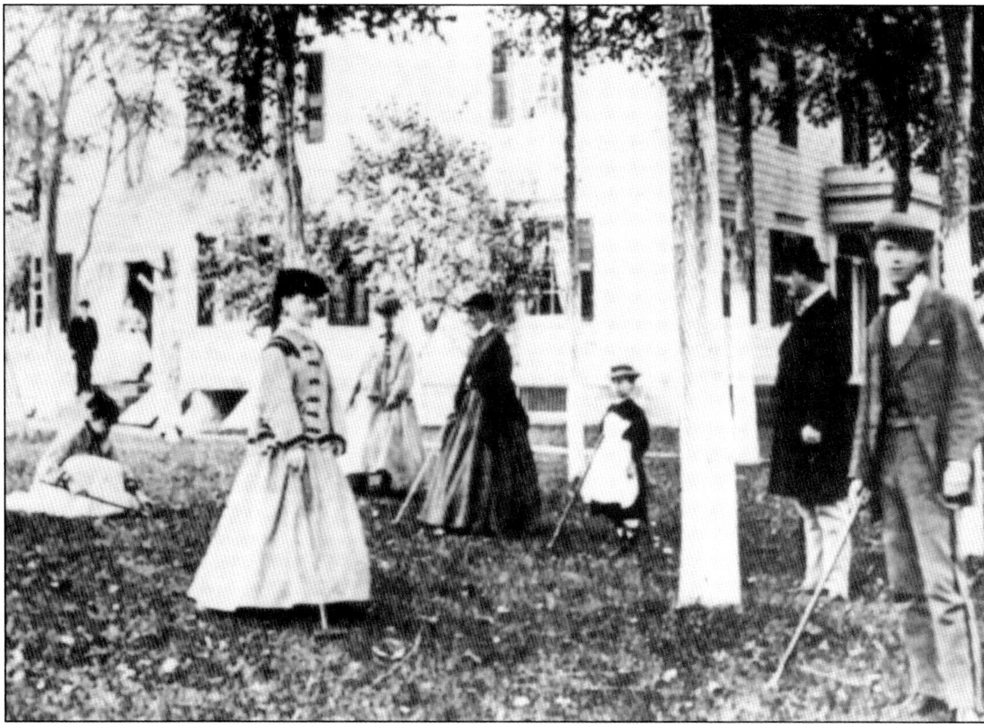

Family members enjoy a game of croquet on the lawn of the Andrew Bulkley house in Southport about 1865.

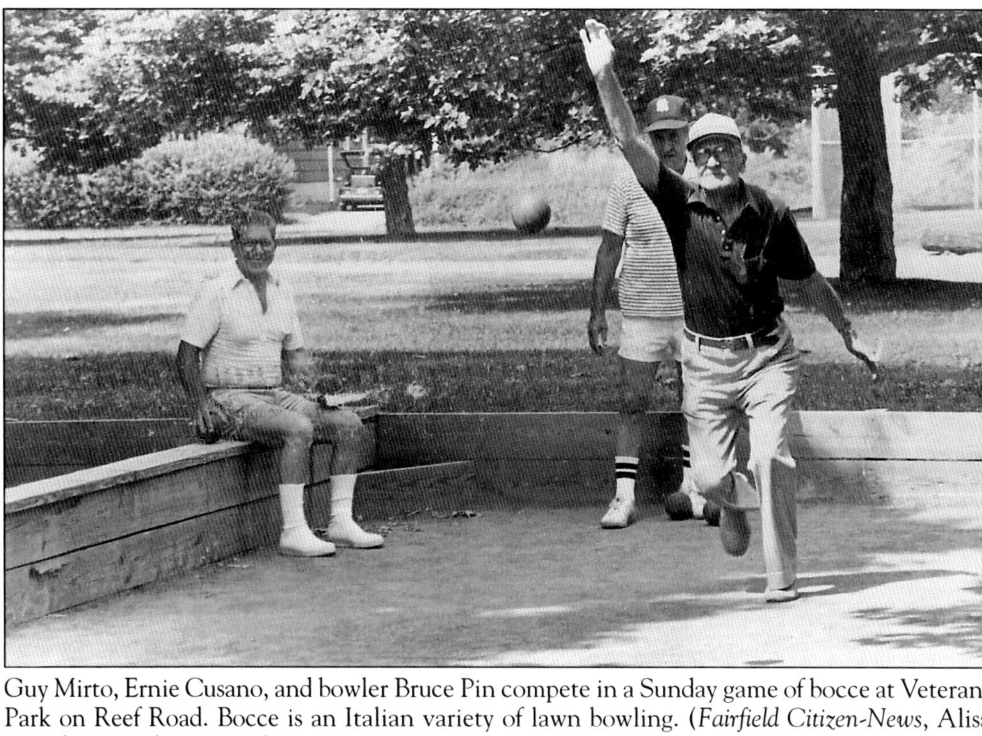

Guy Mirto, Ernie Cusano, and bowler Bruce Pin compete in a Sunday game of bocce at Veterans Park on Reef Road. Bocce is an Italian variety of lawn bowling. (*Fairfield Citizen-News*, Alisa Dix photograph, *c.* 1985.)

Elva Banks, Ada Dunham, and Maria Willis (from left to right) pause in front of the Greenfield Hill Congregational Church to admire Ada's new bicycle in August 1899.

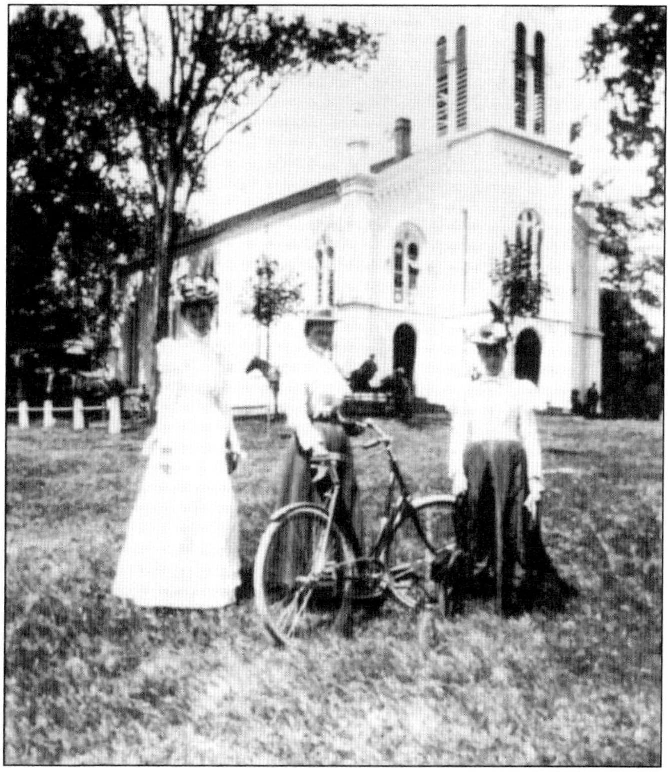

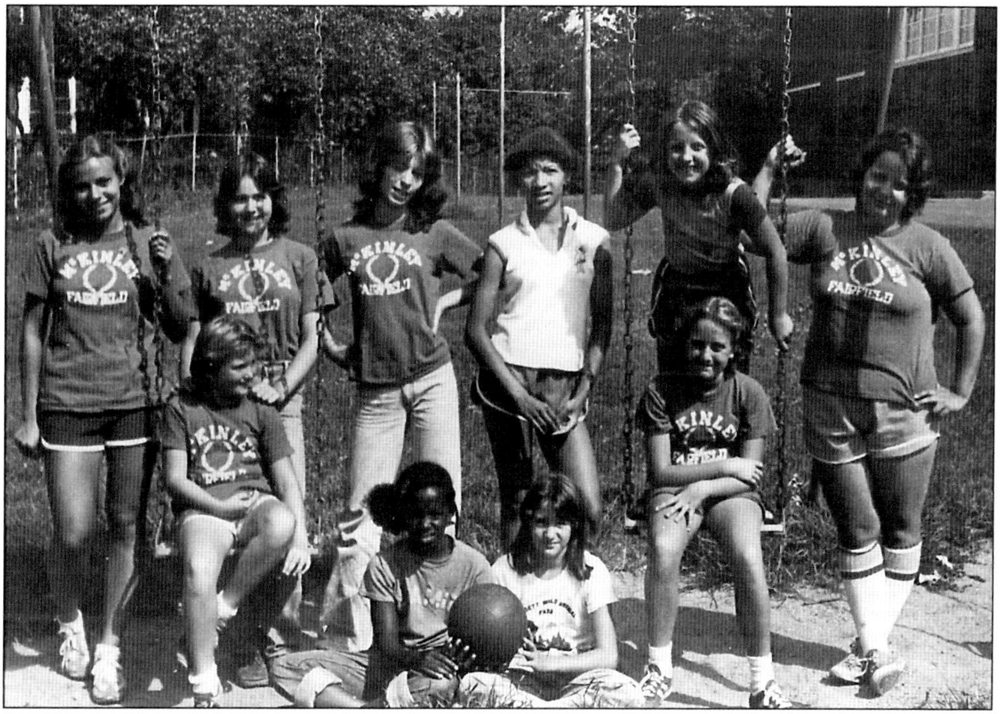

The Fairfield Recreation Department's 1978 kickball champions pose for a group portrait. (*Fairfield Citizen-News* photograph.)

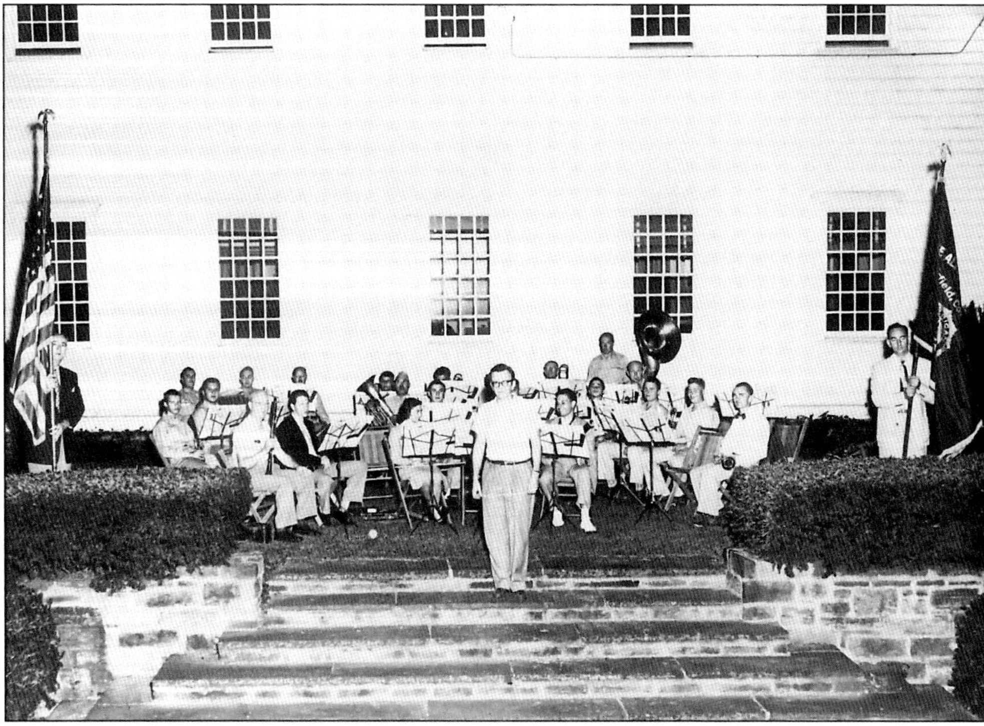

The terrace at the rear of Town Hall was a favorite spot for band concerts and town celebrations until the space was taken for a 1957 addition. Bill Burr prepares to lead the band *c*. 1950. (Frank Romagnano photograph.)

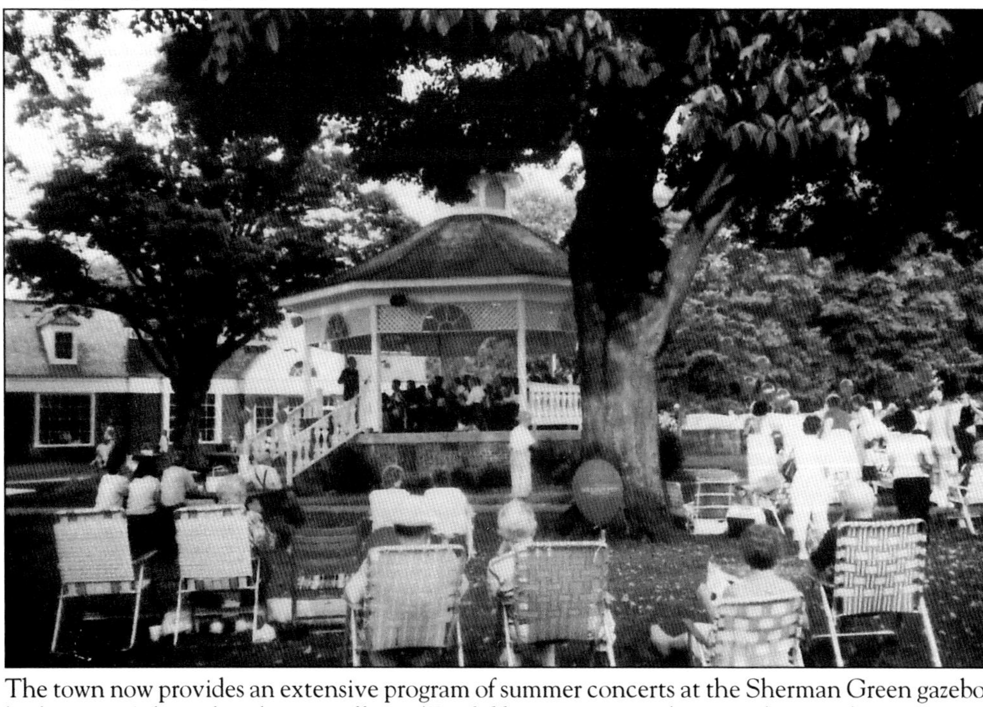

The town now provides an extensive program of summer concerts at the Sherman Green gazebo, built in 1985 through volunteer efforts. (*Fairfield Citizen-News* photograph, 1989.)

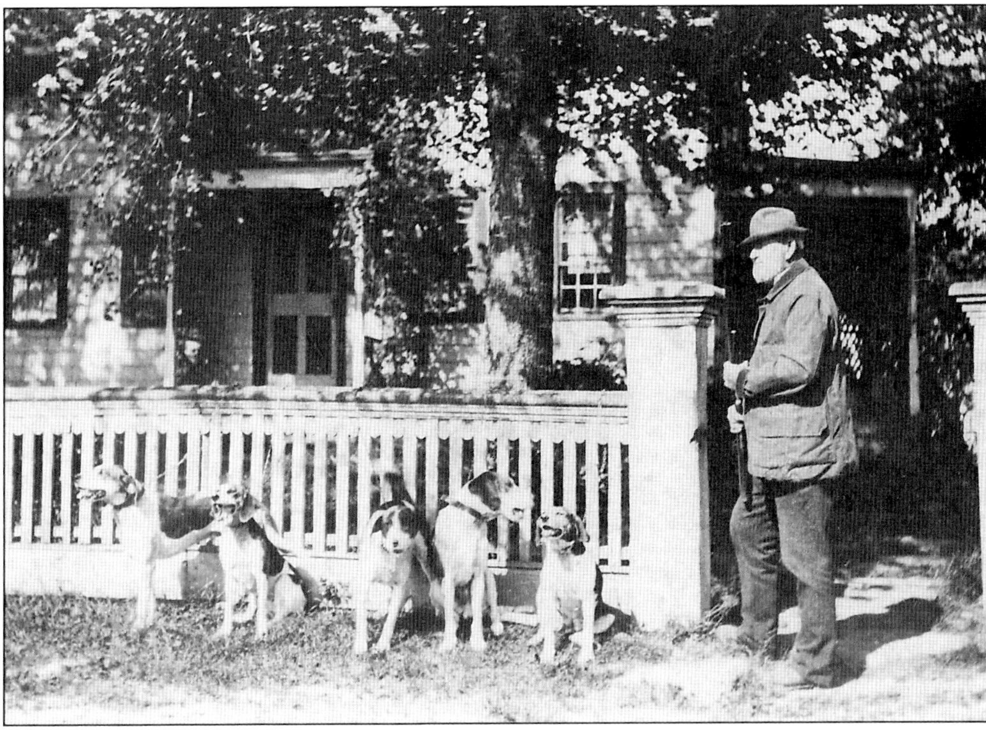

Zalmon Bradley served as president of the Fox Hunters' Club of Fairfield, founded in 1867. He poses with his hounds in front of his house at 5060 Congress Street about 1870.

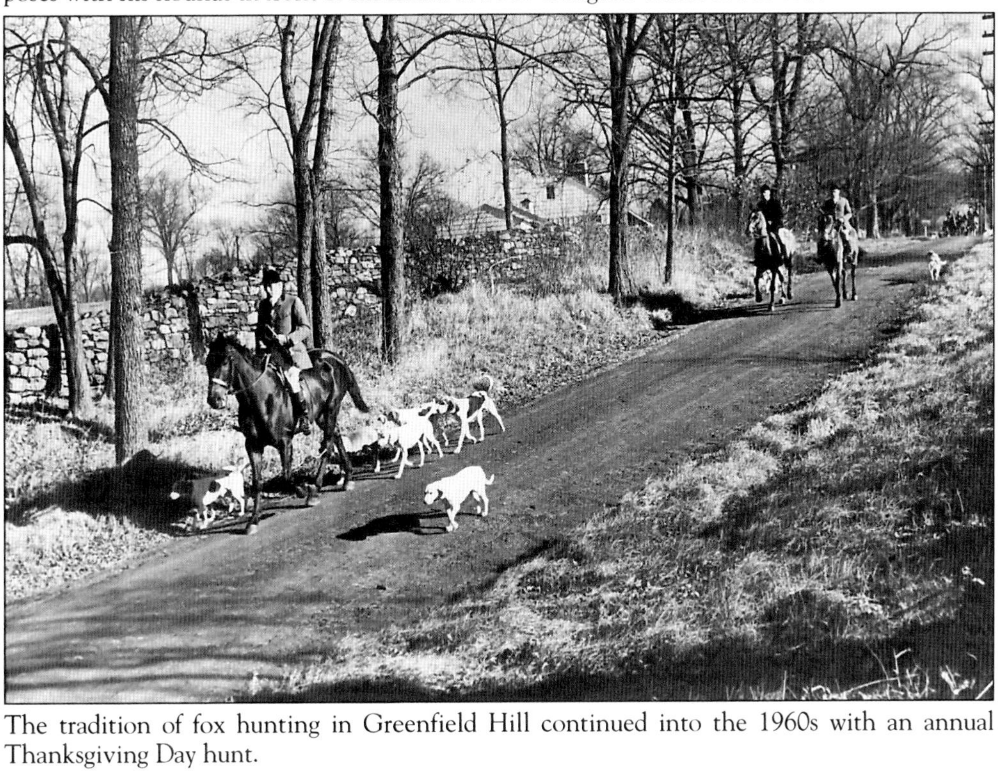

The tradition of fox hunting in Greenfield Hill continued into the 1960s with an annual Thanksgiving Day hunt.

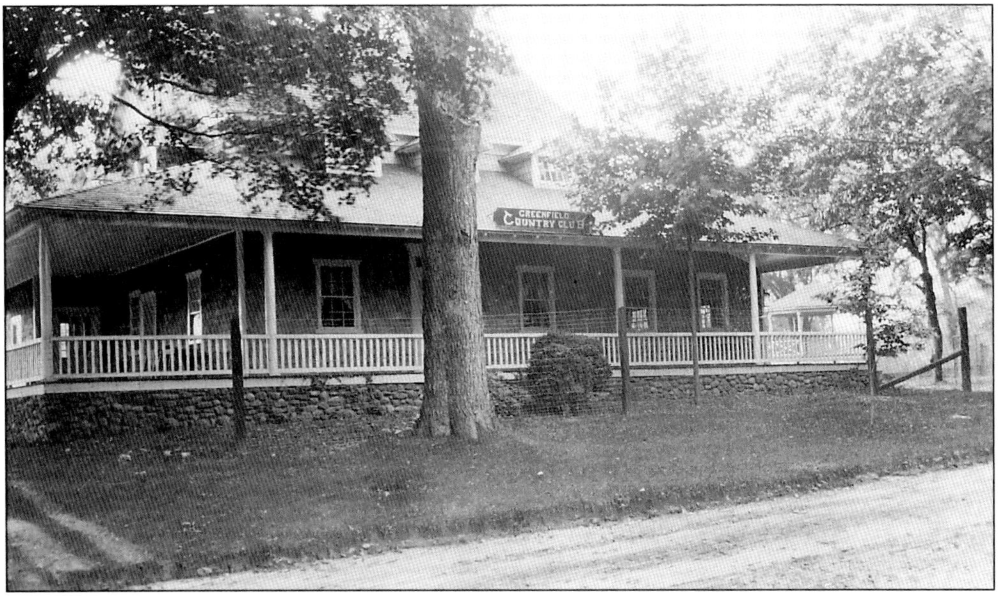

The Greenfield Country Club on Bronson Road, shown about 1905, hosted horse races, oxen pulls, and Farmers' Institutes from 1901 to 1925. The club operated an eighteen-hole golf course from 1925 until the early 1940s. The building still stands and is now a private home.

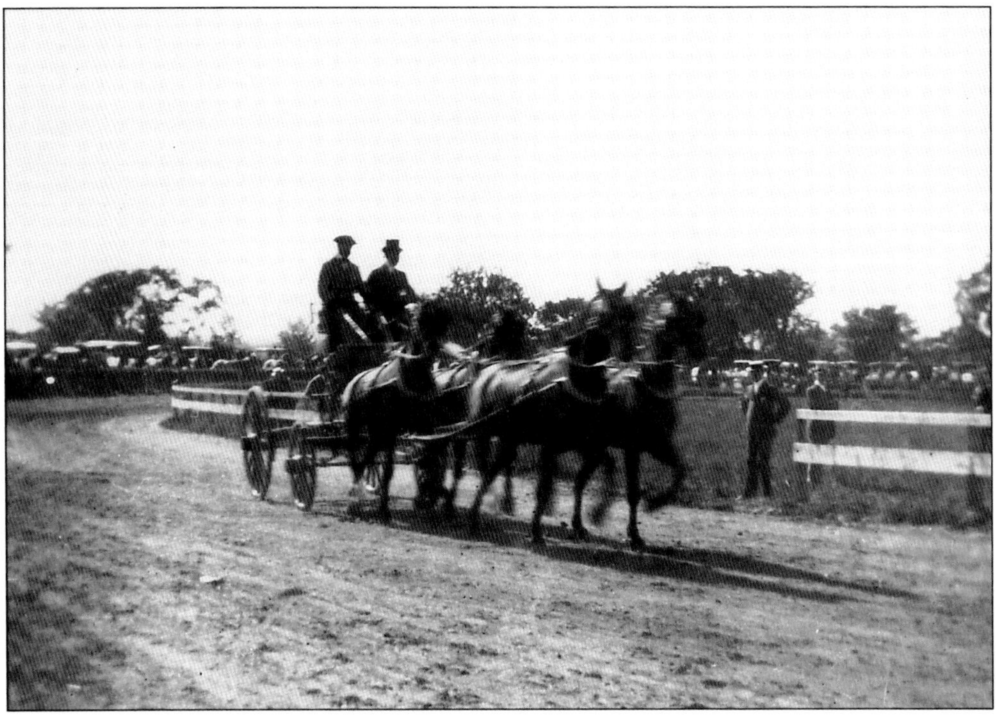

Eight

Celebration and Remembrance

The causes for celebration and remembrance stem from national, state, community, and family events over time, from the arrival of the English in the seventeenth century to the emigration from Eastern Europe and other areas in the twentieth century. Festive, solemn, and religious occasions help form the historical record.

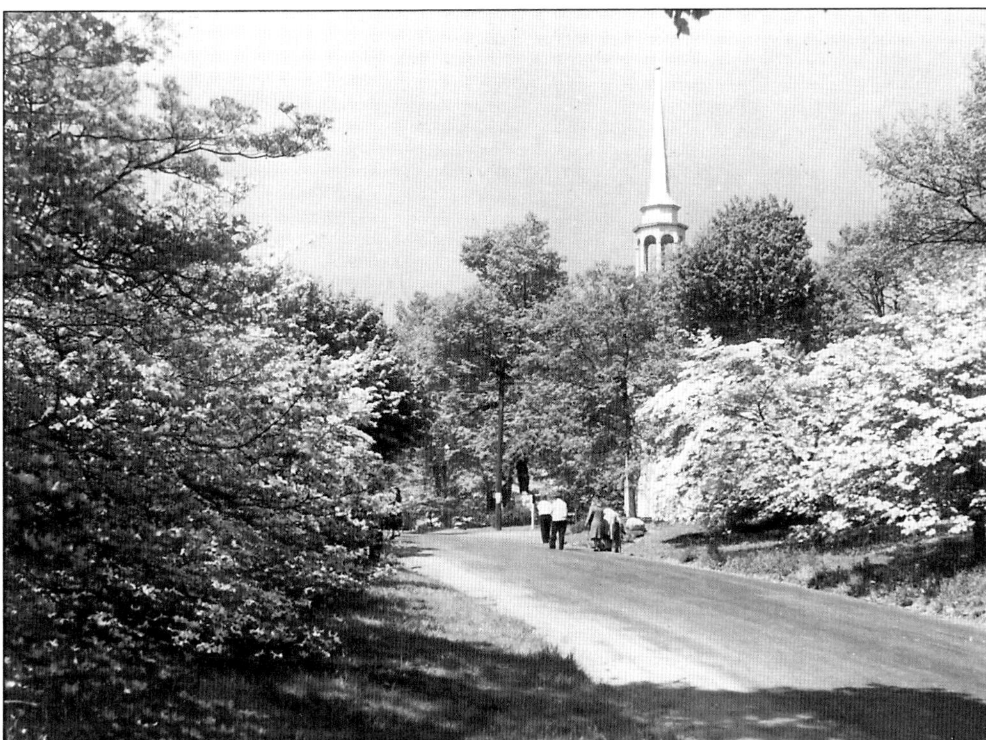

Since 1935 the Women's Guild of the Greenfield Hill Congregational Church has welcomed visitors to the annual Dogwood Festival. The event raises funds for mission projects. Dr. Isaac Bronson planted the first dogwood trees along Bronson Road in the years following the Revolution.

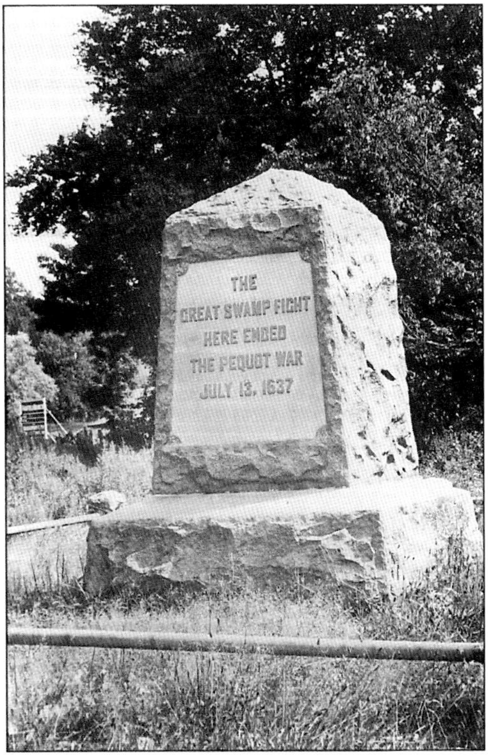

The Great Swamp Fight monument commemorates the site where, on July 13, 1637, a contingent of colonial men defeated a band of Pequot Indians. Connecticut colonists waged an offensive war against the Pequots to drive them from the colony. The first encounter was at Pequot Harbor (New London) and the last stand was at the Great Swamp in what is now Southport.

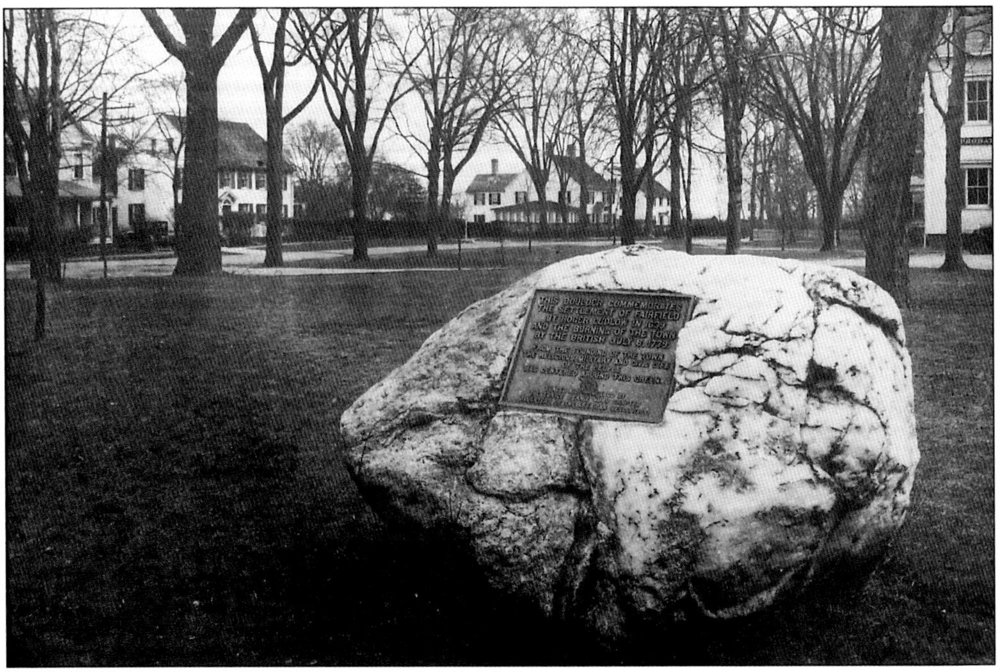

In 1900 the Eunice Dennie Burr Chapter of the D.A.R. dedicated a plaque to commemorate the settlement of Fairfield by Roger Ludlow in 1639 and the burning of the town by the British in 1779. Three houses that survived the 1779 conflagration can be seen behind the boulder on Town Hall Green in this *c.* 1925 picture.

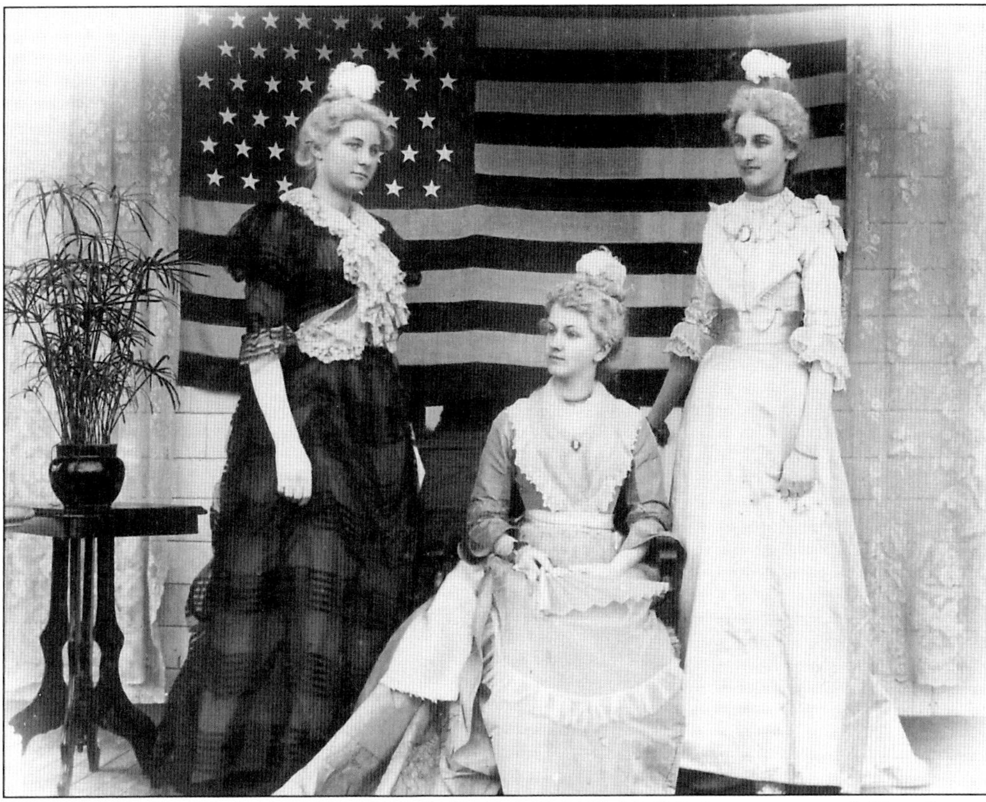

The Lady Washington Tea Party, a benefit for the Greenfield Hill Congregational Church, was held at the home of Simon C. Bradley in 1890. Elizabeth Bradley (left) appeared as Mrs. Custis, Ada Jennings (center) as Lady Washington, and Elva Banks (right) as Mrs. Madison.

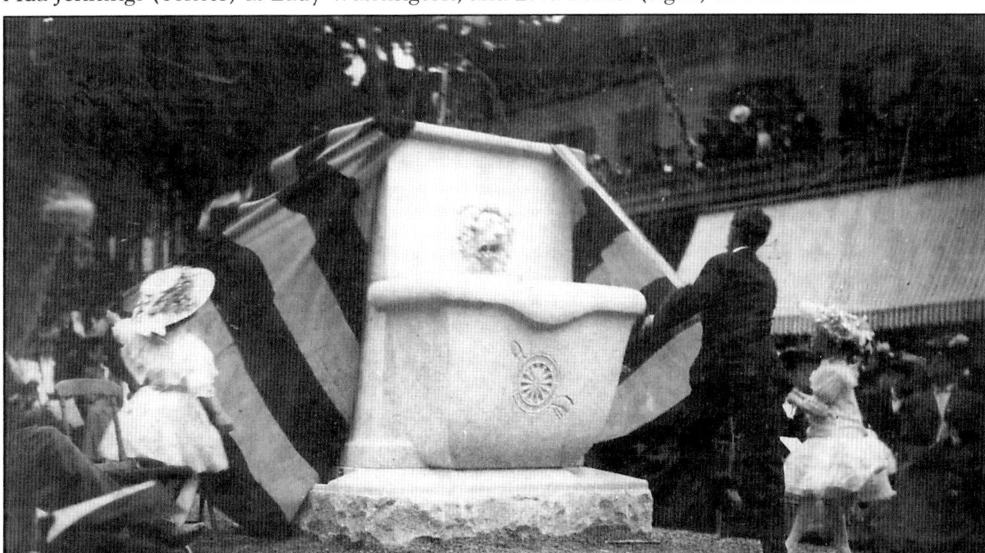

Mr. John Bassett, Miss Alice Curtis (right), and Miss Josephine Wells (left) unveil the Memorial Fountain at Southport on June 17, 1903. The fountain was erected under the auspices of the Dorothy Ripley Chapter of the Daughters of the American Revolution.

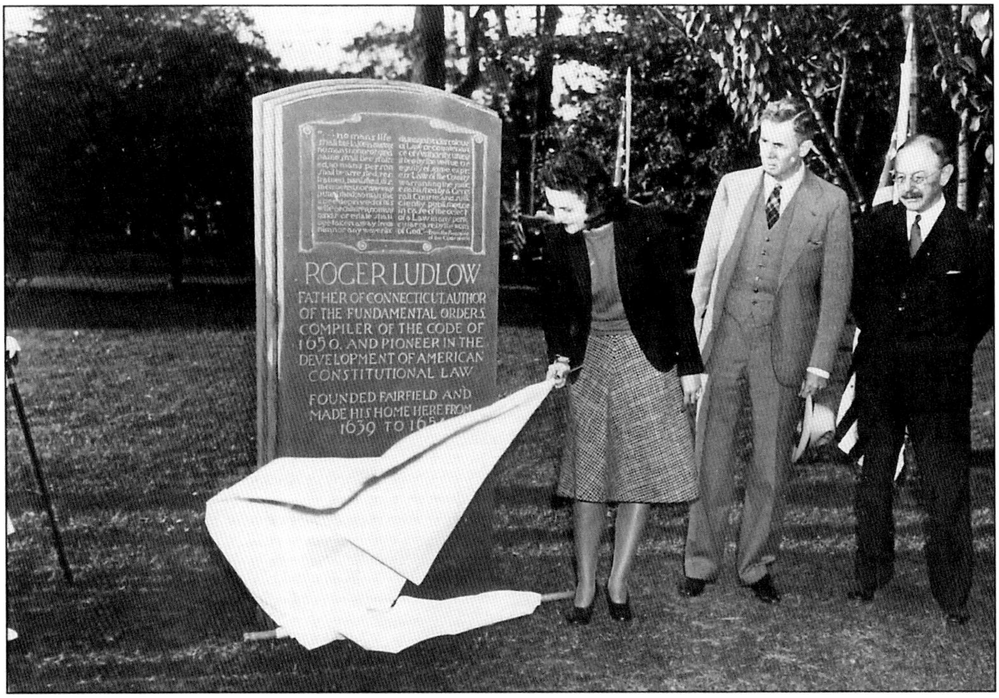

Mrs. Edward Wheeler unveils a monument honoring founder Roger Ludlow on September 28, 1939. Beside her stand two of his direct descendants, R.V. Coleman (center) and Joseph W. Roe. The stone was originally located on Ludlow's home lot at the corner of North Benson Road and Old Post Road and was later moved to the Old Burying Ground on Beach Road.

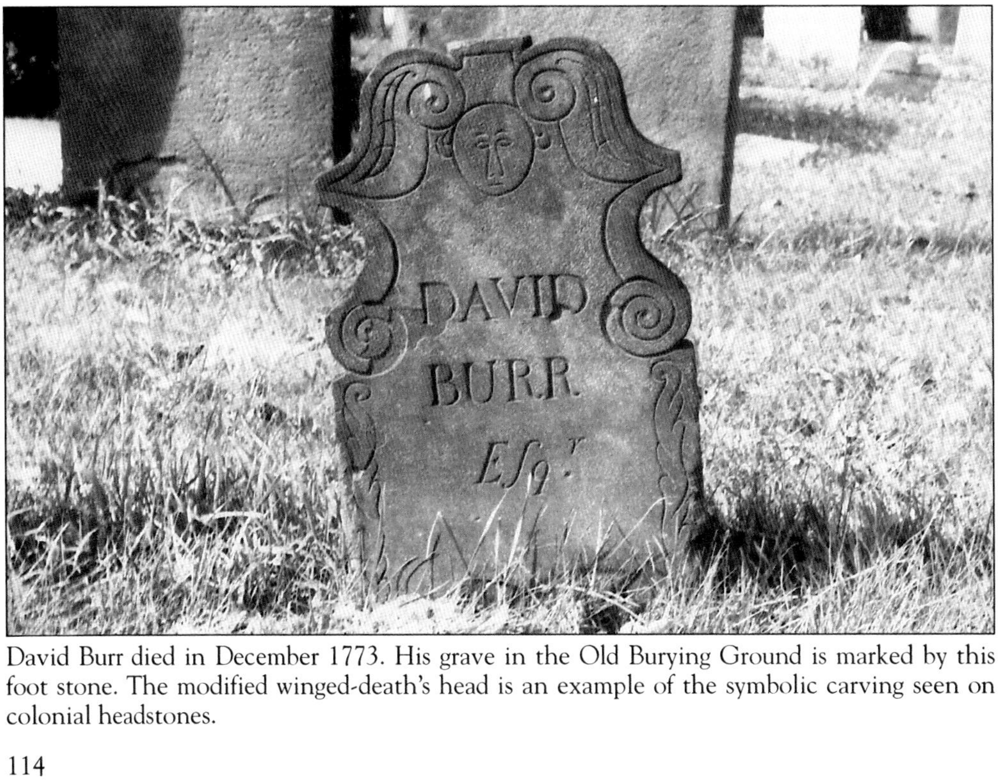

David Burr died in December 1773. His grave in the Old Burying Ground is marked by this foot stone. The modified winged-death's head is an example of the symbolic carving seen on colonial headstones.

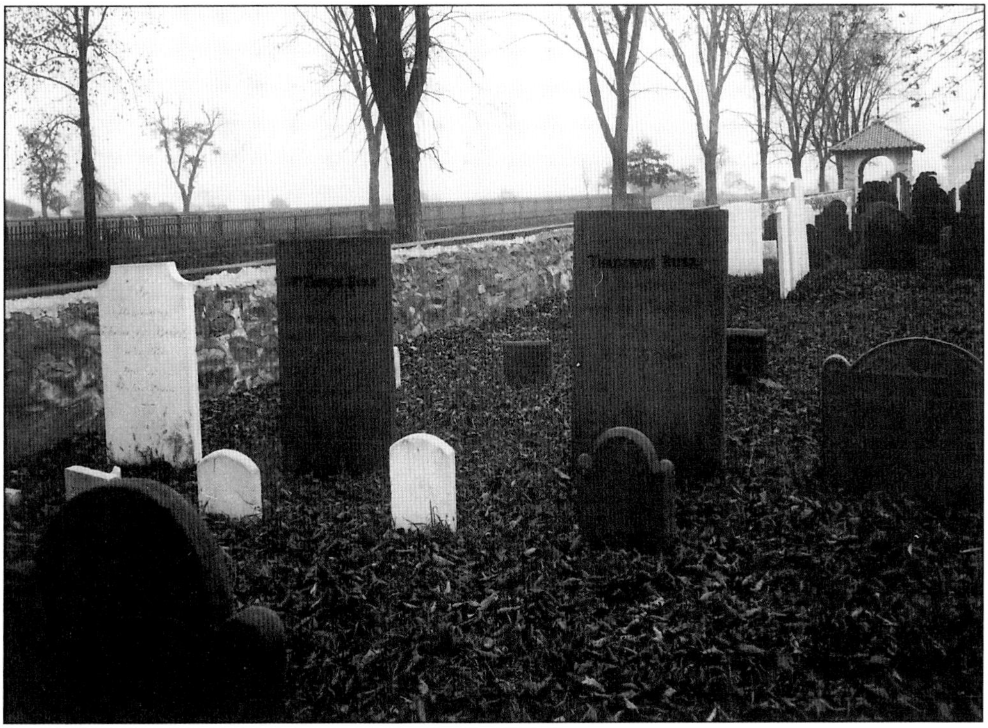

The oldest cemetery in Fairfield is the Old Burying Ground. It is the final resting place for many notable figures in the history of the town and the state. Two of the simpler stones mark the graves of Thaddeus and Eunice Dennie Burr.

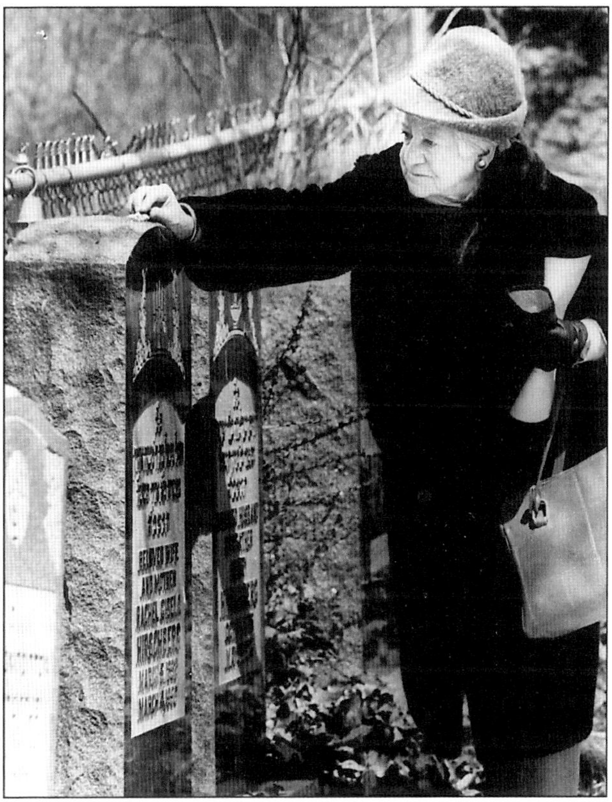

To mark her visit, Gertrude Hirschberg follows Jewish tradition and places a pebble atop the gravestone of Rachel Hirschberg at Workmen's Circle Cemetery on Reid Street. Workmen's Circle is one of several Jewish cemeteries in town. (*Fairfield Citizen-News* photograph, 1978.)

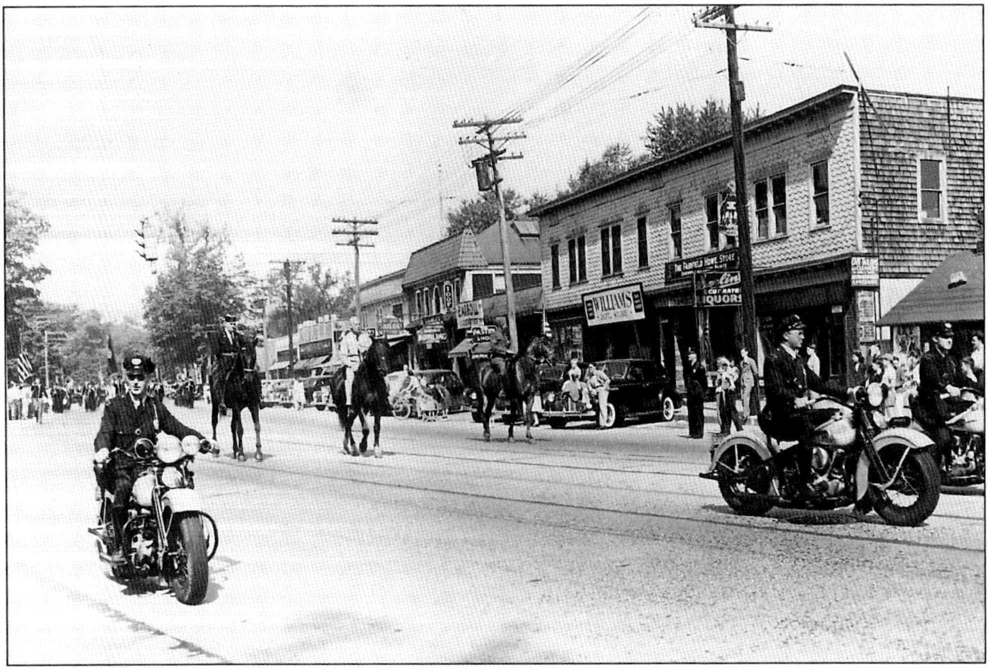

Judge Ned Ostmark, astride the horse in the center, leads a parade along the Post Road in 1947. Although the occasion of this parade cannot be determined, the Memorial Day Parade, consisting of four divisions, is *the* event of the year. (George P. Weising photograph.)

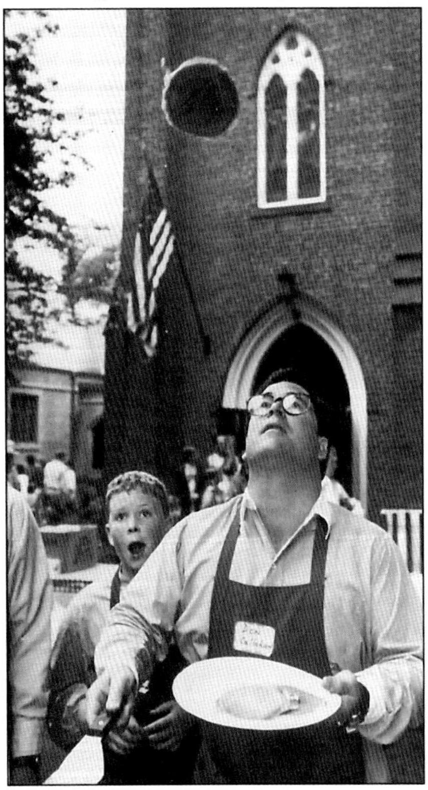

Don Callahan flips flap jacks at the annual St. Paul's Church Men's Club pancake breakfast, near the terminus of the Memorial Day Parade. (*Fairfield Citizen-News* photograph, 1995.)

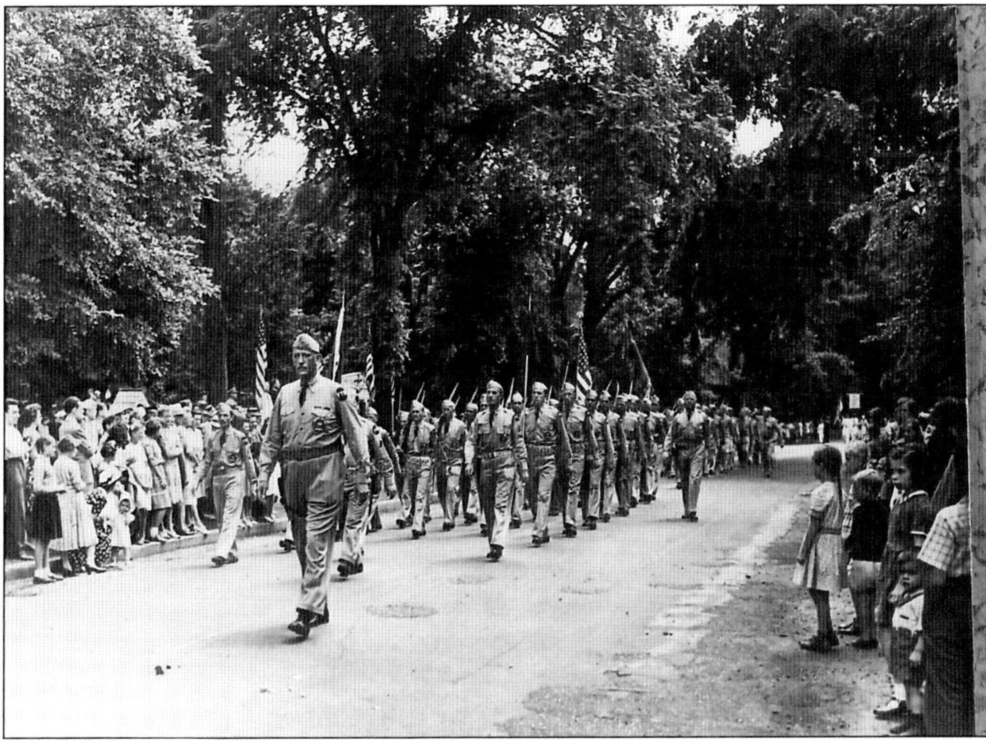

The Fairfield Town Guard marches up the Old Post Road near Town Hall on July 4, 1943, led by Captain Samuel Glover. Glover served as Fairfield's town clerk and as president of the Fairfield Historical Society.

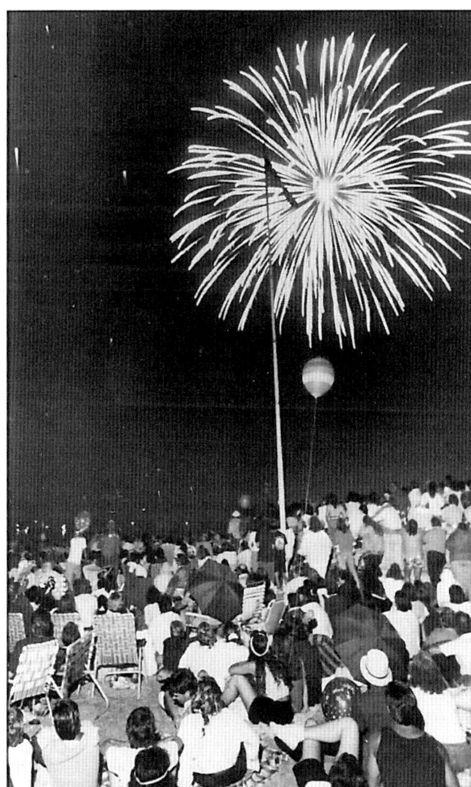

The July 4th fireworks display at Jennings Beach draws hundreds of people. Rockets are launched from a barge anchored in Long Island Sound. Fireworks have replaced the parade as the major attraction for this holiday. (*Fairfield Citizen-News* photograph, 1989.)

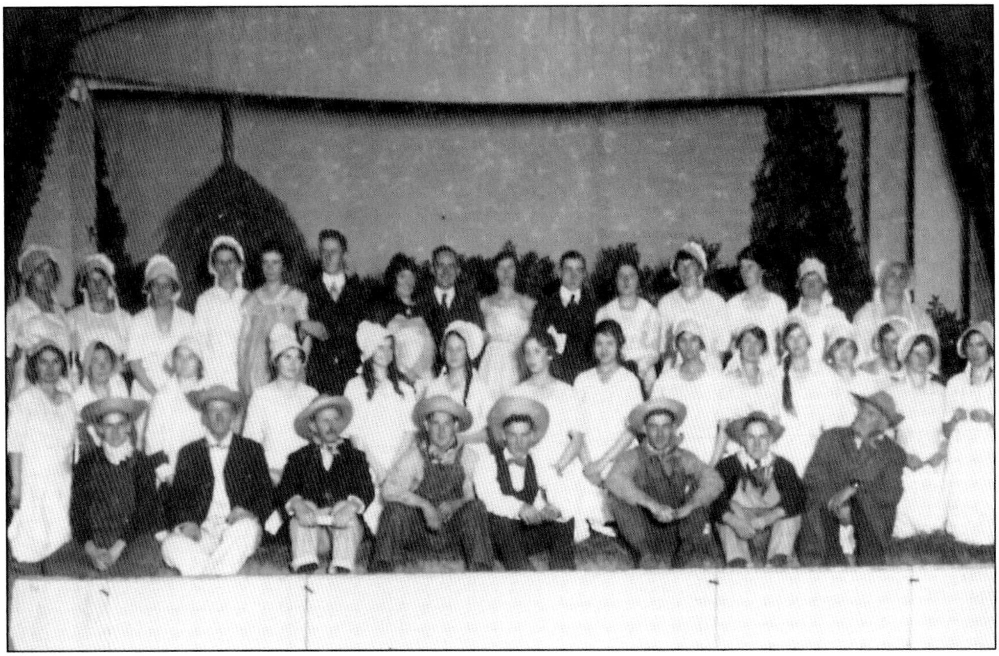

The Greenfield Hill Liberty Chorus raised funds for the American Red Cross with a performance of *Sylvia*, a pastoral operetta. The play was staged at the Greenfield Country Club on October 18, 1918.

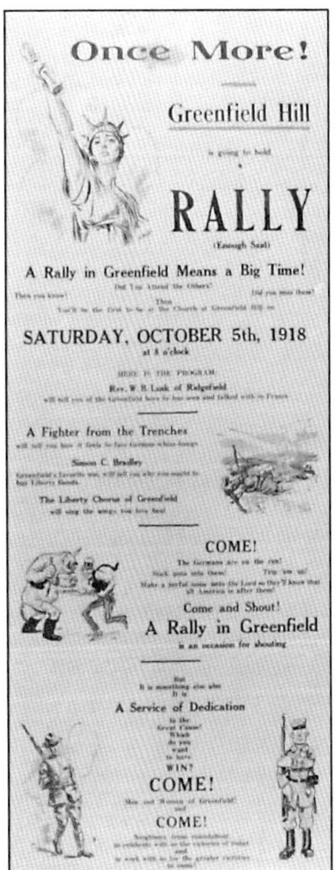

Once More!

Greenfield Hill

RALLY

A Rally in Greenfield Means a Big Time!

SATURDAY, OCTOBER 5th, 1918

at 8 o'clock

HERE IS THE PROGRAM

Rev. W. B. Lusk of Ridgefield

A Fighter from the Trenches

Simon C. Bradley

The Liberty Chorus of Greenfield

COME!

Come and Shout!

A Rally in Greenfield

is an occasion for shouting

A Service of Dedication

WIN?

COME!

COME!

OCTOBER 5th!

The Liberty Chorus also performed at a Liberty Bond Rally at Greenfield Hill on October 5, 1918. (Broadside.)

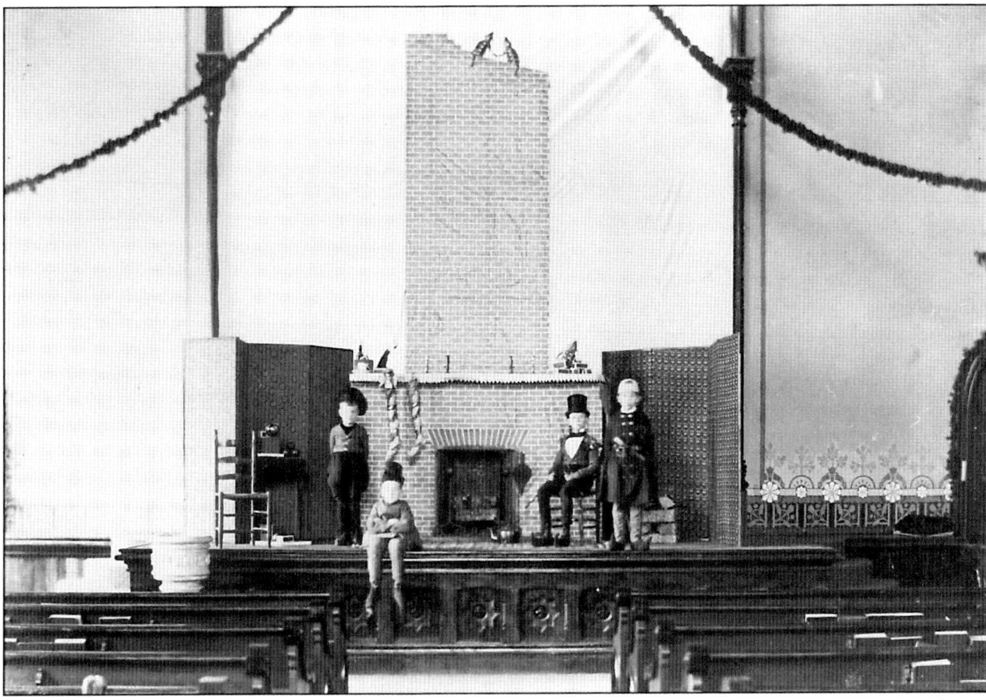

Young members of the Southport Congregational Church, Richard Sherwood, Harry B. Disbrow, Richard A. Perry, and Samuel C. Henshaw, played elves in the 1894 Christmas play.

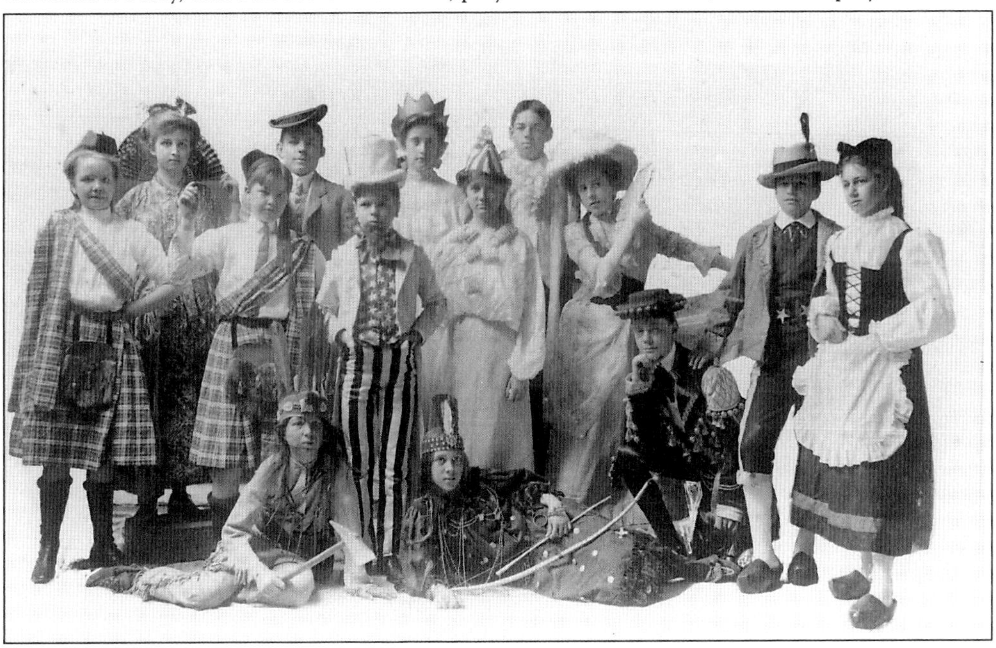

A "Dance of All Nations" revue was presented in 1903, probably at the Brooklawn Country Club. Philo and Katharine Calhoun portrayed Scotland; Harvey Warren and Helen Eames, the United States; Horace Strong and Gertrude Russell, Native Americans; Fred Silliman and Bertha Hitchcock, England; Alfred Fairchild and Mary Howes, France; Celia Pearsons and DeVer Warner, Spain; and Charles Smith and Maude Robinson, Japan.

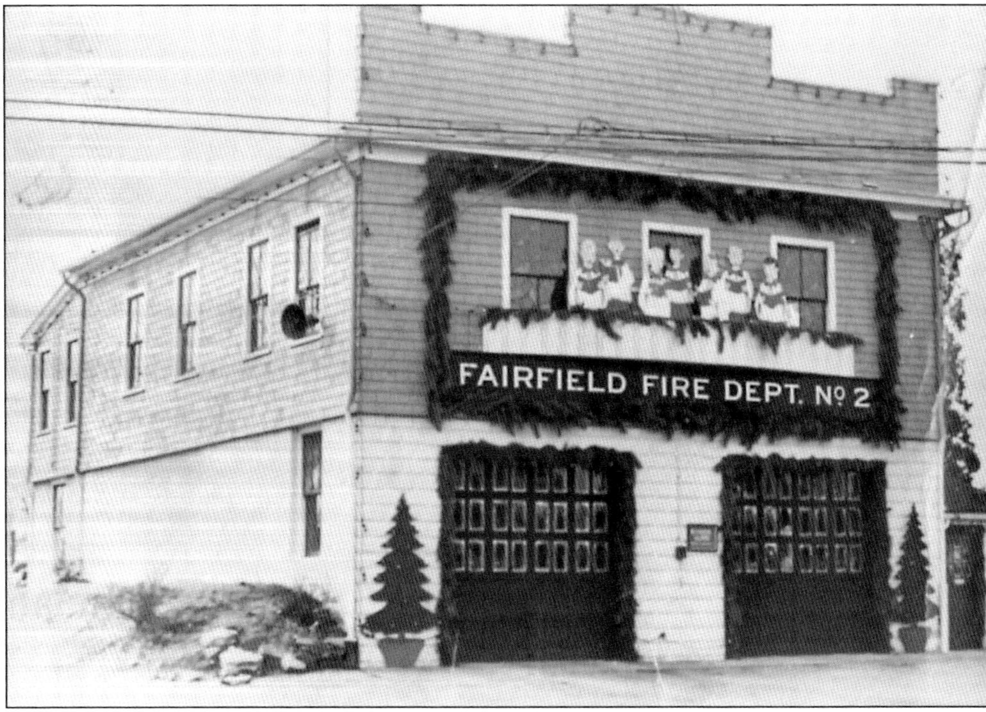

Getting into the holiday spirit, the men of Fairfield's Fire Department No. 2 in the Tunxis Hill area decorated their station for Christmas. This firehouse was replaced by a modern facility on Jennings Road in 1970.

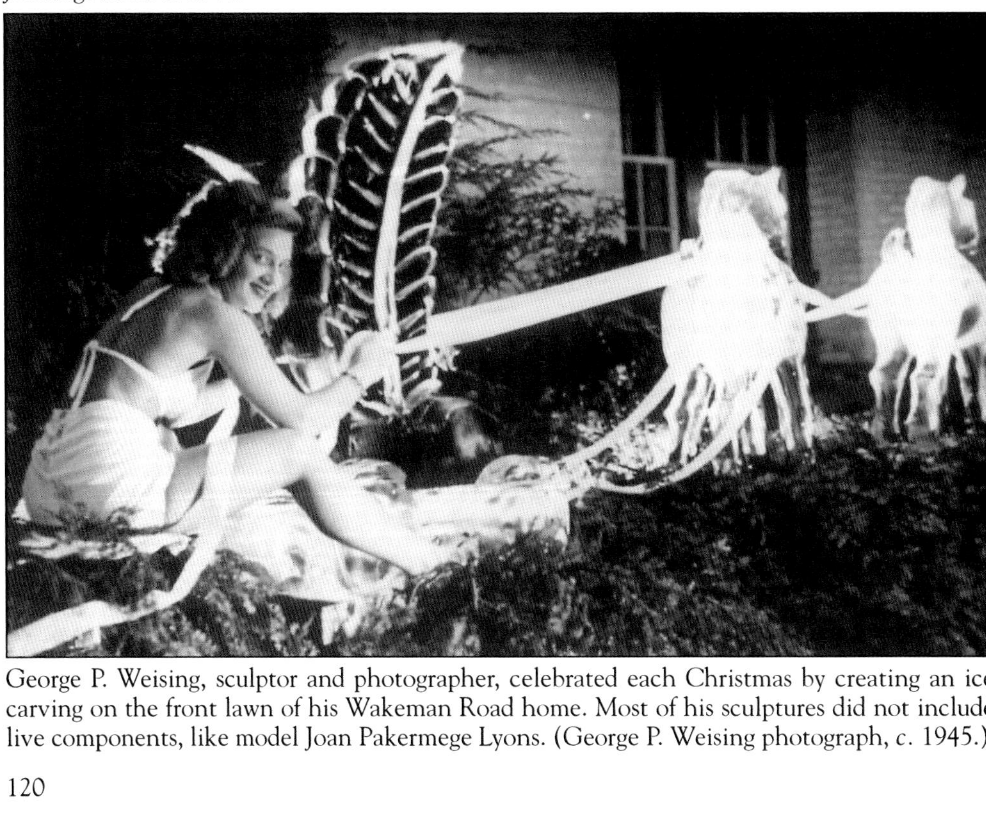

George P. Weising, sculptor and photographer, celebrated each Christmas by creating an ice carving on the front lawn of his Wakeman Road home. Most of his sculptures did not include live components, like model Joan Pakermege Lyons. (George P. Weising photograph, *c.* 1945.)

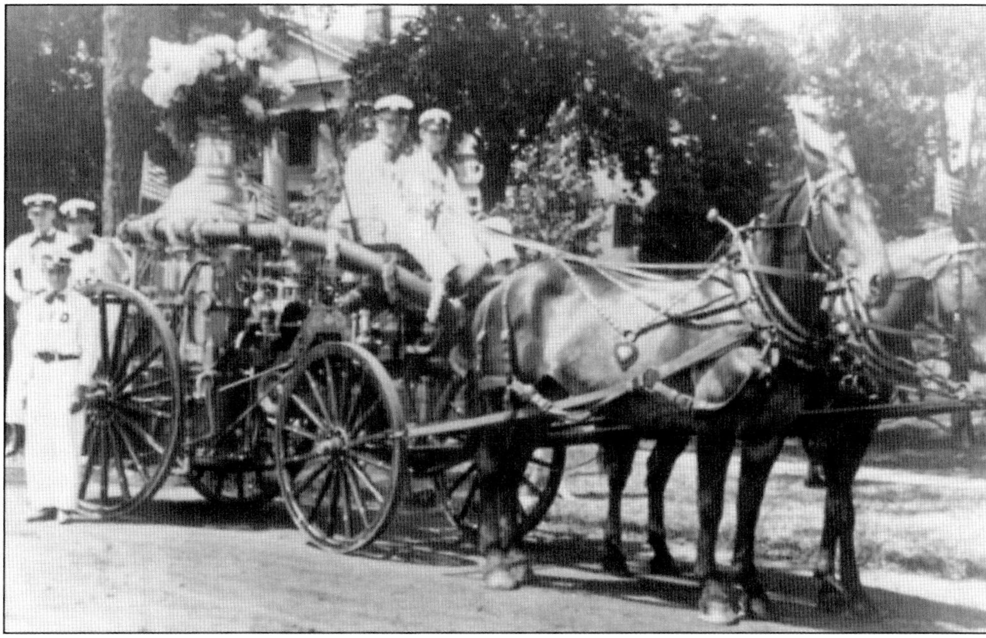

Members of the Southport Volunteer Fire Department decorated their horse-drawn steamer for the 1913 Firemen's Carnival. Henry Sherman lent the horses that pulled the steamer with (from left to right) Ralph Lane, Raymond W. Jones, Wesley W. Lawson, Henry Sherman, and Frank Fallon aboard.

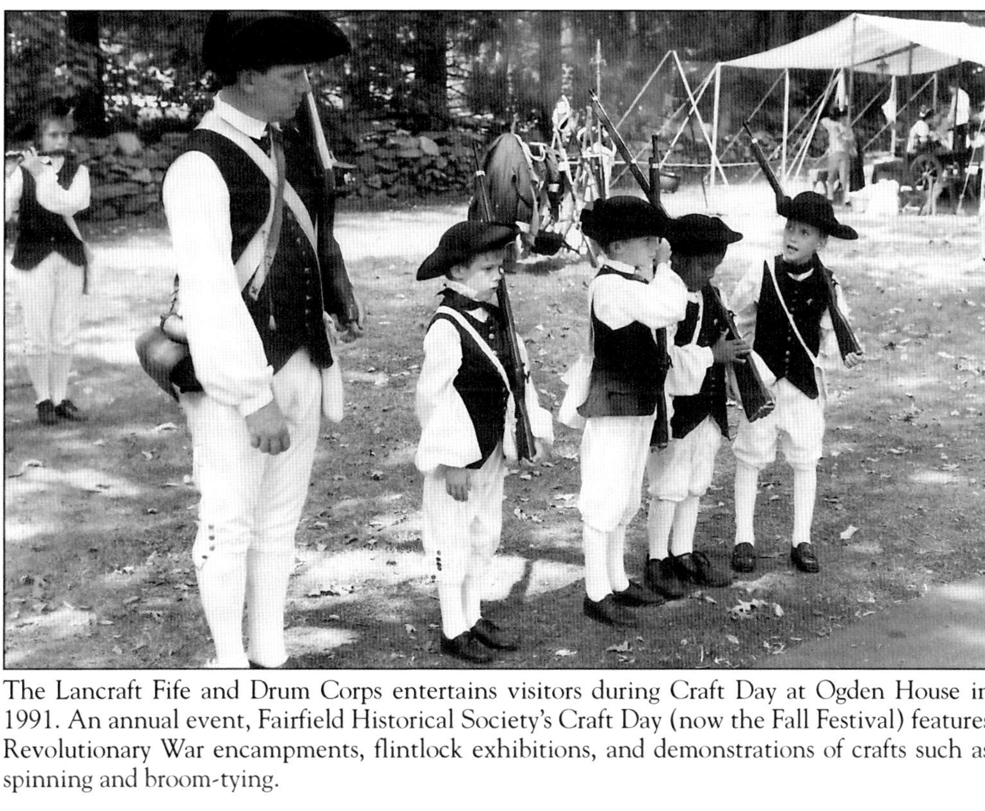

The Lancraft Fife and Drum Corps entertains visitors during Craft Day at Ogden House in 1991. An annual event, Fairfield Historical Society's Craft Day (now the Fall Festival) features Revolutionary War encampments, flintlock exhibitions, and demonstrations of crafts such as spinning and broom-tying.

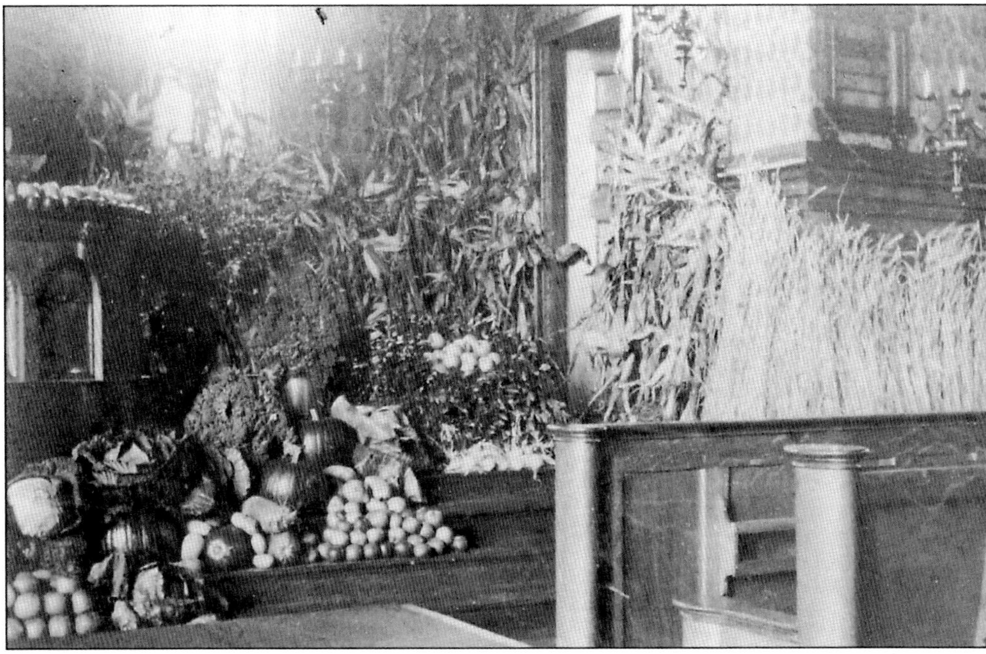

The altar at First Church Congregational bears a sampling of local crops as decoration for a harvest service c. 1885. The abundant variety of produce represents Fairfield's rich agricultural heritage.

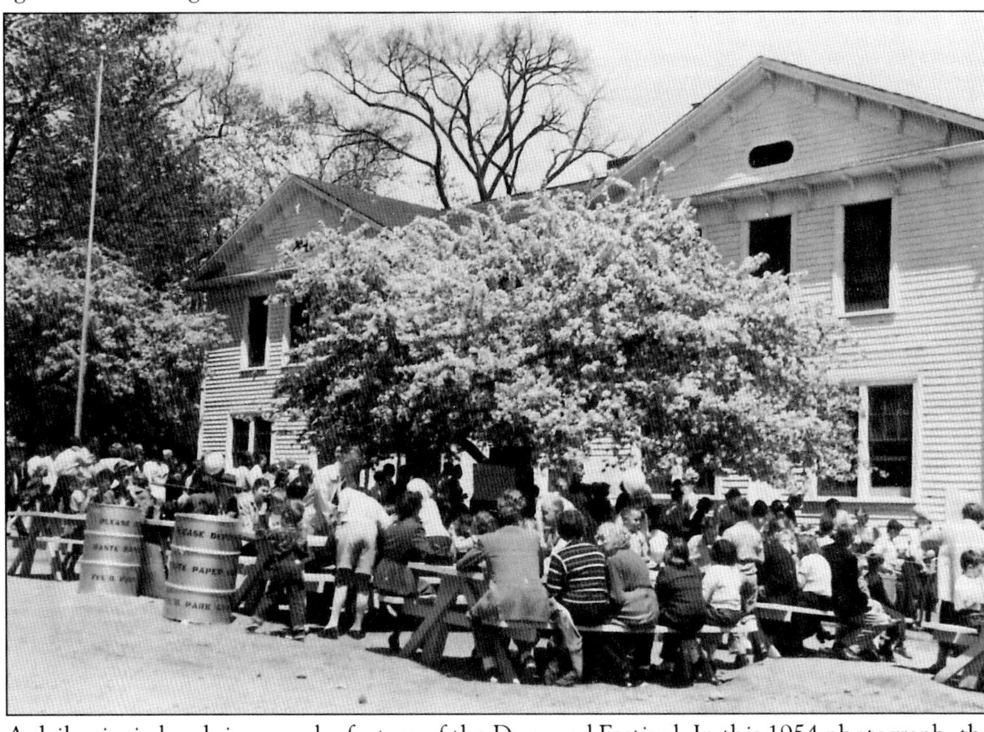

A daily picnic lunch is a popular feature of the Dogwood Festival. In this 1954 photograph, the picnic area is on the grounds of the Dwight School, now demolished. The site became part of the Greenfield Hill Green.

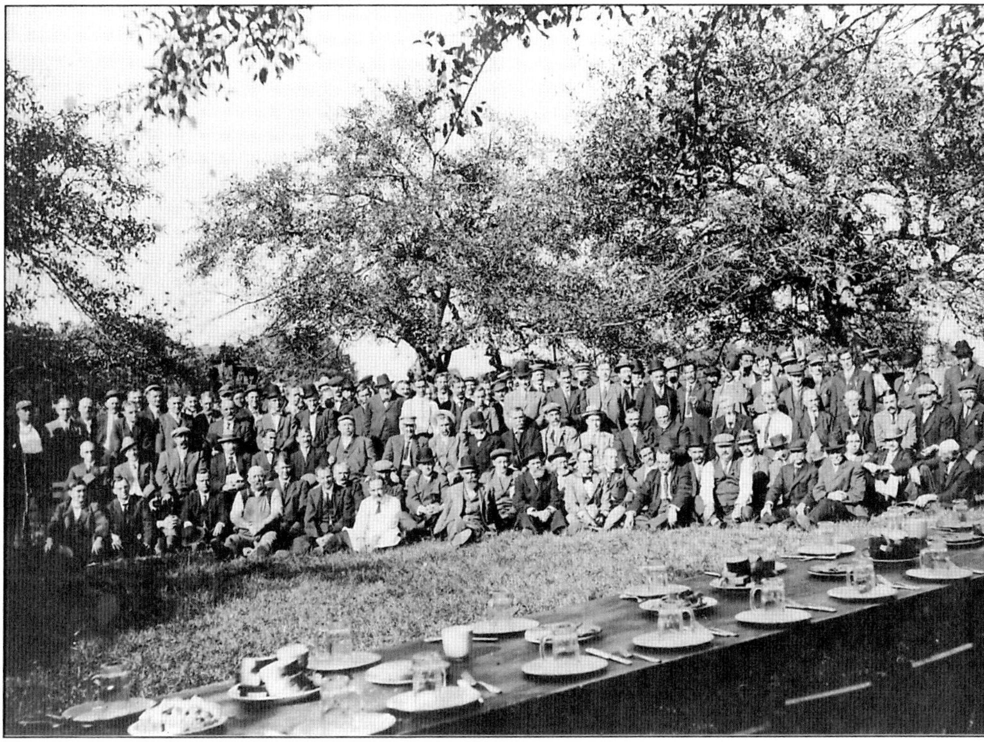

Simeon Pease hosts a Republican clambake at his home on Hillside Road about 1910.

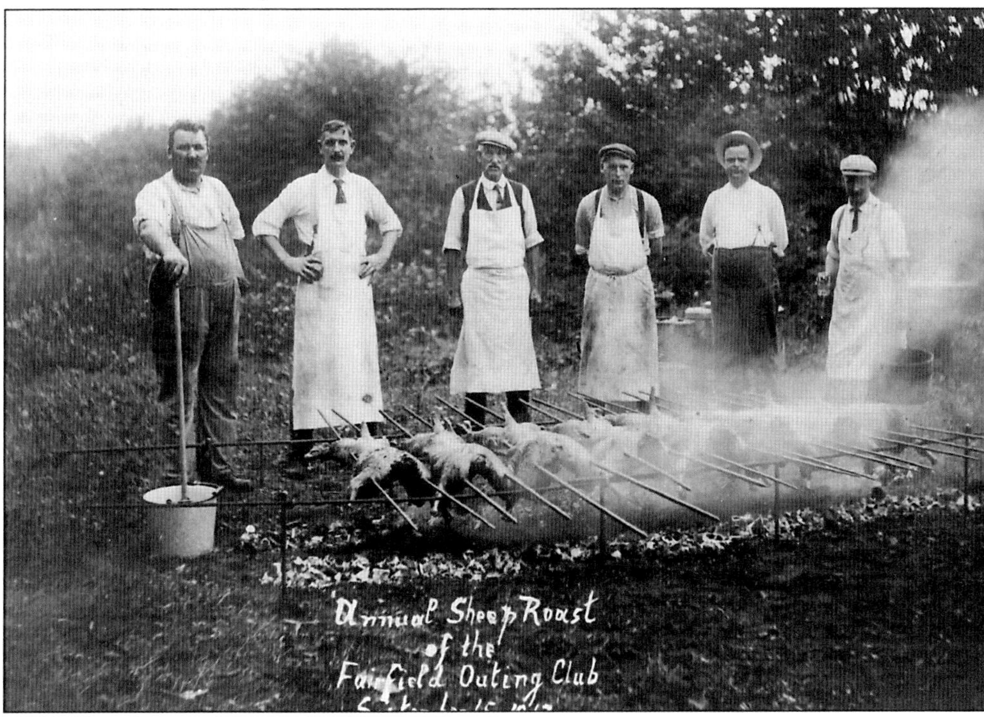

Members of the Fairfield Outing Club prepare the main course at their annual sheep roast on September 15, 1912.

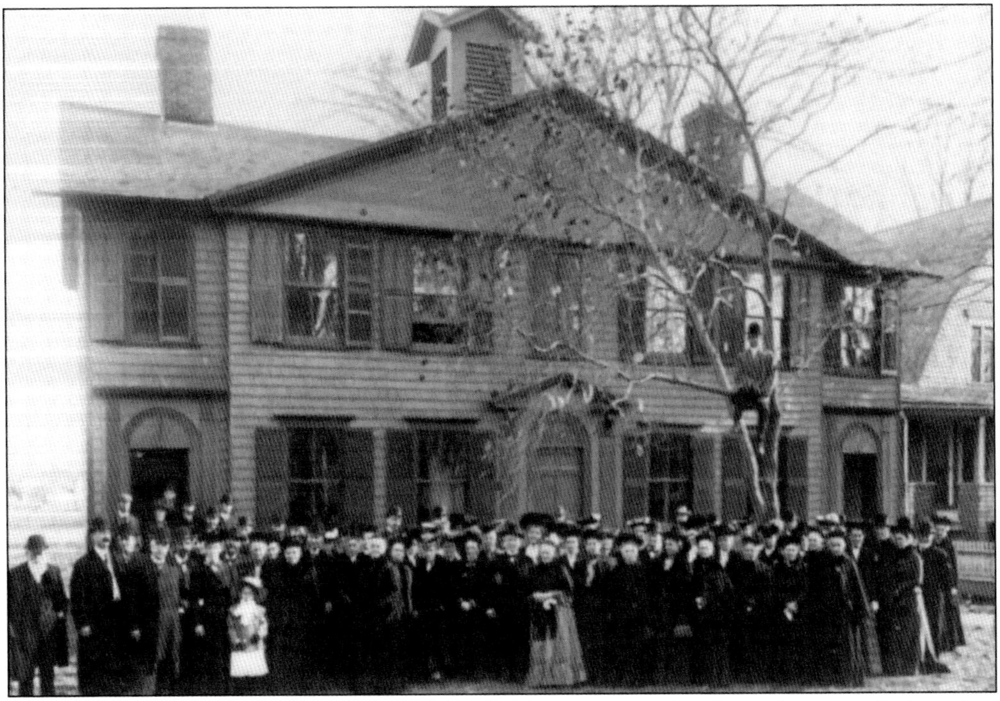

Reunions celebrate educational ties, family heritage, and other shared relationships. Graduates of Fairfield Academy gather for a reunion in 1904 in front of what is now called the Old Academy.

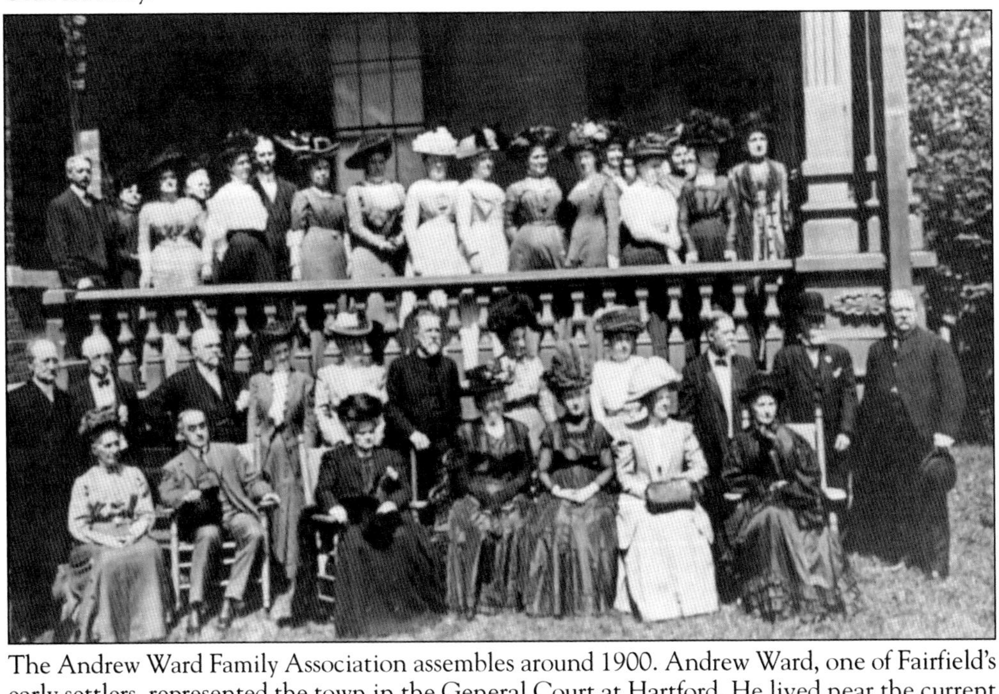

The Andrew Ward Family Association assembles around 1900. Andrew Ward, one of Fairfield's early settlers, represented the town in the General Court at Hartford. He lived near the current Town Hall Green until his death in 1659. Today, descendants of Andrew Ward bear such common Fairfield surnames as Huntington, Wheeler, Child, Wakeman, and Burr.

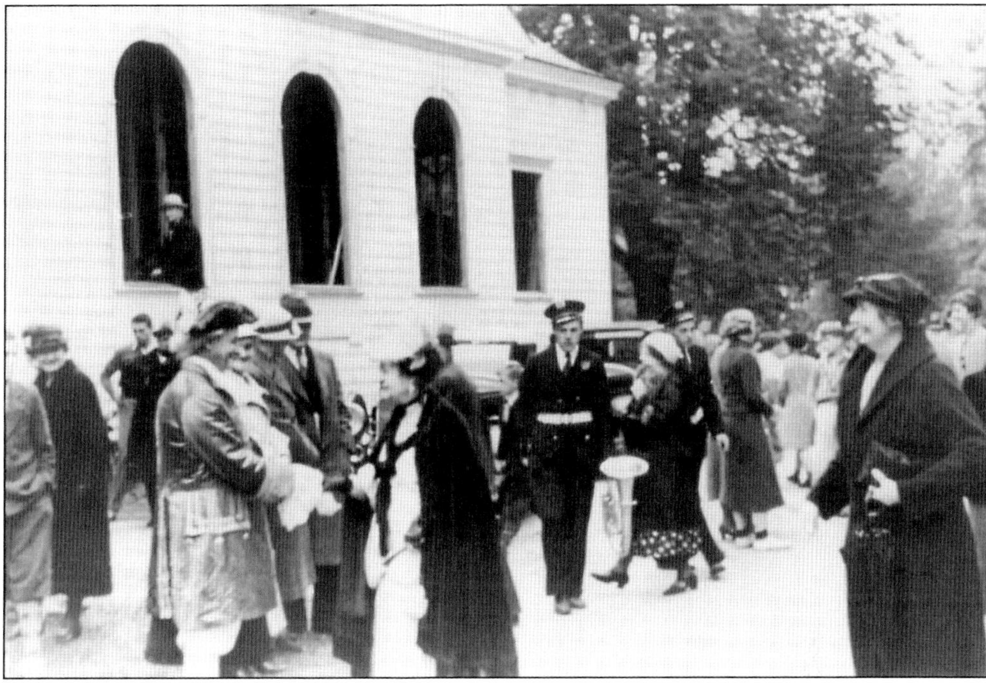

Fairfield celebrated Connecticut's Tercentenary in 1935 with a barbecue on the Town Hall Green. Annie B. Jennings (in the center foreground of the photograph) helped fund the restoration and expansion of the Town Hall, a project evident in the background.

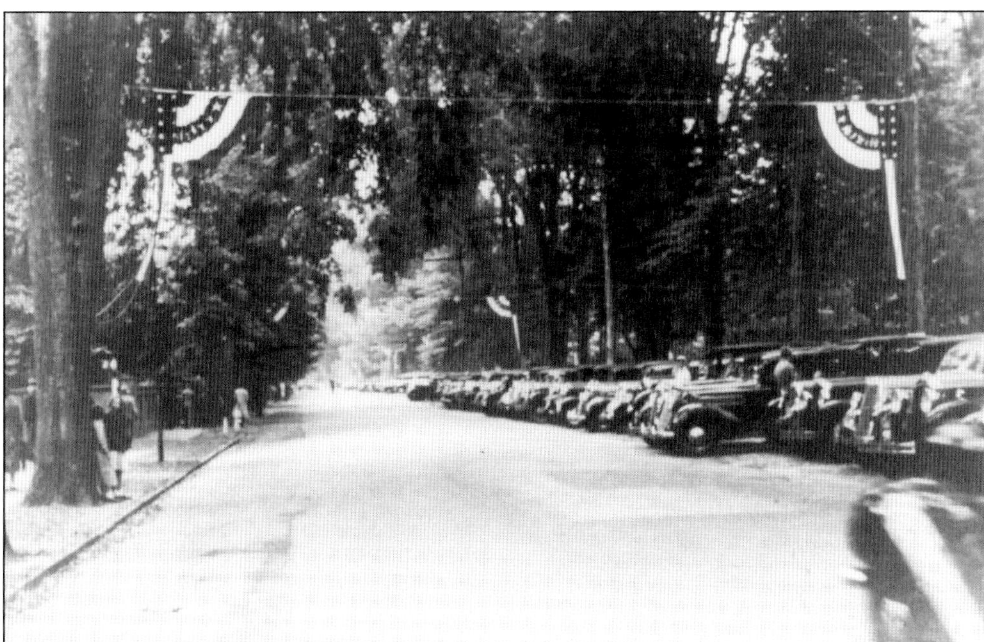

The festivities also included a parade along the Old Post Road.

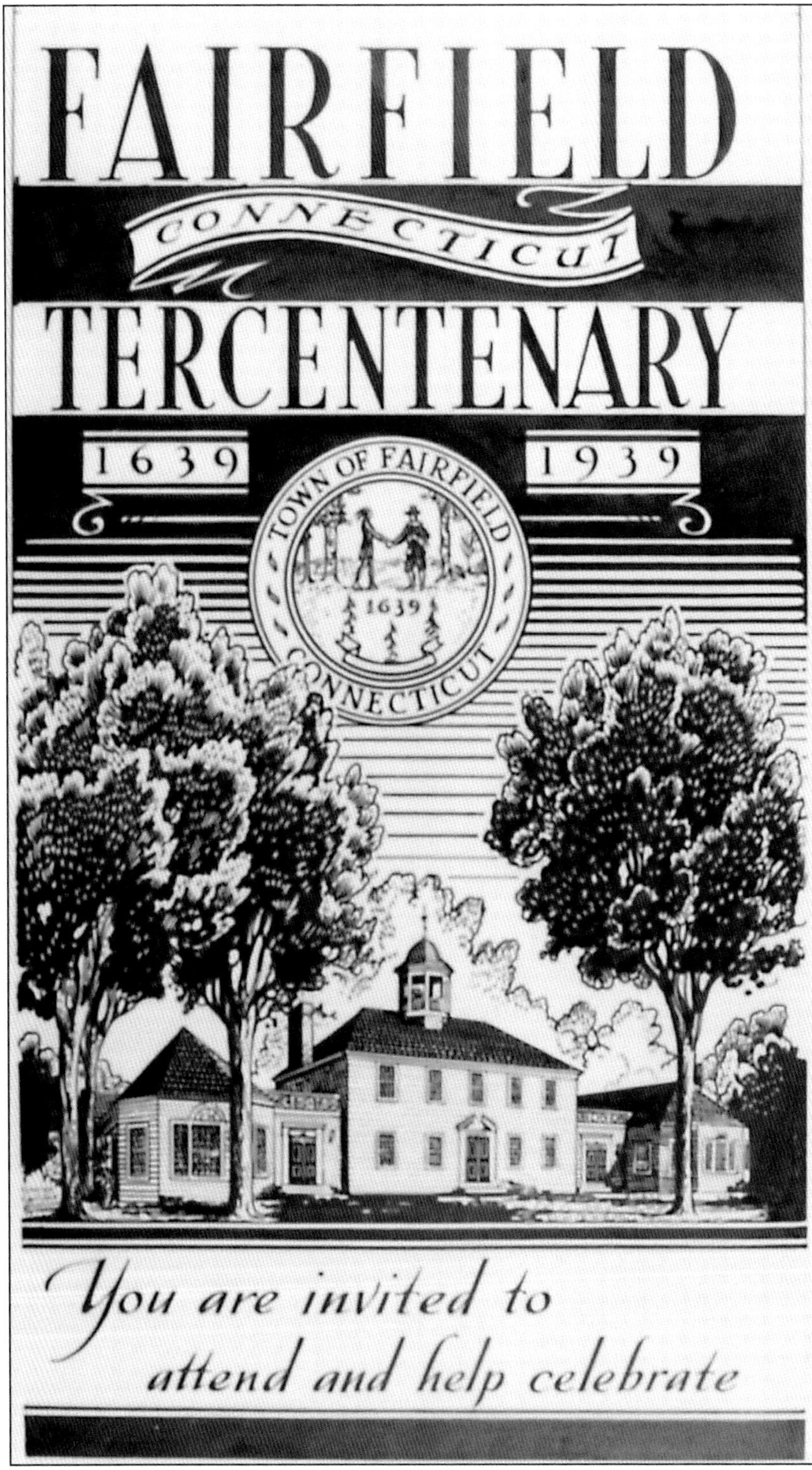

Fairfield is only slightly younger than the state of Connecticut. This poster advertises Fairfield's tercentenary celebration in 1939, which included parades, reenactments, exhibits, and plays.

Bibliography

All titles listed may be consulted at the Fairfield Historical Society. Although the majority are no longer in print, they may be held by the Fairfield Public Library and the Pequot Library in Southport. The related works cited should be more widely available. Other information resources maintained by the society include portrait, photographic, and vertical files; collections of manuscripts and business records; genealogies; maps; broadsides; architectural and landscape drawings; newspapers; oral history tapes and transcripts; videocassettes; and town and church records.

About Fairfield

Banks, Elizabeth V.H. *About the Hill: Greenfield Hill (A History of Its Organizations)*. N.p., 1952.

Banks, Elizabeth V.H. (MacRury). *More About the Hill: Greenfield Hill*. North Haven, Conn.: City Printing Co., 1968.

Banks, Elizabeth V.H. *This Is Fairfield, 1639–1940. Pages from Three Hundred One Years of the Town's Brilliant History*. New Haven: Printed by the Walker-Rackliffe Co., 1960.

Child, Frank Samuel. *Fairfield Ancient and Modern, 1639–1909: A Brief Account, Historic and Descriptive, . . . of a Famous Connecticut Town. . . .* Fairfield, Conn.: 1909.

Child, Frank Samuel. *An Old New England Church: Established Religion in Connecticut. Being An Historical Sketch of the First Church of Christ and the Prime Ancient Society. . . .* Fairfield, Conn: Fairfield Historical Society, 1910.

Cigliano, Jan and Ralph G. Schwarz. *Southport: The Architectural Legacy of a Connecticut Village*. Southport, Conn.: Southport Conservancy, 1989.

Fairfield, Connecticut, 1639–1964. On the Three Hundred Twenty-Fifth Anniversary of the Founding of Fairfield. Fairfield, Conn., 1964.

Fairfield, Connecticut Tercentenary, 1639–1939. Compiled by Historical Publications Committee, Elizabeth L. Child, chairman. Fairfield, Conn.: Historical Publications Committee, 1940.

Fairfield, Connecticut: 350 Years. Fairfield, Conn.: Fairfield House, 1989.

Farnham, Thomas J. *Fairfield: The Biography of a Community, 1639–1989*. West Kennebunk, Maine: Phoenix Publishing for the Fairfield Historical Society, 1988.

Farnham, Thomas J. *The Oak Lawn Cemetery*. Fairfield, Conn.: Oaklawn Cemetery Association, 1993.

Havadtoy, Magdalene. *Down in Villa Park: Hungarians in Fairfield*. Drawings by E. Jean Burke. West Hartford, Conn.: Printed by New Press, Inc. (Division of Imprint, Inc.), 1976.

Lacey, Charlotte Alvord, comp. *An Historical Story of Southport, Connecticut*. Fairfield, Conn.: Fairfield Historical Society, 1927.

A *List of Eighty-seven Old Houses in Fairfield, Connecticut, Marked in Celebration of the Connecticut Tercentenary, 1935–1935*. Fairfield, Conn.: Fairfield Tercentenary Committee, 1935.

Merwin, George H. *The Story of the Dogwood and Greenfield Hill, Past and Present*. Fairfield, Conn.: Ladies Society of the Greenfield Hill Congregational Church, 1938.

Perry, Kate E. *The Old Burying Ground of Fairfield, Connecticut. . . .* Hartford, Conn.: American Pub. Co., 1882.

Schenck, Elizabeth Hubbell. *The History of Fairfield, Fairfield County, Connecticut, from the Settlement of the Town in 1639 to 1818*. 2 vols. New York: Published by the author, 1885–1905. (Note: covers only 1639–1800).

Related Works

Blumenson, John J.G. *Identifying American Architecture: A Pictorial Guide to Styles and Terms, 1600–1945*. Nashville: American Association for State and Local History, 1977.

Garvan, Anthony, N.B. *Architecture and Town Planning in Colonial Connecticut*. New Haven: Yale University Press, 1951.

Griswold, Mac and Eleanor Weller. *The Golden Age of American Gardens: Proud Owners, Private Estates, 1890–1940*. New York: Harry N. Abrams, Inc., in Association with the Garden Club of America, 1991.

Ludwig, Allan I. *Graven Images: New England Stone Carving and Its Symbols*. Middletown, Conn.: Wesleyan University Press, 1966.

Radde, Bruce. *The Merritt Parkway*. New York: Yale University Press, 1993.

Turner, Gregg and Melancthon W. Jacobus. *Connecticut Railroads: An Illustrated History. One Hundred Fifty Years of Railroad History*. Second printing with 1989 addendum. Hartford: Connecticut Historical Society, 1989.

Van Dusen, Albert E. *Connecticut*. New York: Random House, 1961.